Media Ethics

Should journalists be impartial and objective? How should the public's right to know be balanced against an individual's right to privacy? How should the media be regulated? Is there a justification for spin-doctors and cheque-book journalism?

The role and responsibilities of the media are constant subjects of public debate. *Media Ethics* brings together philosophers, academics and media professionals to discuss the pressing ethical and moral questions faced by journalists and the media and to examine the basic notions such as truth, virtue, privacy, rights, offence, harm and freedom, underlying them.

The contributors explore issues of impartiality and objectivity, the ethics of political journalism, the regulation of privacy and media intrusion, and the justification of censorship. They discuss the relationship between journalism and public relations, war reporting and military propaganda in the Gulf War, media portrayals of sex and violence, photojournalism and the tabloid press. *Media Ethics* includes a chapter by Martin Bell on responsible journalism and war reporting in Bosnia.

Contributors: David Archard, Martin Bell, Andrew Belsey, Noël Carroll, Ian Cram, Anthony Ellis, Gordon Graham, Bob Franklin, Richard Keeble, Matthew Kieran, Brian McNair, Mary Midgley, Rod Pilling, Nigel Warburton.

Editor: Matthew Kieran is Lecturer in Philosophy at the University of Leeds. He is the author of *Media Ethics: A Philosophical Approach* and co-author of *Regulating for Changing Values*, a report for the Broadcasting Standards Commission. He has published articles in media ethics, aesthetics, ethics and social philosophy.

Media Ethics

Edited by Matthew Kieran

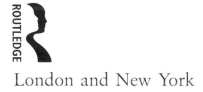

London and New York

First published 1998
by Routledge
11 New Fetter Lane, London EC4P 4EE

Simultaneously published in the USA and Canada
by Routledge
29 West 35th Street, New York, NY 10001

Typeset in Sabon by
J&L Composition Ltd, Filey, North Yorkshire
Printed and bound in Great Britain by
TJ International Ltd, Padstow, Cornwall

British Library Cataloguing in Publication Data
A catalogue record for this book is available from the British Library.

Library of Congress Cataloging in Publication Data
Media ethics/edited by Matthew Kieran.
  p.   cm.
  Includes bibliographical references and index.
  1. Mass media–Moral and ethical aspects. I. Kieran, Matthew, 1968–
P94.M358   1998
175–dc21   97–39544

ISBN 0–415–16837–6 (hbk)
ISBN 0–415–16838–4 (pbk)

Contents

Notes on contributors

David Archard is Reader in Philosophy at the University of St Andrews. He has published *Marxism and Existentialism* (Blackstaff, 1980; Gregg Revivals, 1992), *Consciousness and the Unconscious* (Hutchinson, 1984), and *Children: Rights and Childhood* (Routledge, 1993), as well as a number of articles and book chapters. He has completed a book on sexual consent and is currently researching the concept of community in relation to the family and the nation.

Martin Bell was on the staff of BBC TV news from 1965 to 1997 and during this period covered assignments in over eighty countries, including eleven wars, from Vietnam to Bosnia. He was voted Royal Television Society reporter of the year in both 1977 and 1993, the latter for his work in Bosnia. He became MP for the constituency of Tatton in 1997.

Andrew Belsey is Lecturer in Philosophy at the University of Wales, Cardiff, and a member of Cardiff's Centre for Applied Ethics. He is editor (with Ruth Chadwick) of *Ethical Issues in Journalism and the Media* (Routledge, 1992) and (with Robin Attfield) of *Philosophy and the Natural Environment* (Cambridge University Press, 1994). He is currently engaged on a study of British philosophy of science in the nineteenth century.

Noël Carroll is Monroe Beardsley Professor of the Philosophy of Art at the University of Wisconsin at Madison. He has written widely in aesthetics and film theory; his most recent book is *A Philosophy of Mass Art*, published by Oxford University Press.

Ian Cram is Lecturer in the Faculty of Law at the University of Leeds. His research interests include civil liberties and administrative law. He is currently writing a book on the law and practice of reporting restrictions in criminal trials.

Anthony Ellis is Professor of Philosophy at Virginia Commonwealth University and was formerly Senior Lecturer and Head of the Moral

Philosophy Department at the University of St Andrews. He is the author of many articles in ethics, political and social philosophy and also edits *Philosophical Books*.

Bob Franklin is Reader in Media and Communications at the University of Sheffield. He is the author of many publications, including *Televising Democracies* (Routledge, 1992), *Newszak and News Media* (Arnold, 1997) and *Making the Local News* (with David Murphy, Routledge, 1998).

Gordon Graham is Regius Professor of Moral Philosophy at the University of Aberdeen. He has held visiting positions both in the United States and Europe and his publications include *Contemporary Social Philosophy* (Blackwell Publishers, 1988), *The Idea of Christian Charity* (University of Notre Dame, 1990), *Ethics and International Relations* (Blackwell Publishers, 1996), *The Shape of the Past: a Philosophical Approach to History* (Oxford University Press, 1997) and *Philosophy of the Arts* (Routledge, 1997). He is a regular contributer to *The Scotsman* newspaper, and to BBC Radio Scotland.

Richard Keeble is Director of the undergraduate programme at the Department of Journalism, City University, London. He worked on local papers in Nottingham and Cambridge and edited *The Teacher* from 1980 to 1984. He is the author of *The Newspapers Handbook* (Routledge, 1994) and his study of the press coverage of the 1991 Gulf conflict is to be published by Libbey.

Matthew Kieran is Lecturer in Philosophy at the University of Leeds. He is the author of *Media Ethics: A Philosophical Approach* (Praeger, 1997) and co-author (with David Morrison and Michael Svennevig) of *Regulating for Changing Values: A Report for the Broadcasting Standards Commission* (BSC, 1997). He has also published articles in media ethics, aesthetics, ethics and social philosophy.

Brian McNair is Senior Lecturer in Film and Media Studies at the University of Stirling. He is the author of many books, including *Glasnost, Perestroika and the Soviet Media* (Routledge, 1991), *An Introduction to Political Communication* (Routledge, 1995) and *News and Journalism in the UK* (Routledge, 2nd edn, 1996).

Mary Midgley is a moral philosopher with many publications to her name, including, more recently, *Utopias, Dolphins and Computers* (Routledge, 1996), *The Ethical Primate* (Routledge, 1994) and *Science as Salvation* (Routledge, 1992). Her writings often appear both in the academic arena and national newspapers. She was formerly Senior Lecturer in Philosophy at the University of Newcastle.

Rod Pilling is Head of the School of Media and Communications at the University of Central England and a former journalist.

Nigel Warburton is Lecturer in Philosophy at the Open University, Milton Keynes. He has published articles on the philosophy and history of photography in the *British Journal of Aesthetics*, *Ratio* and *History of Photography* and has edited a book on the photographer Bill Brandt (Clio Press, 1994). His forthcoming book, *The Philosophy of Photography*, is to be published by Routledge. He is also the author of *Philosophy: The Basics*, *Thinking from A to Z* and *Philosophy: The Classics*, all published by Routledge.

Introduction

The media clearly have a strong and complex influence upon how we understand and shape our world. From news reporting and investigative journalism to the broadcasting of soaps, dramas and films, they provide us with information, entertainment and seek to enhance our understanding of the world. Hence, in often indirect ways, the media engage with and affect our beliefs, values and fundamental commitments. Naturally, then, given the media's increasing presence and influence within our world, there arise a host of ethical and social questions that need to be addressed.

Indeed, there has been increasing public debate about such matters, usually motivated by outrage against some perceived wrong committed by a section of the media. Accusations of bias, press cynicism, media manipulation, condemnations of journalistic intrusions into privacy, worries about the damaging or distortive effect of the televisual medium and hotly contested pronouncements about the appropriate forms of media regulation or censorship have all hit the headlines with ever greater frequency. The aim of this collection is to focus upon some of the key questions about the media's ethical responsibilities and rights. For only by critical reflection upon what, rationally, we may legitimately demand of the media, in terms of their duties and responsibilities, can we hope to arrive at any substantial basis for claiming that a particular press intrusion or media programme is immoral.

As most of the readers of this collection will notice, the majority of the essays in this collection are philosophical. This is for a good and important reason. Although sociology, psychology and legal studies are informative, for example, about what people's actual preferences are, how those preferences come about and how legal restrictions actually apply, they are, essentially, non-normative. They do not and cannot tell us what, for example, people's preferences ought to be and why, rationally speaking, this is so. It may be that many people assume political spin-doctoring, cheque-book journalism or the broadcasting of pornography on satellite channels are immoral and thus should be prohibited. But even if there were a social consensus about such matters, it does not follow that these things are indeed wrong. For, as we are all aware, people's preferences and moral judgements can be mistaken. Hence, in order to understand what the ethical issues involved are, what responsibilities, rights or duties exist and how they might conflict, we need to pursue a philosophical analysis of things like the nature of objectivity, privacy, the influence of sexual and violent programming and censorship. As it happens, as a recent report for the Broadcasting Standards Commission has shown,[1] there isn't even a consensus on such matters, except perhaps regarding the public's views on rights to privacy, so there are pressing conceptual and pragmatic reasons for trying to resolve such issues rationally. This is not to deny that other disciplines have something to contribute to such matters. They do. But, as can be seen from the nature of the collection, their primary role is to explain what is actually happening and why. Such considerations are important since they need to be taken into account when reasoning philosophically about such matters. After all, if privacy or state censorship laws are clumsy instruments, then this must be taken into account when considering, philosophically, whether they are justified or not.

The first article, by Andrew Belsey, focuses on whether it even makes sense to think we can make ethical demands of journalism. For journalism, by necessity, seems to involve muck-raking, deceit and intrusions into privacy, amongst other things, in order to achieve the function of getting the all-important story. Perhaps we have good reason to exempt journalists from the ethical responsibilities, such as the duty to tell the truth, which obtain in ordinary life. But despite such considerations, and the recognition that journalism is a major industry, Belsey argues that journalism's responsibilities, as well as special rights, arise from appropriately conceiving of journalism as occupying a distinctive facilitating role in the democratic process. Hence journalists must serve the public interest in a virtuous manner. Unethical journalistic activity, such as habitual muck-raking or deceit, will undermine the public's trust in the media and without that relationship of trust journalism's democratic function cannot be fulfilled.

This theme clearly relates to the next two articles, by Martin Bell and myself, which focus on the assumption that journalists should aim to be impartial and objective. Bell argues that far from being distanced, neutral observers, journalists are implicated within the events they are reporting and should not avoid making and reporting evaluative judgements about them. But, though understood by some as an argument against objectivity, it is no such thing. For, as I argue, objectivity is a matter of arriving at the appropriate report, interpretation *and* evaluation of a state of affairs. Impartiality, unlike neutrality, does not preclude evaluative judgements. For good journalism should not just describe how and why an event happened but seek to show its true nature; and often what is most important is to highlight, in the case of a war massacre for example, the truly evil and horrific nature of what has been perpetrated. It is through the symbiotic process of reflective equilibrium, rationally considering one's judgements in regard to the basic principles of interpretation and evaluation, that objectivity can be achieved. To deny this would be to reduce, falsely, all journalism to the status of propaganda – which is a perversion of journalism proper. For journalists do indeed have a duty to strive for impartiality and thus objectivity.

Such considerations tie in with Mary Midgley's article because the culture of journalism seems to presume, falsely Midgley argues, that impartiality requires journalists to focus upon the failings and possibility of hidden motives in public characters. Midgely traces how such cynicism has evolved from Strachey's revolution in biography. Yet, as Midgley points out, hypocrisy is not always vicious. A failure to live up to publicly espoused ideals may only reflect human fallibility rather than vicious hypocrisy. Indeed, even where the hypocrisy is vicious, it may be of greater social value to concentrate on a public character's good aspects rather than his failings in order to avoid, falsely, damaging a valuable cause.

Such issues, of course, are particularly pertinent when considering the interrelationships between journalism and politics. A consideration which may cut against Midgley's argument, in the sphere of party politics, is the emerging network of systems contemporary political parties use to get the most favourable 'spin' on a story for their respective party. Although many complain about the media's confrontational style of political journalism, and the presumption of cynicism, McNair argues that if we understand the game properly, it is clear that journalists need to maintain this approach to combat the politicians' attempts to control the news agenda in a way which serves their interests, as distinct from the public's.

In the light of these arguments concerning matters of impartiality, objectivity and the public interest, Richard Keeble's article serves as a warning that such values may be very difficult to realise. In focusing upon the media coverage of the Gulf War, as personalised in the figure of Saddam Hussein, Keeble argues that the media played a distorting role in constructing our understanding of the war. Hence, at the very least, we always ought to ask whose interests are served by reporting an event in this way. A failure to do so can only reinforce the false assumption that we are always told the truth – something which, if Keeble's analysis is plausible, turns out to be a very dangerous assumption indeed.

Moving on to the issue of privacy, David Archard outlines concerns about the nature of privacy and the public interest justification for infringing it. Indeed, where the right to privacy is trumped by considerations of public welfare, it is far from clear that a right has been infringed at all. However, most of us assume that where there is no direct public interest, construed in terms of harm, there can be no justification for media intrusion. Yet, interestingly, Archard sketches an argument which cuts against this presumption. Gossip, for example, can and does play a significant role in the moral life of a community, by reinforcing the normative dispositional force of certain moral prescriptions and prohibitions. Thus, for example, perhaps the perverted sex life of a private individual ought to be exposed, not merely for his or her own good but to stand as an example of what flourishing human sexuality should not aim towards. Moreover, exposing the private lives of the rich and powerful can reinforce a sense of egalitarianism which tends, rather healthily, to dissolve their mystique, which can so easily be abused.

Nonetheless, despite Archard's powerful argument, some people may remain worried about the moral nature of gossip as such and, more importantly with regard to the media, the effects such intrusion may have upon the private lives of celebreties and royals alike. The deaths of Diana, Princess of Wales, Dodi al-Fayed and their driver in August 1997 tragically highlighted the way such figures are often hounded by the news media to the extent that they can have little privacy or peace regarding even the most intimate aspects of their lives. It may be thought that such media intrusion is far from justifiable. But to challenge Archard's argument it must be shown that there is a clear division between the public interest and what the public is interested in. If, however, there is a link between the two, as Archard suggests, then the media attention devoted to the lives of the royals and celebrities is morally justifiable (even though we may rightfully deplore the form such intrusion may take in a particular case).

Ian Cram's article outlines how the piecemeal nature of the legal protection of privacy interests was found wanting by the Calcutt Committee report and the nature of its recommendations. Cram argues that, given a lack of political will to institute a direct right of privacy, enforceable by the courts, it is worth paying greater attention to the non-legal forms of privacy protection provided by regulators and current codes of media practice. Importantly, Cram goes on to consider how the European Convention on Human Rights and Fundamental Freedoms could, if incorporated into domestic law, provide the most substantial means by which to protect privacy.

Bob Franklin and Rod Pilling's article examines whether there has been a discernible move towards more tabloid orientated journalism and how this has affected both contemporary news values and the role of proprietors and regulatory authorities in attempting to curb such market-driven excesses. They go on to examine the likely effectiveness of increasing legal restrictions and the costs and benefits of self-regulation. Especially when gossip comes to be seen to constitute news as such, the problem arises as to the forms of redress ordinary people, unable to avail themselves of the legal and regulatory avenues open to those better off, have open to them when their privacy and lives have been abused by the press.

Nigel Warburton switches focus to ethical problems arising from the nature of the photographic medium. Many people are worried about the ethical problems which new media technology seems to raise. For example, the possibility of creating flawless images may undermine the trust we place in photojournalism as bearing faithful witness to an event as it happened. But Warburton argues that such worries are based on a mis-understanding of the nature of the photographic medium and a naïve presumption that, prior to the electronic age, photographs could not be manipulated and thus were, in a straightforward sense, transparent windows on to the world. What it does show, however, is that news photographers must retain a commitment to retaining the causal link from the resulting image back to the originating event. For the point of photojournalism is to retain a link to the actual world so that we can understand what was true of an actual event.

Noël Carroll's concern, by contrast, is a cluster of misgivings people have voiced about the nature of the televisual medium. These worries basically amount to three claims. Firstly, that television's realistic nature carries with it, falsely, a certain rhetorical force. Namely, that it cultivates in viewers, falsely, the assumption that how things are depicted is, in fact, the way things must be. Secondly, that television indulges a fantastical, morally dubious form of escapism. Thirdly, that as a medium television precludes the use of our imagination. But, Carroll argues, these worries turn out to be unfounded. Essentially, they fail to take account of the complex ways in which we understand and respond to television, or rely on an overly simplistic view of the nature of our emotions. Thus, Carroll concludes, the television medium or image is not inherently immoral though we may nonetheless have worries about the content of certain programmes.

Gordon Graham's target is the form of argument that suggests that representations of sex and violence, both in reporting and fiction, cause harm. The premiss that watching such programmes will cultivate a ten-dency to be violent is, Graham argues, highly debatable for all but a very few. Moreover, even were harm to result from such programmes, this would not legitimate censorship. After all, we know that allowing cars on the road will directly lead to the deaths of a number of individuals each year. But the freedoms at stake are more important than the resultant harm. The interesting point about reports or films which make gratuitous use of violent or sexual imagery, Graham argues, is their failure to engage our interest in order to deepen our understanding. Thus we should, perhaps, ask why it is that our artistic and journalistic communities are failing us.

The last article in the collection, by Anthony Ellis, follows on to address arguments over censorship and the media. Obviously freedom of speech is valuable and ought to be protected, to some extent, against government interference given the primary importance of individual freedom. Ulti-mately, he argues, the harm involved in such restrictions is so great that even proven harm resulting from free speech should not be prohibited unless it is of a very high degree. But Ellis also goes on to consider whether not just harm but offence can constitute grounds for prohibition. Yet the notion of offence is intrinsically tied to morality. Given this link, at least within a liberal framework, offence cannot constitute sufficient grounds for censorship because the liberal state has no business in legislating for morality. Indeed, deeply held beliefs and moral convictions often need to be attacked. Legislation to protect the feelings of those who cherish certain beliefs is, at best, mistaken, and at worst, deeply pernicious. A culture that legislates against offence is one that not only fails to protect our basic freedoms as individual persons but one likely to stagnate and infantilise its citizens.

The articles in this collection show that there are some deep ethical and social issues in journalism and the media which require careful thinking through, with regard both to their philosophical complexity and to their pragmatic aspects. Of course, the arguments here do not constitute the last word. But they do at least help to elucidate some of the central ethical issues in the media and provide arguments which must be taken into account in justifying our judgements. Thus, at the very least, they help us to understand more deeply what responses are rationally open to us and what the ethical responsibilities of the media are. It is to be hoped that the collection may play a small part in focusing the debate and emphasising the need for rational justification in such matters, as opposed to the rhetoric, prejudices and emotional responses that so often seem to hold sway.

I would like to thank all the contributors for accepting the invitation to contribute to this collection and for responding courteously to editorial requests. I would also like to thank all the speakers and participants at the media ethics conference held at the University of Leeds, in September 1996, from which this collection sprang and gratefully acknowledge sponsorship for the conference from the Society for Applied Philosophy and Yorkshire and Humberside Arts.

Matthew Kieran
Leeds, May 1997

Note

1 See Matthew Kieran, David Morrison and Michael Svennevig, *Regulating for Changing Values* (London: Broadcasting Standards Commission, 1997).

1 Journalism and ethics
Can they co-exist?

Andrew Belsey

Introduction

Both the image and the essence of journalism are hard to pin down because each appears to contain contradictory strands. By 'image' I mean the way in which journalism is generally regarded by the public. By 'essence' I mean the reality that lies behind (or apart from) the image. It is well known that journalism has a poor image with the public. They do not regard it highly. They are suspicious of journalists and the way they practise their trade. Journalists are regarded in much the same way as politicians, as disreputable, untrustworthy and dishonest, pushing a personal or sectional interest rather than the facts of the case. If people are told that the essence of journalism is truth-telling, they will react with some scepticism or derision. If they are told that the practice of journalism is founded on ethical principles they will either laugh or, if they are prepared to take the matter seriously, point out that the typical tabloid story is trivial, scurrilous or invented.

But all this is contradicted by another image of journalism, illustrated by the most extraordinary event of the British General Election of May 1997. This was the election of Martin Bell as Member of Parliament for the Tatton constituency. Until about a month before the election, Mr Bell was a television journalist – a respected journalist, let it be said – working for the BBC, reporting from the war-torn zones of the world with an immediacy and an integrity that made a considerable impact. To cut a long story short, Mr Bell stood as an anti-corruption (or as the media put it, 'anti-sleaze') candidate against Neil Hamilton, the previous MP for the constituency, who was alleged to have been involved in financial dealings ethically incompatible with the status of a Member of Parliament. When Mr Hamilton refused to stand down and was renominated by his party, the candidates of the other major parties withdrew to give Mr Bell a clear run, and he was elected as an Independent with some ease.

This was an unusual situation. It is unusual for non-party candidates to be elected to the House of Commons. It is even more unusual for major parties to stand aside to assist a non-party candidate. But what was most unusual was that this non-party candidate, standing on a platform of public and political honesty, was a journalist, a member of a profession usually mistrusted as much as politicians themselves. But here was the public, or at least that part of it represented by the electors of Tatton, putting their trust in Mr Bell as the right person to stand up against political corruption, or any suspicion of it.

Part of the reason for this is the character of Martin Bell himself, as he is well known to the television audience who have been able to assess him as a person of integrity. But there is more to it than this. It is not that there is a general mistrust of journalists, but with Martin Bell as the sole exception. There is a different and competing image of journalism, which can indeed be focused on reporters like Martin Bell. Journalists who, for example, stand in bullet-strewn areas at considerable risk to themselves, telling the viewers via the camera what exactly is going on, are regarded as brave and honourable, and almost certainly doing their honest best to present an objective and truthful account of what is happening and why.

There is, perhaps, a difference between television and newspaper journalism here. Many people rely on television as the main source of information for news, current affairs, world events, consumer matters and the like. Being able to see the journalist or presenter and whatever else is on the screen means that the audience can to some extent trust its eyes rather than rely solely on the word. Of course, in one sense this means that there is even greater scope for manipulative propaganda if the control of television broadcasting is in the wrong hands, so the audience will also take the source into account. In the United Kingdom the BBC is more trusted than channels with purely commercial (profit-seeking) interests, which is one reason why the maintenance of public service broadcasting is socially and politically important. Still, although of course anyone would be foolish to place absolute trust in anything that appears on television, there is a contrast with the newspaper world, where there is the suspicion among readers, justifiably based on actual cases that have been exposed, that journalists sit in their offices and invent stories. Newspapers are also known to be politically biased and to treat their readers unscrupulously, so why should they be trusted? But it is not just intentional bias that is regarded as a danger. Although both television images and written stories are taken in through the eyes, there is an enormous difference in their reception, for words are known to be deceptive, always at a remove from a reality that can be depicted directly.

It would, however, be a mistake to rely on there being an intrinsic difference between television and newspaper journalism. Although stories have been invented by some newspapers, it is usually other papers that have exposed these deceptions of the public. And the alleged corruption against which Martin Bell offered himself as a symbol was brought to light by a lengthy and sustained campaign by newspaper journalists, and one that was legally dangerous, given the severity of British libel law. And as for the deceptiveness of the written word, this is not the place to go into this ancient and extraordinarily deep philosophical issue, so let me just say that it is a problem that we mostly manage to overcome at a pragmatic level in our daily lives. Whenever we are offered information, whether by newspapers, television, the Internet or any other source, we have no option but to use our everyday intelligence to assess it for reliability. This applies as much to a depiction as to a word or written text.

There is then no general assurance of the soundness of journalism. Just as nowadays the practice of television journalism is satirised on television, so there is a long tradition of satire against the foolishness of the newspaper industry before the television age (Evelyn Waugh's *Scoop*, for instance). But there have always been journalists who have stood out from the crowd because their virtue (if not always their judgement) seems unimpeachable. There are examples this century from George Orwell and James Cameron down to the investigative journalists of recent years, who have recognised that the proper practice of journalism must sometimes be subversive and anti-establishment, and expose what those in power would rather keep concealed from the public to whom they should be accountable.

The point, however, is not that there are exceptional individuals like Orwell, Cameron and Bell who escape the public suspicion and distrust of journalists. It is rather, as I have already hinted, that there is a different and competing image of journalism, one that contradicts the low esteem in which journalism is held. No doubt there is a good deal of Hollywood in this image, but it is more than a myth. This alternative image presents the journalist as the fearless investigative reporter standing up against the mob or the dishonest city boss, determined to expose the corruption because 'the public has a right to know'. More generally this is an image which sees journalism as serving a useful, even indispensable function in society, providing the information, the analysis, the discussion and the comment without which a modern complex society could not operate. This takes us straight to the underlying political justification for the existence of journalism and for such notions as 'the freedom of the press', that the free circulation of news and opinion is a requirement of a democratic society.[1]

Journalism as an industry

Corresponding roughly to the double image of journalism is a two-sided reality but one in which the two sides contradict rather than complement each other. On the one hand journalism is an industry, a major player in the profit-seeking market economy, and journalists are merely workers in that industry, driven by the need to make a living. On the other hand journalism is a profession, a vocation founded on ethical principles which direct and regulate the conduct of the practitioner. Since trying to live in both these realities is difficult, if not contradictory, deeper explanation and analysis is called for.

There is no doubt that journalism is a major industry. Indeed, journalism is too narrow a term: this is the age of the media. The media are multifarious, transnational and interlinked: newspapers, magazines, television, radio, film, video, cable, communication satellites, the Internet are increasingly coming under the control of a handful of corporations which are based nowhere and everywhere and which seek greater market share, greater profits and greater global influence. In spite of the variety the media is, in defiance of grammar, a singular phenomenon, and one which has universal effect. Once upon a time social theorists were concerned with material production and with the means of production, the farms, forests, factories, fleets and mines which constituted the economy. Today we are sometimes urged to forget these old-fashioned concerns and to realise that this is the age not of production but of information, and that it is the means of information that now dominate economic and social life and provide an insight into its heart and mind.

In such an industry media workers are like any other workers. They are concerned with getting a job, job security, working conditions, future prospects, and, quite rightly, personal satisfaction. They are under the usual pressures of work in the 1990s: line management, downsizing, deskilling ('shorthand not required') and reskilling ('Windows 95^{TM} and PageMaker^{TM} required'). It is market share and the 'bottom line' that rule, and sales figures, circulation figures, audience figures and keeping the advertisers happy dominate the thoughts and actions of the executives who manage the various branches of the corporation. This ethos soon permeates the whole structure of the media industry, including, it must be stressed, that part of it still theoretically devoted to the public service. In a competitive market audience figures and the urge towards growth are as inescapable in 'non-commercial' organisations as in the explicitly profit-seeking ones.[2]

Let me admit that this is not the whole story, for, whatever other age we live in, it is also nominally the ethical age, not just in medical ethics and other traditional areas of moral concern but in environmental ethics, professional ethics, business ethics. Corporations – not necessarily from the best of motives but because they recognise and fear the power of the concerned consumer – include ethical objectives in their statements of principle, and emphasise their commitment to environmental responsibility, the rights of indigenous people, meeting the needs of the customer, personal (or personnel) development, parental leave, crèches, and all the other symbols of the modern caring corporation. But while admitting all this it is not too much of an exaggeration to say that overall it has little effect against the overwhelming demands of competition and the requirement for growth as the only means to survival in a heartless world. The market is either amoral or immoral (or perhaps both at different times), and this affects the media industry as much as any other.[3]

What then of ethics in the media? Inasmuch as workers of all sorts are required to 'perform', financial objectives predominate and there seems to be little scope for ethics, irrespective of the worker's own personal motives and desires. Perhaps it could even be argued that in journalism the situation is worse, because the doctor who exploits a vulnerable patient for sexual favours can be struck off and lose the privilege of practising, and an accountant who steals from clients can be sent to prison, but a journalist who misbehaves may get a scoop and a promotion. The theoretical and practical difficulty, however, lies in deciding what constitutes journalistic misbehaviour.

There are two contradictory pressures on journalists. On the one hand they are subject to the attention of the lobbyists and the publicity-seekers, who not only want their story told but want their own slant on it. This is an ethically-fraught area (especially if the lobbyist happens to be also the owner of the newspaper or television channel). But it is the other hand which is even more ethically interesting and puzzling here, because a lot of journalism consists of discovering and printing information about something or some situation that those involved in would rather keep secret. (Sometimes, of course, the two hands come together: journalists are deliberately given a misleading story to print but recognise it for what it is and have to investigate for themselves what the real story is.)

To make the situation even more complicated, this second aspect of journalism can itself be divided into at least two parts. First, much of the practice of discovering and printing information that some people would wish to keep secret is absolutely and legitimately central to journalism. Investigative journalism, finding out what is really going on in society, keeping people well informed about political, economic and other matters, providing information, analysis and comment, is precisely what a responsible press is supposed to do in a democracy in order to serve the public interest. But where are the boundaries of the public interest? That is the question. They do not coincide, as has often been pointed out, with what the public is interested in.

The second part of discovering and printing what some people would prefer to keep secret often involves information that the public is interested in, but should not be, from an ethical point of view. This is what is not legitimately part of journalism. This can involve any combination of ethically dubious content, presentation and investigation. The content may be what is properly secret, or at least private (the two are not the same).[4] Thus personal privacy should be respected, and although it is difficult to draw the line, there are some things clearly on the wrong side of it, like invasions of private grief and suffering. But well beyond this private people are entitled to a private life; the difficulty is always in deciding who are these 'private people'.[5] Then there is the question of presentation. Dubious material is usually presented in dubious ways, involving trivialisation, sensationalism, obscenity, vulgarity, racism, sexism and homophobia. But even legitimate material can be presented in ways that are ethically offensive, a point often overlooked in discussions of media ethics.

Methods of investigation have traditionally received more ethical attention. There are technological aids, like long-range cameras, telephone taps and electronic eavesdropping devices of all sorts, used to spy on people and pry into their affairs. Of course, modern technology cannot be blamed for unethical journalism, since deception, lying and trespass have always been open to journalists. We know, of course, that journalists often behave in such unethical ways, and if it is unethical, then they should not do it. It is as simple as that.

If only it were as simple as that! The point is that words like 'deception', 'lying' and even 'spy' and 'pry' have the ethical evaluation, the condemnation, built into them. But should activities like this, only without the condemnation, be contemplated by journalists? Let us revisit the distinction between the content, the material of journalism, and the method of investigation. Could the end justify the means? In the investigation of crime or corruption, or just incompetence, perhaps the journalist has to resort to some deception.[6] These are areas where the people involved would rather keep things secret but where the public really does have a right to know. There is a long and honourable tradition (perhaps dying now) of investigative journalism, in which the journalist cannot come straight out with the questions. Much investigative journalism (like much police work) is not glamorous but consists of the minute analysis and comparison of thousands of documents. But then some first-hand investigation might be called for, in which a bit of deception, a touch of electronic eavesdropping, is the only available means – but with words like 'deception' and 'eavesdropping' shorn of their condemnatory ethical undertones.

But can we play about with the meanings of words like this? In this context the question is part of a much larger and central ethical issue about the relation of ends and means, and the related problem of dirty hands. Can we do good by doing bad? If we are doing good, then perhaps we are not doing bad. The issue usually comes up in discussions of issues much more difficult than journalism, like war and violence. Is bombing a city justifiable if civilians will be killed? Is it morally right to assassinate the evil dictator?[7] (It is worth remembering, however, that for journalists not lucky enough to work in liberal democracies, this last question might be practically pressing rather than merely theoretical, especially when the dictator is not only willing and able to assassinate them, but preparing to.) But even in liberal democracies journalists can find themselves investigating evil and ruthless people, when prudence if not morality calls for deception. But how can the gangster, the drug pusher, the corrupt politician, the fraudulent businessman be exposed, except by methods which in other contexts would be questionable? Perhaps in these journalistic contexts such methods are morally required.

So far in this section I have been concerned with 'industrial' journalism, in which journalism is just a job and the journalist is subject to all the usual pressures to 'perform' for the sake of the corporation. I have already strayed into ethical matters but will postpone further discussion of them until the next section, when I shall deal with them more directly. Before that, what can we conclude about industrial journalism? Corporate pressures, the search for sales, the search for audience, promote the production of material that the public is interested in, rather than that which is in the public interest. So as not to appear too unconspiratorial, I should say that 'what the public is interested in' is not fixed, a given, eternal, immutable fact of nature. The appetite is rather, and largely, constructed by the very media that feed it, in a glorious circle of supply creating demand and demand creating supply.

One symptom of the resulting trivalisation of social life and the representation of it in the media is the failure to distinguish between secrecy and privacy, and a resulting failure to understand the ethical significance of the distinction. Neither term is well defined, and I do not intend to stipulate once-and-for-all definitions of them, but instead to try to bring out the differences significant in the context of journalism. Although private individuals can have secrets, I take secrecy in the political sense to be the concealing of information by those public individuals and organisations with power, when it ought to be available to ordinary people as part of the democratic process, for reasons of accountability. Privacy, on the other hand, although the term is often misused in connection with what organisations try to keep hidden,[8] is something that only individual persons can have, and only in so far as they are engaged in private and not public activities.

These definitions solve few problems; there is an element of circularity, and they do not provide criteria for distinguishing what may be kept hidden legitimately, whether it be a matter of secrecy or privacy. Just as there are no doubt legitimate areas of privacy for individuals so no doubt there are legitimate areas of secrecy for organisations, but they are much smaller than is often taken for granted. (Consider the long struggle in the United Kingdom against official secrecy and for freedom of information.) But industrial journalism, in league with supposed public demand, too often confuses the two areas, and connives with the powerful to keep secret what ought to be exposed, while invading the privacy of those who neither wish for nor deserve such treatment. This is an over-generalisation, of course. Lots of individuals love the attention of the media and are quite willing to be on the receiving end of the publicity. And at the other end of the scale there is still serious journalism dedicated to serving the public interest and to keeping the public informed as part of the democratic process. But the reality of industrial journalism is to be found largely inhabiting an ethics-free zone.

Ethical journalism

So journalism is just a job in a market economy in which the usual pressures of work discourage practice based on ethical principles. But there is another reality in which journalism is a profession based on ethical principles, indeed constituted by ethical practice. However exaggerated the claims about this reality have sometimes been, it is not just a myth, a self-serving piece of propaganda put about by those with lots to hide and lots to gain. Nor is it just an ideal, never to be attained. It is a reality illustrated (rather than proved) by the experience of Martin Bell in Tatton, a journalist getting the support and confidence of the public in direct competition with a politician. Ethical journalism even has a sort of physical embodiment in the *Code of Practice* issued by the Press Complaints Commission (as well as in similar codes all over the world), even though such codes fail to be sufficient from an ethical point of view.[9]

But before fully considering the claims of journalism to have an ethical existence, we should look at the question of professionalism.[10] Ethics and professionalism are often seen as co-requisites. What then is a profession? Traditionally a profession involved the giving of a service by a certified expert to an individual client, for a fee and on the basis of mutual trust and respect. In areas like law and medicine the client has to trust the expertise and the good faith of the practitioner, who in turn respects the needs and vulnerability of the client. The professions are policed in the sense that a practitioner who transgresses against the ethically based standards of practice is punished in some way, with expulsion from the profession as the ultimate sanction.

On this account journalism doesn't sound like a profession, but then neither do many other occupational areas that today claim professional status. (Almost every occupational area claims professional status.) Even the traditional professions often fail to match their traditional image, as social, economic and technological changes alter the relationship between the service-seeker and the service-provider. Perhaps then the emphasis should be on the ideas of ethical practice and adherence to an ethical code. Indeed, it is the proliferation of such codes among occupational groups that is used to justify the claim to professional status. Presumably, the spread of such codes, inasmuch as they have a genuine and serious effect, should be welcomed, as it means that the idea of ethical practice permeates further into society. But if all occupational groups are code-based professions, professional status no longer points to any significant ethical distinction between one occupation and another.

A further (yet related) account of professionalism is in terms of each profession's essence, which links the practice of the profession to the attainment of some intrinsically worthwhile end. Thus it is claimed that the essence of medicine is the promotion of health, of accountancy the insistence on financial probity, of law the pursuit of justice, of social work the enhancement of client autonomy, of the Church the cure of souls, etc. On this approach the essence of journalism is telling the truth, or, to put it in different terms, journalism is constituted by truth-telling. Essentialism of any sort is not these days universally popular as a method of explanation and illumination, and these examples show some of the reasons why. For a start, we might expect all the transactions of everyday life to be based on telling the truth, so there is nothing distinctive about journalism on these grounds. Furthermore, while we might be able to deal with the truth and nothing but the truth, the whole truth is altogether more difficult. All information is selected from an infinite whole, and all information has to be presented in one way or another. And then much journalism is concerned with opinion, argument, debate and discussion, where notions of objectivity and fairness are central, rather than truth. Furthermore, essentialism of this sort is not very helpful because it is over-general and thus somewhat vague. It provides no way forward when the rights and interests of different people conflict. There is a very great deal in the practice of medicine, for example, which is not illuminated by generalities about the promotion of health. This so-called essence does not help much on questions about abortion and euthanasia. Similarly, the notion of truth-telling in journalism does not answer the problem, already discussed, of using dubious methods to obtain the truth. This does not, of course, suggest that telling the truth is not important in journalism.

We have not, so far, tracked down what is meant by speaking of journalism as a profession, except in so far as ethical practice is necessary, but not sufficient, for a profession. But this should be of little concern, as it is the ethical practice and not the designation 'profession' that is important. So long as any occupation, or indeed any activity, is based on sound ethical principles, why should we worry whether it is a profession or not? As I have already suggested, professional status tends to be a self-awarded honorific these days, a fact that is of more sociological than ethical significance. What clearly is of ethical significance is the ethics of the activity, whether it be journalism or anything else.

What then of the reality of ethical journalism? Analogies with traditional professions obstruct rather than assist understanding. A journalist is not (except perhaps in a very few, exceptional cases) an individual service-provider with an individual client. Nevertheless, journalism can best be thought of as providing a service. Journalists provide a vital service to society as a whole, but it is a political service. Journalism is part of the political process. Now of course there are dangers in such a statement. Journalists are not legislators and neither are they governors. It is bad for society and for journalism if journalists are tempted to be either. They should be considered, rather, as facilitators, to use the jargon of the modern age to make a very traditional point.

They facilitate the democratic process. It is not true that we have just moved into the information age, because even the drafters of the American Bill of Rights recognised that information oils the wheels of democracy when they laid down that 'Congress shall make no law . . . abridging the freedom of speech, or of the press' (First Amendment to the Constitution of the United States of America (1791)). Autocratic governments control information, and regard secrecy as a important weapon – and not only autocratic governments. But if a government is to be accountable to the people it must know what is going on; if the people are to cast their votes wisely and rationally they too must know what is going on. Information is necessary (though not of course sufficient) for a successful democracy, inasmuch as it requires the free circulation of news, opinion, debate and discussion. Hence the incorporation of freedom of expression and freedom of information in international charters like the Universal Declaration of Human Rights. A democratic necessity is transformed into a human right.

As commentators on the American Constitution have pointed out, the traffic is not one way, and the privileges guaranteed to journalists by the First Amendment should be reciprocated by the responsibilities of journalists.[11] The privileges are granted to enable journalists to facilitate the democratic process without hindrance, and so they license conduct which is directed towards actually facilitating it, and not just any old conduct. It is in this political area that the reality of ethical journalism is located, since journalism as part of the democratic process can only be ethically informed journalism. The point is obvious, in that the ends of democracy cannot be served by media that are full of untruths, lies, invasions of privacy, scurrility, obscenity, triviality, distortion, bias and all the other sins that industrial journalism actually exhibits. All the virtues associated with ethical journalism – accuracy, honesty, truth, objectivity, fairness, balance, respect for the autonomy of ordinary people – are part of, and required by, journalism as located within the democratic process.

If the media are to be part of the democratic process because of their role in the origination and circulation of information and opinion, then the quality of that information and opinion is going to be a vital issue. Quality here is meant in a typically ethical sense, so that the ethics and the politics of the media are not really different or separable issues. Ethical journalism serves the public interest. One good reason for putting the point in terms of virtues is that although virtues might become ingrained dispositions they are not arbitrary or irrational but based on sound ethical principles. Virtues are not algorithms, but the very nature of their principle-based flexibility enables them to deal more successfully with novel situations than can a set of rules embodied in a code of practice. And a democratic society, especially one in a technological age, will constantly produce situations and opportunities which are ethically novel.

This then is the reality of ethical journalism, journalism based on the idea of virtuous conduct, facilitating the democratic process and serving the public interest. Cynics will say that this is myth-making and that there is no reality behind it. The less cynical might say that it is an ideal of what ought to be, and a long way in advance of what actually is, although we might aspire to make some further progress towards the ideal. The cynic, I wish to argue, goes too far, although given the nature and power of industrial journalism one can understand why there is an apparent justification for such cynicism. The lesser cynic is correct in approach, although, as I have argued, ethical journalism is not just an ideal but a reality, just as much a reality as industrial journalism.

Journalism is a two-sided reality, in which the two sides contradict rather than complement each other. Is this a helpful way of putting the point? I hope so. Industrial journalism exists, and so does ethical journalism. They both co-exist and contend, battling for supremacy in a recreation of an ancient and eternal struggle. Each is armed with different weapons. Industrial journalism can call on the amoral power of the transnational corporation, but ethical journalism is undefeated, being able to rely on the undiminished strength and perennial appeal of virtue.

Co-existence?

But enough of these Manichean metaphors! What is the ordinary journalist to do in his or her everyday working life? No doubt journalists, especially when young and entering the profession, wish to be good journalists, to do a good job, and to obtain at least some degree of personal satisfaction. But they will have mixed motives and expectations, some material, some ethical. It is unlikely that many journalists are motivated directly by a desire to serve the public interest, yet they are likely to have some such notion occupying an underground area of their thoughts.

The pressures of work keep it underground, mostly. Journalists do behave unethically. Yes, they have invented stories, invaded privacy, harassed the unfortunate, used sexist images and generally behaved badly. The image of journalism held by the public, according to which journalists are a shifty, untrustworthy bunch of unprincipled self-servers, has plenty of justification. And yet not all journalists suffer from this image, as is shown by the example of Martin Bell, not only in his habitual role of respected journalist but also in his unexpected role of victorious politician. There is a delicious irony in the fact that it was a journalist who stood for and was elected to Parliament on an ethical ticket.

The pressures of work that prevent ethics from having a firm place in journalism are not all that different from the pressures on anyone else.

There is a job to be got, promotion to be obtained, so the story has to be written and the methods necessary to obtain the story used. The story must sell, the managers must be satisfied, the growth targets met. The market must be chased, so there is a constant temptation (more than a temptation) to print trivial stories, salaciously presented and obtained by suspect methods. Personal beliefs and desires do not come into it. Journalists are often thought to be hypocrites when those who are committed Labour voters work for or even edit newspapers that are little more than Conservative Party propaganda sheets. This has happened, and probably the other way round as well. How can they do it, people wonder, failing to recognise that the necessity of making a living makes a mockery of most people's highest ethical aspirations. Compromise is part of living in the world as it now is.

Does this mean that there is no place for moral integrity in journalism? No, I am far from arguing that, having claimed that ethical journalism is as much a reality as industrial journalism. But of course ethical journalism is under pressure, as is ethics in almost any walk of life, because we live in a world dominated by economic considerations and an economy driven by market forces. Moral motivations and moral intentions are good, but they can be powerless in practice, or misled. They are powerless when the pressures of the system are too great for them to prevail against. They are misled when, for example, journalists find themselves justifying their unethical conduct in terms of their own unblemished intentions to do good, though employing dubious means. This is the doctrine of the double effect, and it is as fallacious in journalism as it is everywhere else.[12]

But fortunately it is not necessary to draw a totally pessimistic conclusion. In spite of all the pressures ethics is entrenched in journalism, and so it will never disappear completely. There is a tradition of truth-seeking, objective reporting and fair and reasonable presentation which is sufficient to challenge if not to defeat industrial journalism. There is also a tradition, though not one that is as strong as it should be, of reasoned discussion of such matters. It is an interesting coincidence that the same Martin Bell, shortly before his sudden transformation into a successful politician, was attracting media attention not because of his own work in the media but because of his theoretical discussion of some of the principles on which it was based. The point he was making was that there is not the conflict that many people assume must exist between objectivity in reporting and commitment to values, because journalists should not try to take a neutral stand between right and wrong. The war reporter in the world of today cannot avoid witnessing an appalling collection of atrocities, massacres, torture and other crimes, and must not pretend that these are neutral events of no moral significance. Such pretence involves a failure to be objective.

This is surely correct, and it illustrates some of the problems of ethical journalism. It is relatively easy for journalists based in liberal democratic countries to be objective about unsavoury military dictators in other parts of the world, but objectivity does not come so easily when the unsavoury character is your own boss. The case of Robert Maxwell demonstrates both the farcical and the tragic side of this. The sight of the sycophants of the living Maxwell intoning moral condemnations over his corpse was amusing for the uninvolved spectators but not for those whose pensions disappeared with Maxwell over the side of the boat.

But there is, I fear, no resolution of the contradiction, no solution to the paradox of industrial journalism co-existing with ethical journalism. Yes, good intentions are fine, but they can only operate within the existing system. But systems are rarely monolithic and thus they fail to be monopolistic. There is scope for good intentions, after all. But good intentions are not sufficient, as they need to be matched by corresponding good actions. This is why I put the emphasis on virtue in journalism, as virtue is a disposition to act in ethically correct ways, even in novel situations. And whatever the difficulties caused by co-existing with industrial journalism, there is still scope for the tradition of ethical journalism to live and develop.

Notes

1 See Judith Lichtenberg (ed.), *Democracy and the Mass Media* (Cambridge: Cambridge University Press, 1990).
2 For a wide-ranging discussion of the issues raised in this paragraph, see James Curran and Jean Seaton, *Power without Responsibility: The Press and Broadcasting in Britain*, 4th edn (London: Routledge, 1991).
3 The current state of business ethics is surveyed in Peter W. F. Davies (ed.), *Current Issues in Business Ethics* (London: Routledge, 1997).
4 See Sisela Bok, *Secrets: On the Ethics of Concealment and Revelation* (Oxford: Oxford University Press, 1982); and F. D. Schoeman (ed.), *Philosophical Dimensions of Privacy* (Cambridge: Cambridge University Press, 1984).
5 This is discussed further in my article 'Privacy, publicity and politics', in Andrew Belsey and Ruth Chadwick (eds), *Ethical Issues in Journalism and the Media* (London: Routledge, 1992), pp. 77–92.
6 See Bok, *Secrets*, pp. 249–64; and Jennifer Jackson, 'Honesty in investigative journalism', in Belsey and Chadwick, *Ethical Issues in Journalism*, pp. 93–111; and on the wider issues, Sisela Bok, *Lying: Moral Choice in Public and Private Life* (Brighton: Harvester, 1978).
7 Jonathan Glover provides an illuminating introduction to such moral issues in *Causing Death and Saving Lives* (Harmondsworth: Penguin Books, 1977). See also Richard Norman, *Ethics, Killing and War* (Cambridge: Cambridge University Press, 1995).
8 See Bok, *Secrets*, esp. p. 13.
9 Press Complaints Commission, *Code of Practice* (London, Press Complaints Commission, September 1994). There is an analysis of the PCC Code in Andrew Belsey and Ruth Chadwick, 'Ethics as a vehicle for media quality', *European Journal of Communication* 10 (1995), pp. 461–73. See also Nigel G. E. Harris, 'Codes of conduct for journalists', in Belsey and Chadwick, *Ethical Issues in Journalism*, pp. 62–76.

10 See Ruth Chadwick (ed.), *Ethics and the Professions* (Aldershot: Avebury, 1994).
11 This issue is discussed in Stephen Klaidman and Tom L. Beauchamp, *The Virtuous Journalist* (New York: Oxford University Press, 1987), esp. pp. 5–14. My thinking on ethics and journalism owes a great deal to the clarifications and insights of Klaidman and Beauchamp's book.
12 See Glover, *Causing Death and Saving Lives*, esp. pp. 86–91.

2 The journalism of attachment

Martin Bell

I write as a war reporter of some antiquity – that is, more than thirty years in the business, from the killing fields of Vietnam to the *barrios* of Nicaragua to the savage hills and valleys of central Bosnia. It was not a calling that I ever chose; rather, I would say that it chose me. One day a long time ago in a BBC newsroom, I happened to be the reporter nearest the door when a foreign war broke out. Having survived one war zone I would then be asked to take my chances in another – and then still more, until today I have discovered that a journalist can be typecast just as much as an actor. I am well on the wrong side of 55 and had wished to end my career with a stint as peace correspondent, if such a job were to exist; but sadly I have concluded that it does not. I even tried to resign, but was vigorously dissuaded.

Have the wars themselves changed? Hardly at all. The modern high-tech high-intensity conflict exemplified by the Gulf War was probably the exception. The Bosnian War was more typical; in it civilians were targeted on a massive scale and the weapons used were essentially those of the First World War battlefields: rifles, machine guns, mines, trench mortars and artillery. They were just as lethal: an old trench mortar can ruin your day just as effectively as a bright shining new cruise missile. Sometimes as I stood amid the mud and barbed wire of these wasted emplacements it seemed to me that we had learned nothing and forgotten everything, and that we were revisiting history all the way back to 1914, pausing only to fail to absorb the lessons of 1938. The only new ingredient was television.

But our way of reporting the wars has changed fundamentally, and not only because of television and its satellite dishes, those concave discs which we pitch almost on the front lines themselves and which uplink all our tragedies and bind us to them. Our attitudes and ways of working have also changed. When I started out as a war reporter in the mid-1960s I worked in the shadow of my distinguished predecessors and of a long and honourable BBC tradition of distance and detachment. I thought of it then as objective and necessary. I would now call it *bystanders' journalism*. It concerned itself more with the circumstances of wars – military forma- tions, tactics, strategies and weapons systems – than with the people who provoke them, the people who fight them and the people who suffer from them (by no means always the same categories of people).

I am no longer sure about the notion of objectivity, which seems to me now to be something of an illusion and a shibboleth. When I have reported from the war zones, or anywhere else, I have done so with all the fairness and impartiality I could muster, and a scrupulous attention to the facts, but using my eyes and ears and mind and accumulated experience, which are surely the very essence of the subjective.

This is not an argument for campaigning or crusading journalism. That has its place, from William Cobbett in the last century to G. K. Chesterton, George Orwell, John Pilger and many others in this, but its place is in political and polemical literature and not in the daily chronicling of the news. I am old-fashioned enough to insist on the distinction between them. Besides, it is my experience that the campaigners and crusaders tend to find what they are looking for, ignoring inconvenient evidence to the contrary and the unstructured complexity of what is actually out there. Rather, I have found it useful to do the opposite and seek out the unfavoured spokesmen of unpopular causes, whether the Afrikaners in South Africa, the loyalist paramilitaries in Northern Ireland, or the Serbs in Bosnia; they will often hold the key to a conflict and its possible resolution.

In place of the dispassionate practices of the past I now believe in what I call the *journalism of attachment*. By this I mean a journalism that cares as well as knows; that is aware of its responsibilities; that will not stand neutrally between good and evil, right and wrong, the victim and the oppressor. This is not to back one side or faction or people against another. It is to make the point that we in the press, and especially in television, which is its most powerful division, do not stand apart from the world. We are a part of it. We exercise a certain influence, and we have to know that. The influence may be for better or for worse, and we have to know that too.

In my one and only book, which was mainly about the Bosnian War and which touched on this issue, I cited a story from Sarajevo which I hope is apocryphal but I believe is not.[1] It was about a journalist who wished to write a profile of a front-line sniper. It did not matter on which side the sniper operated, because both sides had them and each feared the other's as much as it valued its own. The reporter made his arrangements with the man's commander and visited the front line. The sniper was peering out from between two bricks in his forward defences. The reporter asked, 'What do you see?' The sniper replied, 'I see two people walking in the street: which of them do you want me to shoot?' It was at this point that the reporter realised, too late, that he had embarked on a project which was inherently lethal and which he should not even have considered. So he urged the sniper to shoot neither of them, made his excuses and turned to leave. As he did so, he heard two shots of rapid fire from the position just behind him. He turned and looked, questioning. 'That was a pity,' said the sniper, 'you could have saved one of their lives.'

I use this example because, even at the level of theory or hypothesis, it disposes of the myth of the journalist as neutral observer and witness, the candle-holder who looks on. There are other instances which occur almost daily in the known, real world of war reporting. Which of us has not, during a tour of the trench lines in quieter times (which is when such facilities are usually offered), been asked by a soldier whether we would like him to blaze away, with rifle or machine-gun, for the camera's sole benefit? On one occasion an entire battery of 105 millimetre field guns would have been fired for my benefit, had I wished. To have accepted the offer would greatly have increased the marketability of what I had to offer my news editor later in the day. But the answer to all such invitations had to be a firm and principled 'No'.

Is that always the case? I somehow doubt it. I am fortunate in having worked for a news organisation, the BBC, in which – despite all its trials and travails – a culture of truthfulness still prevails, and which is not driven by the commercial imperative of maximising profits. (The interesting comparison here, not on the point of truthfulness but of profit-chasing, is with another great but troubled institution, Reuters.) The differences which have arisen between the BBC and myself, one of its foot soldiers in the trenches of news – differences on a range of issues from 'objective' reporting to rolling news to the censorship of real-world violence – are essentially a falling out between friends on matters of perspective rather than principle.

These are exactly the same differences that occur, on a field of battle, between an army's front-line soldiers and its staff officers. We see things that they do not see. We know things that they do not know. We have been where they have not. Yet they command and deploy us. This discrepancy of view is even greater in television, because of the technical advances in recent years that have so much extended its reach, if not its grasp. Our staff officers – the programme editors and network executives – are on the receiving end of such a flood of information both verbal and visual that they *think* they see and they *think* they know and they *think* that they have been there. The news itself takes on an aspect of virtual reality; it may be that the problem lies partly in the proliferation of computer screens, and in journalists whose eyes are directed downward at the screens in front of them, rather than outward at the wider world beyond. So the screens become screens also in the traditional sense, of blocking the view and filtering out the light.

The differences between us were brought home to me most forcefully in November 1996, when I attempted to explain my 'journalism of attachment' to an audience of television news people in Berlin. I was invited, not by the BBC but by my friends in German television, to take part in a session on the ethics of television journalism; I contributed a few brief, and moderate, remarks about the limits of objectivity. I was not in fact proposing anything new and revolutionary, although there were some present who saw it as that, but merely articulating a change in the practice of news reporting. I pointed out that the BBC's guidelines require its reporters to be objective and dispassionate. I am no longer sure what 'objective' means: I see nothing object-like in the relationship between the reporter and the event, but rather a human and dynamic interaction between them. As for 'dispassionate', it is not only impossible but inappropriate to be thus neutralised – I would even say *neutered* – at the scene of an atrocity or massacre, or most man-made calamities. I was not dispassionate at Ahmici in Bosnia in 1993, just as Jeremy Bowen was not at the bombed bunker in Baghdad in 1991, and for that matter even the great Richard Dimbleby himself was not at the liberation of Belsen in 1945 (and he was operating in a much more restrictive broadcasting climate).

There is a time to be passionate and a time to be dispassionate – a time and a season for all things; and I would not report the slaying of innocent people in the same tone and manner that I would use for a state visit or a flower show or an exchange of parliamentary insults.

It is a matter of common sense. It is also a matter of tone and tact rather than language, for television resists the flourishes of rhetoric and fine writing. It is a cool medium which answers best to understatement and requires the sparest of commentaries, especially alongside powerful and emotive pictures. Adjectives themselves are hardly necessary, since our images are our adjectives. Lately I have come to be merciless even with the verbs. The hardest technical discipline of all is the writing of silence.

I was in the process of explaining some of this to my colleagues in Berlin, when I was set upon from the floor by a middle-ranking BBC executive who clearly saw me as a heretic and backslider from long-established truths. He compared me to a priest who had grown weary of the long years of celibacy and had resolved to explore the carnal pleasures hitherto denied. (The term that he used was less felicitous, but executives do not necessarily rise through the ranks by having a way with words.) He then countered my argument for a principled journalism with the old and Shakespeare-derived notion of the function of news being to hold a mirror up to nature, or in this case to events in the world about us.

But the analogy is, of course, a false one. It is false for this reason, that the mirror does not affect what it reflects, the television image does. This is a clear and consequential distinction. One of its consequences is that journalism – not only in the war zones and amid human suffering, but perhaps especially there – is not a neutral and mechanical undertaking but in some sense a moral enterprise. It must be informed by an idea of right and wrong. It operates frequently on morally dangerous ground. It makes a difference. It has to be aware, as in the story of the reporter and the sniper, of what that difference might be.

I happen to believe – and I admit this to be a comforting, even convenient belief – that especially in the case of television the difference is mostly benign. I know there are critics who hold otherwise, and that in situations of incipient riot and civil commotion the very presence of television can be inflammatory. This certainly has been so on some occasions, though people tend to hold to their own realities. I remember a long time ago during a serious loyalist riot in East Belfast being approached by an old lady who bore down on me, with voice and umbrella raised, through a hail of missiles. She accused me of filming something that wasn't happening. She had her reality, I had mine: we were apparently not even witnesses of the same event.

But for most of the early 1990s I spent my working life in an environment rather less agreeable than civil commotion: the projectiles were harder edged and moving faster. I make no exaggerated claims here; but that time served in the war zones has left me with the settled conviction that the effect of television, even as its impact and influence have grown, has been to make things a little *less worse* than they would have been without it.

To take the simple example of prisoner exchanges: there was no deal between the three peoples and armies of Bosnia more likely to be undone, no business or transaction between them more fallible, than the handing over and retrieving of prisoners. It brought out their deepest dislike and distrust of each other, as well as a distinctively Balkan sense of the value of human life. So it was that at quite an early point in the war they came to insist on the presence of a foreign television crew at the handover point, as a means of holding each other to honour agreements already reached. Sometimes it worked and sometimes it didn't. But the television camera made failure less inevitable.

On a broader canvas, I would argue from experience that the presence of television in the satellite age makes war crimes harder to commit, and certainly harder to get away with than in the darker ages preceding it. This may seem a difficult case to make from a war which was waged with peculiar brutality and included the massacres at Srebrenica, Ahmici and Uzdol (only one of these, incidentally, involving the Serbs); but it was one of the many lessons of the Bosnian War that, in this decade of the dish, a military victory can swiftly turn into a political defeat. So it was with the Serbs. Their siege of Sarajevo held, and their enemies' attempts to break it were beaten back repeatedly and at terrible cost. But the killing and maiming of civilians, under the eye of the camera, left the Serbs friendless and isolated. The major bombardments of Sarajevo over a three and a half year period were viewed all over the world on the day that they happened. The counter-attacks, by Bosnian government forces, were either not viewed, or seen as acts of defence by a people cruelly besieged. The Serbs' case was lost in the court of world opinion before ever a war crimes tribunal was even mooted.

Of course in all such cases a tide of lies will wash over the airwaves; the perpetrators of war crimes will attempt to cover their tracks; and as television grows more consequential it will find itself increasingly blocked, cajoled and manipulated. But sooner or later the truth will come out, or a sufficient outline of it, as most notoriously it did many months after the massacre at Srebrenica. The war crimes will do most damage, over the long term, to those who commit them.

The same applies to the indiscriminate targeting of civilians; a point may actually have been reached where television is changing the conduct of wars and the ways in which they are waged. The British Army's staff college regularly introduces into its war games (the theoretical scenarios of future conflict) an element of media intrusion, in which an alliance's cohesion or an army's willingness to fight may be weakened by a public relations disaster: the bombing of an orphanage, perhaps, instead of an arms dump. 'Collateral damage' – as dreadful a euphemism as 'ethnic cleansing' – can now be decisive in a military campaign. This may be a heretical notion to introduce, but I have come to wonder whether, had satellite television existed in 1945, the carpet-bombing of Dresden and Hamburg by the British and Americans would have been politically possible; or would the tens of thousands of civilian casualties have turned allied opinion against the prosecution of the war by such ruthless means? Further back still, could the sacrificial strategies of the Battle of the Somme in 1916 even have been contemplated? They would be unthinkable today.

In our own time, much ink has been spilled on the relationship between television and diplomacy – the so-called 'CNN effect', which for reasons of regimental pride I should prefer to call the 'BBC effect'. That there is such a connection is now accepted by all but a few unreconstructed British diplomats of the old school. I remember an American colleague telling the story of President Bush's Chief of Staff, usually a man of meticulous punctuality, arriving late for his appointment with him; he explained that CNN had just screened some dramatic footage from Kurdistan, and the administration was therefore revising its policy towards the Kurds.

The British establishment tends to resent such pressures as an impudent challenge to its wisdom by an upstart medium. When Douglas Hurd was Foreign Secretary, he pointed out that murder, warfare and the forced migration of peoples were nothing new; they had always been with us. What was new was that, mainly through television, they were much more widely known than they had been before; and so politicians were challenged to take action on issues that were not of their choosing, and on priorities set by the box in the corner of the living room. Mr Hurd was rather scathing about the 'Something Must Be Done Club'.

He was speaking with the Bosnian example specifically in mind. I am, I suppose, a founder member of his 'Something Must Be Done Club'. I find the company I keep there more honourable, and easier to live with, than those who associate with the opposing faction, the 'Nothing Can Be Done Club'. Besides, I never openly advocated intervention in Bosnia (except once, and inferentially, with a parallel exposition of the risks). I did not need to. The images did it for me. But if, as a result of the television reporting from Bosnia, governments were moved to take action which they would not otherwise have taken, and people were helped who would not otherwise have been helped, I see nothing there for which we need apologise. For all the failures and retreats of the UN's involvement there, it probably saved a hundred thousand lives. Is anyone maintaining that those lives were not worth saving?

To me this is another case of television doing more good than harm. But since I am concerning myself here with the moral ground on which it operates, I will add a note of warning about a tendency which, if it persists, could do more harm than good. I am not referring here to the ratings-driven downmarket drift of the news agenda, especially on the commercial and satellite channels, although that is troubling enough. I mean the representation of real-world violence.

It is a long-running argument. What we should show and what we should not show are issues that cause more difficulty to a television reporter in a war zone than any others, except getting access in the first place. I have even wondered, occasionally, whether it isn't easier to deal with the warlords than the editors. At least I am face to face with the warlords and understand them; we are sharing the same slivovitz. The editors are a thousand miles away; they are cautiously determined not to cause offence; we are negotiating about raw footage that I have seen and they have not, and working to guidelines that are vague and variable.

I find myself at one end of this argument, and usually standing alone. I do not believe that we should show everything that we see. Some images of violence – as for instance most of the pictures of both the market-place massacres in Sarajevo – are almost literally unviewable and cannot be inflicted on the public. But people have to be left with *some* sense of what happened, if only through the inclusion of pictures sufficiently powerful at least to hint at the horror of those excluded. To do otherwise is to present war as a relatively cost-free enterprise and an acceptable way of settling differences, a one-sided game that soldiers play in which they are seen shooting but never suffering. The camera shows the outgoing ordnance, but seldom the incoming.

This actually connects with the sort of world in which the old-style 'dispassionate' war reporter could ply his craft quite comfortably. No need to be unflinching, because nothing is left in the coverage that he has to flinch from. No need to be compassionate, because nothing is left in that he has to care about. What remains? Neither evil nor suffering nor bloodshed nor grief, nor anything from the darker shores of the human condition – but just a passing show, an acceptable spectacle.

The argument is more one of degree than of principle. But I believe that we have retreated too far, certainly in British television – practices vary from country to country and network to network – and that a measure of course-correction is now in order. We should flinch less. We should sometimes be willing to shock and to disturb. We should show the world more nearly as we find it, without the anaesthetic of a good-taste censorship. And if we do not, then perhaps we should ask ourselves whether we are merely being considerate, or *indifferent*. And in a world where genocide has returned in recent years to haunt three continents we should remind ourselves that this crime against humanity requires accomplices: not only the hatred that makes it happen, but *the indifference that lets it happen.*

I have a friend, a Bosnian soldier who spent more time in Bosnia than any other, who chides me for having let the Bosnian War get at me too much. 'There you go again,' he says when he sees me at work, 'bleeding all over your typewriter.' (Yes, I still use a typewriter: it keeps me honest.) Maybe he is right. It is certainly easier to take the reporter out of the war zone than the war zone out of the reporter. But the soldiers themselves have also been deeply affected by what they have seen there, and are not less effective as soldiers because of it. We, and they, are battle-softened veterans of a foreign war.

These are issues which seem to me to deserve more attention than they commonly receive. Should we really be expected, in the most powerful news medium ever devised, to be indifferent to its consequences? Is objectivity even possible? Should it be one of our imperatives not to upset people? What do we believe in? What in the end is our vaunted technology *for*? And what is the justification for a disengaged journalism which would requires its practitioners, as special people with special privileges, to close their hearts to pity?

This is a phrase with a certain historical resonance. There was in this century a military commander who urged his generals to do just that – to close their hearts to pity. He enjoyed a measure of success for a while. His name was Adolf Hitler.

Note

1 Martin Bell, *In Harm's Way: Reflections of a War Zone Thug* (London: Hamish Hamilton, 1995).

3 Objectivity, impartiality and good journalism

Matthew Kieran

Introduction

It is a commonplace assumption of journalism that the media have a fundamental duty to be impartial in order to achieve the goal of an objective report or analysis of current events. Of course, certain kinds of feature journalism or polemical programming do not have such a duty but I am unconcerned with those here. Rather, my focus is upon news reports, investigative journalism or current affairs programmes. This supposed duty, to impartiality and objectivity, arises from conceiving of the media as an unofficial fourth estate.[1] One of the functions the media must fulfil is to report and evaluate, appropriately, events that affect our lives as members of society. Hence, for example, the media must inform us about significant political matters, criminal proceedings, social affairs, corruption and vicious hypocrisy. Thus, in covering such matters appropriately, it seems to follow that the media must be impartial in their approach in order to arrive at and report upon what is, in fact, the case. This explains precisely why, above all else, journalists prize their reputation for impartiality. To accuse a journalist of being biased is to impugn his journalistic integrity in the deepest possible sense. For it is to claim that a journalist is, intentionally or otherwise, not adhering to the truth-respecting methods required for him to achieve the proper goal of journalism: arriving at the truth of the matter. Hence when Nick Robinson, a BBC political correspondent, heard rumours that media managers in the Labour Party were whispering that he had his own political motives and agenda his response was the following: 'I've had ten years as a journalist in the BBC and nobody's ever accused me of bias and if they do I'll pursue it.'[2]

However, it has become increasingly fashionable, within cultural, media and even journalistic studies, to dismiss claims concerning objectivity. Infamously, at the time of the Gulf War, Baudrillard claimed that the war was only a media event.[3] In a similar vein Glasser claims that journalists striving for objectivity rely, falsely, upon a 'naively empirical view of the world, a belief in the separation of facts and values, a belief in the existence of *a* reality – the reality of empirical facts.'[4] Of course, construed in one sense, such claims are clearly false. There are facts of the matter which can be faithfully reported. The Gulf War did happen and any report which claimed it didn't is obviously false. However, we can construe the claim in a more interesting fashion. The basic thought is that news events inevitably give rise to a number of different legitimate reports which are not reducible to one underlying complete and consistent report. This is because news reports rest upon commitments to fundamental moral, social and political principles. Yet these principles are not themselves open to dispute but are presumed to be inaccessible to critical questioning.[5] One could hold to this claim on the grounds that fundamental beliefs are ideological and thus determined by the socio-economic structure or discourse we are implicated within. I believe this presumption to be typically false but will not examine it here.[6] A more interesting argument which might underwrite such a position can be derived from the work of Richard Rorty. The basic thought is that since our most fundamental beliefs and values are contingent, they are not amenable to rational justification:

> As long as we think that there is some relation called 'fitting the world' . . . which can be possessed or lacked by vocabularies-as-wholes, we shall continue the traditional philosophical search for a criterion to tell us which vocabularies have this desirable feature. But if we could ever become reconciled to the idea that most of reality is indifferent to our descriptions of it . . . then we should at last have assimilated what was true in the Romantic idea that truth is made rather than found, and that truth is a property of linguistic entities, of sentences.[7]

The subjectivity of interpretation

News is essentially value-laden. Given that journalists bring to bear their fundamental value assumptions in making a report, any event is open to innumerable redescriptions in different terms. Thus it is pointless to seek rational justification in order to privilege one news report over any other. For, the claim is, description is interpretation-laden and interpretation itself is evaluatively driven. Any given event is open to many possible interpretations which are appropriate given different kinds of evaluative concerns and commitments. So journalists who claim to search for 'the right' description, interpretation and evaluation of states of affairs are, on such a view, misguided and misleading. Much of the force of the critique of objectivity derives, in relation to media analysis, from the way it apparently captures the nature of journalism's pre-reflective practice. For over different newspapers, broadcast bulletins, individual journalists and the time-span of a story we seem to end up with divergent reports of the same event. The nature of an event, it is claimed, partly depends upon those who interpret it.

Consider, further, the following example. When the ceasefire in Northern Ireland was announced on 30 August 1994, there was obviously a huge demand for stories about the ceasefire that would symbolise the incipient hopes for the peace process. On the day itself Crispin Rodwell, a photographer acting for Reuters, was asked to get an image to go with the hopeful news. He spent some time traversing Belfast and came upon a freshly painted slogan, 'Time for Peace, Time to Go.' So he started photographing the slogan whilst people walked by. Whilst he was doing so a young boy started playing brick-a-bat against the wall, which he managed to capture on film (see Figure). He then sent a batch of the photographs through to Reuters, including one of the boy in front of the slogan. Now, importantly, Rodwell cropped the photograph so that the second half of the slogan, 'Time to Go', did not appear. Reuters's executive editor rang Rodwell to check that the photograph had not been artificially set up in some way, for example by paying for the slogan to be painted. Once satisfied that this was not the case, Reuters syndicated the photograph around the world and it was the predominant image used on the front pages of most British newspapers to go with the story about the ceasefire.

Now, of course, however one interprets the image and its use, certain low-level descriptions of what the photograph is of are true. The slogan had been painted on the wall and the boy had played brick-a-bat against it.

Figure

But, we might think, such low-level descriptions can be interpreted and evaluated in rather different ways. Thus journalists generally are not so much after *the* rational assessment and report of a story but, rather, different ways of interpreting and evaluating the same event in ways in which the relevant audience will find appropriate.

The point is that, as Rodwell and the Reuters executive editor presumably knew, 'Time for Peace, Time to Go' is an oft-used Irish Republican slogan. It is, in such a context, tantamount to writing 'Brits Out'. The slogan effectively asserts British troops should withdraw from Northern Ireland if there is to be peace. But through the cropping of the image and its subsequent use, next to headlines announcing the ceasefire, the same slogan came to symbolise the hopes, both in the province and Britain, that the ceasefire would lead to permanent peace. The very same slogan, depending on the use to which it is put, seems to give rise to different interpretations and evaluations. On this view, it is not the case that one interpretation is 'the' right one. For both interpretations can appeal to objective features of the image and basic beliefs or evaluative commitments. Rather its meaning seems to depend upon its use and the context it is placed within. The meaning of the image, and of events generally, so it is claimed, depend upon how they are framed by the interpretative and evaluative commitments of those who are reporting upon it.

It is important to recognise the exact claim being made here. One should not confuse it with a far weaker epistemic claim: namely that though there is a truth of the matter, over how an event should be interpreted and evaluated, we might not know what that truth is. For example, in the Bosnian War many claims and counter-claims were made about massacres by both sides. But the media were often not able to find out whether they really had happened or not. But, reasonably enough, you might think, we presume there is a truth of the matter; there either was or was not a massacre at Srebrenica. Similarly, we might be unable to determine whether increasing violence on television bears a causal relationship to increasing violence in society. This may be because there are so many other factors, variables and multiple causes that research will never be able to prove the matter one way or the other. Yet we might presume that there is a truth of the matter, it's just that we cannot determine what it is.

But the critique of objectivity involves a much stronger claim. Obviously events are significantly independent of us, so certain low-level descriptions are true of them. But, the claim is, how we should interpret the image or event, and construe its significance, depends upon the categories, interpretative framework and evaluative commitments we bring to bear upon it. Thus the meaning of Rodwell's photograph depends upon the conceptual context and framework it is placed within. Of course, we can still evaluate the different possible interpretations and evaluations in terms of their consistency, coherence and adequacy to the low-level descriptions. But where interpretations differ, because of different basic beliefs and evaluative commitments, there is no resolvable dispute.

The subjectivity of evaluation

Such disputes are irresolvable because there is no morally neutral stance from which the distinct sets of basic commitments can be impartially weighed up and evaluated. Hence when there are contradictions in news media coverage that run down to the foundational level they are irresolvable. So (according to Rorty), once we recognise 'that anything can be made to look good or bad by being redescribed' we should renunciate 'the attempt to formulate criteria of choice between final vocabularies' and must perforce become committed ironists.[8] We should, on this view, recognise that 'the truth of the matter' is relativised to the basic commitments involved.

On such a view we should not be surprised that news media reports often diverge over both how certain facts and which facts are salient. Consider, although it is not clear cut, the US media coverage of the O. J. Simpson trial. Apart from the shift of focus in media attention due to the ebb and flow of the legal process, there were striking differences in the coverage of the trial, depending on who reported it. The mainstream media concentrated on the circumstances of Simpson's initial arrest, whether he had received favourable treatment because of his star status and what the circumstantial evidence was. Conversely, the black media focused upon possible racial angles to the case and whether Simpson had been set up because of his colour and star status. By contrast, the women's press made much of the allegations of wife beating and abuse by Simpson of Nicole Brown. It would seem, then, that the same event affords a plurality of different possible legitimate news reports which cannot be meaningfully contrasted with one another in terms of some higher-order interpretative principle. For the radical divergence in news reports merely reflects something fundamental about the basic interests and values concerned.

If the critique of objectivity is sound then it obviously has fundamental consequences for the nature and practices of news reporting. Journalism proper aims at the appropriate description and interpretation of current events. Hence a journalist's news report should aim to persuade the audience that his or her description and interpretation is the rational and appropriate one. But given that what constitutes appropriateness is, on this view, relativised to fundamental beliefs and evaluative commitments, we cannot distinguish between reasons as causes of belief change and other non-rational causes. Although we can distinguish between rational and non-rational forms of persuasion relative to our foundational commitments, ultimately which beliefs and values we assent to is a contingent matter. Hence a Rortian journalist would be someone who fulfils three conditions: (1) she has radical and continuing doubts about the final vocabulary she currently uses, because she has been impressed by other vocabularies, vocabularies taken as final by people or books she has encountered; (2) she realizes that argument phrased in her present vocabulary can neither underwrite nor dissolve these doubts; (3) in so far as she philosophizes about her situation, she does not think that her vocabulary is closer to reality than others.[9]

Rortian journalists who recognise the contingent nature of their fundamental values and vocabularies are committed to the claim that ultimately the distinction between good and bad news coverage, like the commitments it depends on, is contingent, wholly arbitrary and thus an illusion. Hence they cannot be committed to conveying 'the' truth about world affairs but only deeply sceptical about the validity of any news report, including their own. To condemn a particular news report as shoddy, irrelevant or inappropriate would only serve to point out that we do not share the news values being addressed rather than to claim there is a fundamental mismatch between the report and the actual nature of the event being covered. For all reports, on this picture, are necessarily contingent and biased. Thus if objectivity is, as a matter of principle, impossible then the news media can't in any meaningful sense have a duty to be objective.

Objective constraints upon interpretation

However, though the critique of objectivity may seem plausible there is good reason to think it flawed. Let us return to Rodwell's photograph of the slogan 'Time for Peace, Time to Go'. Pre-reflectively we might well ask why we should presume that just because the media have used it in a certain way that it is appropriate to do so. After all, if the slogan was intended to have a certain meaning, and was publicly understood to have that meaning in the relevant context, then surely to present it as if it had a different meaning is surely to misrepresent it. I remember reading, when I was younger, *Bright Lights Big City*, a novel by Jay McInerney about New York yuppies, literary sets and their cosmopolitan nightlife. Throughout the novel the central character made various detours to the restroom in several clubs. I thought it highly civilised that clubs in New York had rooms where people could go and rest, away from all the noise of the music, chat and take their drugs. But it was only years later when I actually went to the United States and found myself wandering around the airport looking for the toilet that I finally realised that 'restroom' actually meant 'toilet'. The point here is that though the words in the novel could give rise to the interpretation I had given them, this is only because I did not have the relevant background knowledge. Had I possessed the relevant background knowledge I would not have misconstrued the semantic meaning of the word. Similarly, readers who interpreted the slogan in Rodwell's photograph as concerning the ceasefire lacked the relevant background information about what the slogan was intended to and taken to mean. The slogan's meaning is not altered, but rather misrepresented, by the new context and use to which it is put. Meaning is not straightforwardly reducible to use. For we can misuse and misinterpret the meaning of something, whether because we lack an understanding of the appropriate context or because we misunderstand the publicly governed rules which determine how a concept or term ought to be applied.

Of course, there is something to the thought that what the image is expressive of is determined by its context and use. Even though the slogan itself clearly means 'Brits out', nonetheless the image of the boy playing brick-a-bat against the phrase 'Time for Peace' does seem to express the hopes many had for the peace process at that time. But it is crucial to note the difference between something's meaning and what it can be used to be expressive of. Clearly such use in and of itself does not change the meaning of the slogan. But the image of the slogan was adapted to reflect the hopes of the newspapers' readers. Before an after-dinner speech in January 1994, John Major had his head in his hands in order to think out his speech in verse. The correct interpretation of what John Major was doing concerns what his intentions in acting thus were. But the photographs of him in this pose were used by the media to express the general perception that both he and his government were in trouble. Representations of events can be used to express general perceptions, hopes and fears. But, used as such, the image should not necessarily be understood as an interpretation and evaluation of the nature of the event it is of. To construe the use of Rodwell's photograph as conveying the meaning of the slogan is to misunderstand what it's being used for. The slogan's meaning, and the appropriate interpretation of it, is an objective matter in the sense that one can be mistaken or misrepresent it. Indeed, one might think that had such images as 'Time for Peace, Time to Go' not been used so prolifically in the way they were at the time of the ceasefire, and had people understood that the photograph was merely expressive rather than relaying what was actually meant, then the British public would not have been so naïve about the prospects for the ceasefire.

The Rorty critique of objectivity falsely reduces all journalism to the status of propaganda. But propaganda is a perversion of journalism proper. Propaganda, as can be seen from the history of journalism in the old USSR, covers events in terms of assumed basic commitments and values which are not considered open to critical revision.[10] Hence even when a propaganda report is true it does not constitute good journalism because truth is conceived of merely as a contingent means for the promotion of the presumed basic commitments. A propagandist need not be a liar but cannot be, as journalists should be, committed to truth-respecting methods. The idea that what is true is somehow constituted out of the news report itself naturally and viciously lends itself to thinking of all news as exercises in rhetoric: it is only a question of whose rhetoric is, ultimately, more powerful. Whichever type of news coverage wins out will, according to Rorty, effectively remake reality in its own image: a chilling thought reminiscent of George Orwell's *Nineteen Eighty-four.*

But the thought is only chilling precisely because what people may be told and come to believe can, *pace* Rorty, come apart from what is actually the case. The fact that, in *Nineteen Eighty-four,* the chocolate ration is reported to have gone up does not make it so. Commonsensically we do draw a distinction between good and bad news reports on a rational basis in a non-arbitrary manner. For our understanding of the news media as committed to reporting the truth entails a distinction between non-rational means of persuasion and rational ones. The fact that there may be fundamental differences between news reports driven by distinct beliefs and values does not entail that the resultant reports are equally sound. Of course, different news reports might focus upon different aspects of a story because they are addressed to different concerns and audiences. But even news reports that speak to different concerns ought to cover the central aspects of an event which make it a news story. Hence we can and do sometimes criticise news reports for failing to focus upon the central facts and issues of a story whilst distracting readers with peripheral features. That there may be distinct emphases in news reports and analyses of events shows at most that news stories may legitimately speak to the distinct social concerns of different groups. The Rorty critique of objectivity is inherently flawed because it fails to allow for the possibility of misinterpreting an event (and thus precludes the possibility of much substantial media criticism).

Objective contraints upon evaluation

Conflicts in news reporting usually occur because there are differences in judgement as to what really constitutes a news story, how a story should best be covered and what the public ought to have their attention drawn to. The end of journalism itself, relaying the news about events that affect and concern the public, is hardly disputed and it is unsurprising that differences in coverage reflect differences in social values and commitments. But none of the news media involved, including the most radical ones, will dispute that what they are after is the appropriate description and analysis of the news story. Only by recognising the goal internal to journalism can we make sense of the claim that certain reports might be mistaken or inadequate in focus or tone.

What must be emphasised is that there are facts and features of an event which are independent of the reporting of them and the foundational commitments involved. Hence any report must attempt to take account of the facts about the events they are seeking to cover. News reports are diagnostic, in that they seek to identify the essence of the story and possible underlying causes, and prescriptive, in that they suggest what the significance of the event is and even sometimes how such an event might be prevented again. Of course, some events may only be construed as news given a certain agenda or be news by virtue of the news media's role. But it doesn't follow from this that news coverage is wholly determined by foundational values in a way that is immune to critical analysis. The standards by which we assess the value of a news report concerns adequacy to the facts and the cognitive virtues of rational coherence, plausibility and explanatory value.

Returning to coverage of the Simpson trial, the different reports should be conceived either as emphasising distinct aspects of the case or, if each asserts that its report is the appropriate and complete description, in direct conflict. Thus black media reports, whilst dwelling on the strain of racial issues running through the case, need not deny or occlude the central question of Simpson's guilt or innocence. However, where reports do conflict each is committed to the claim that the others are inadequate to the facts, misconceived or biased. Such conflicts are, in principle, testable by adducing the known facts and evidence for the report, the reliability of sources, the consistency, coherence and plausibility of the reasoning involved. Hence the responsibility of journalists to make clear their attribution of sources, provide evidence for their report, make clear the reasoning involved, relevant background beliefs and the possible motives of key players. Then the public has a clear basis for judging for themselves whether the report appears to be objective, i.e. it relies upon an impartial evaluation of the facts and bears the mark of an appropriate description of the events concerned.

The core features of a news story which should structure the journalist's report are fixed (let us number these features F1 . . . F12). A news report, and the claims made within it, are assessable as true or false by drawing on the chronology of events, the motives and nature of the characters involved, source attribution, the historical background and the norms and wider beliefs implicit in the report. Hence we can and do make sense of the claim that reports can be mistaken. Thus the radical diversity of news reports concerning the same event is merely apparent. Indeed, it is striking that news reports of most events, as distinct from feature articles, hardly diverge at all except in atypical cases such as the Simpson trial. Monism in news reporting is the rule rather than the exception. A thorough news report, unhindered by exigencies of time, production constraints and different audience interests, would explain the diversity of the news coverage in terms of a fundamental comprehensive report.

Of course, this still allows for different possible reports as legitimate. For we might be interested in distinct aspects of the same story, say the racial issues in the Simpson case (F1 . . . F4), which constitute only a cluster of the story's features. But although the emphasis and tone of different legitimate reports may be distinct, as in the news coverage of

the Simpson case, nonetheless they may all be correct in some respect.
They may be true regarding what is covered but fail to refer to other
relevant aspects of a story, say questions of Simpson's actual guilt or
innocence, the wife beating angle or his true character (F5 . . . F12),
hence they are incomplete. Such incomplete reports can be combined, as
a matter of principle, into one single complete report. Thus, in principle at
least, we could capture the single correct interpretative framework which
fits a news story in a way which would include the specification of the
distinct aspects open to the journalist to focus on in making his report.
The plurality of different correct reports of a story are the upshot of
incomplete reports which can be subsumed under a minimal, empirically
grounded, coherent and comprehensive report. Thus the different legitimate reports are, essentially, not different interpretations at all but incomplete sketches of the correct report.

It is important to emphasise that I am not claiming that a clear appre-
hension of the facts of the matter are necessarily sufficient to yield the
correct interpretation and evaluation of the relevant states of affairs. Given
that our understanding is necessarily mediated by our interpretative and
evaluative frameworks the facts of the matter underdetermine the correct
report. However, we clearly can and should critically examine the relevant
facts, our considered judgements concerning them and our general principles of interpretation and evaluation. For our construal of the facts,
judgements and even general principles of interpretation and evaluation
may be inconsistent or incoherent. In applying our principles of interpretation and evaluation we can symbiotically examine our judgements and
assessments in the light of each other. The process of reflective equilibrium
enables us to strive for a position where our considered judgements and
assessment cohere with our considered principles of interpretation and
evaluation.[11] Where this is so the report will be able to explain what the
relevant facts are and their relationship to one another in a consistent,
coherent and explanatory manner. Indeed, such a process should be able to
help the reporter explain why alternative possible assessments may be in
error. Now it may be true that even having gone through such a process
convergence on the same report has not been achieved. But this is merely to
recognise that objectivity does not necessarily guarantee convergence. It
may be that given all the relevant facts and critical reflection the event may
legitimately admit of more than one possible evaluation which, on their
own terms, are equally consistent, coherent and explanatory. Hence reasonable disagreement can still arise. Nonetheless, a strong degree of
objectivity still pertains to both reports and, moreover, the possibility of
one correct report remains. It is just that the correct and complete report
would specify both those alternative assessments which are reasonable and
rationally grounded.

This is not to say that journalists must always capture the complete
story in their report or even always aim to do so. For the nature of

journalism, in getting information about events out quickly, is necessarily a time- and production-bound business. We cannot expect anything other than rough sketches of history. But it is crucial that we do not confuse the pragmatic constraints on arriving at an understanding of the truth of an event with the false claim Rorty would have us believe, that there is in essence no truth to be had. This claim leads dangerously close to conflating fact and fiction: something which would only serve the interests of governments, public figures, business men and those in positions of power and influence with something to hide.

True, as Rorty points out, we cannot reason from nowhere. But the fact that we must reason from somewhere does not entail that foundational beliefs and journalistic reports are unamenable to rational assessment. At any given time certain beliefs and presumptions must be taken as given, otherwise journalistic practice could not get going and news reports would be interminably long and tedious. But these presumptions and beliefs are open to examination in the light of other beliefs and values we hold, hence reason can lead to a change both in fundamental commitments and the way a news story is being covered. Hence the news media in the USA during the Vietnam War came to reassess and modify their evaluative commitments, leading to a shift in coverage from the uncritical acceptance of US policy to often downright hostile news reporting.[12] Closer to home the shift in the way the bovine spongiform encephalitis scandal has been covered in the mid-1990s provides an interesting example of how, in the light of increasing evidence and critical reflection, journalists shifted from dismissing warnings about human contamination as the allegations of cranks to talking of a credible potential disaster. Seeking consistency, coherence, simplicity and informative explanations in news reports may have to start from somewhere, but it does not follow that the implicit beliefs and values are immune to critical revision.

Objectivity, impartiality and good journalism

This is not to claim that the questions at issue are simple or easily resolvable. For example, only late in the Simpson case did it become obvious to many that the racial strand to the story was very important indeed. Yet it is a feature of news events that they are highly complex. But this is due to the messy nature of human reality and not to some putative incompatibility between the basic values and commitments implicit in different news agendas. In other words we may not be able to know in some cases which of the conflicting reports is the most accurate and we may remain ignorant about relevant facts. But this is an epistemological matter, a question of whether we can find out what is the case, and does not touch the point that there is a truth of the matter which journalists properly aim at.

Of course, there may be fundamental disagreements in how to cover a story. For example should, in covering the Gulf War, reporters have worked with the military pool groups or, like Robert Fisk, worked independently? Journalists have different techniques, strategies and methods of uncovering stories and, if nothing else, they are driven by commitments to both the means and ends of their journalism. Similarly, at the broader institutional level, the in-depth coverage of politics by the worthy broadsheets and the tabloid concentration upon the rich and famous reflect different emphases. Yet although journalists must bring to bear their own understanding, assumptions and values in reporting an event, it does not follow that there are radically different correct interpretations of the world. Take the *Sunday Times* report about Michael Foot's alleged spying activities.[13] What the *Sunday Times* 'discovered' was that Michael Foot had met a KGB agent and spied for the USSR. Obviously the natural interests, agenda and prejudices of the *Sunday Times* were driving the reporters' perception of the facts they had available. But we do not think that the actions of Michael Foot in this regard are open to a plurality of interpretations. Rather, we recognise that the facts of the case – how he was approached, how he acted, what his motives were – determine which of the ways in which his actions should be construed. In journalism, as distinct from fiction, there is a truth of the matter and this is what objectivity in journalism aims at. Thus how a journalist reports a news story may come apart from what the story actually is. Hence it is not just illegitimate but immoral to reconstrue news events merely because a journalist's prejudices, interests or news agenda suggests things should be otherwise. So, in the Michael Foot case, we should condemn the *Sunday Times* not just for being mistaken but for, at best, only carelessly respecting the journalistic practices that aim at objectivity, and for allowing their own assumptions and thirst for a good story to override the proper journalistic goal of aiming at the truth. It is precisely because we can and should understand journalism as aiming toward an objective report upon states of affairs, and thus what we have good reason to believe, that we can criticise the news media where this goal is clearly not aimed at or where a report fails to realise this goal through carelessness or lack of critical assessment.

Of course, in recognising distinct aspects of journalism's internal goal we should not lose sight of the idea that there are different means of informing the public about their concerns and interests. This is why, in some ways, the craft of journalism is akin to an art rather than a science. Nonetheless, like science, journalism as a practice aims at truth and it is relative to this fundamental aim that we classify news reports as good or bad. Good journalism aims at discovering and promoting the audience's understanding of an event via truth-promoting methods. This is, indeed, why impartiality is important. For a journalist must aim to be impartial in his considered judgements as to the appropriate assessment of particular events, agents' intentions, why they came about and their actual or potential significance. A failure of impartiality in journalism is a failure to respect one of the methods required in order to fulfil the goal of journalism: getting at the truth of the matter.

Conversely, bad journalism is truth-indifferent and fails to respect truth-promoting practices. Whether the *Sunday Times*'s Michael Foot story was bad journalism depends not just upon its falsity but whether claims concerning their poor research and methodology are sound. If speculation was treated as fact, if their research and methodology were poor, then truth-promoting methods were abandoned and the truth was not sought. Honesty, discipline and impartiality are required to be a good journalist. The danger of taking Rorty's critique of objectivity to heart is not just an abstract one, but very real. Where reporting turns away from the goal of truth and journalists treat events as open to many interpretations, according to their prejudices, assumptions, news agenda or the commercial drive toward entertainment, the justification and self-confessed rationale of journalism threatens to disappear. The intelligibility and rationality of the practices and activities of news journalists themselves depend upon recognising journalism's internal goal, informing the public about significant events in the world, and this goal requires journalists to strive to be impartial and thus objective.

Notes

1 See, for example, Matthew Kieran, *Media Ethics: A Philosophical Approach* (Westport, CT: Praeger, 1997), ch. 2, and John Locke's *A Letter Concerning Toleration* (New York: Prometheus, 1990) where he stresses that citizens need to know how they are being governed in order to judge the actions of those who exercise power on their behalf.

2 Quote taken from a 1996 BBC *Panorama* programme on political spin-doctors and the media.

3 Jean Baudrillard, 'The Reality Gulf', *Guardian*, 11 January 1991.

4 Theodore L. Glasser, 'Objectivity and news bias', in Elliot D. Cohen (ed.) *Philosophical Issues in Journalism* (New York: Oxford University Press, 1992), p. 183.

5 See, for example, Richard Rorty, *Contingency, Irony and Solidarity* (Cambridge: Cambridge University Press, 1989), Paul Ricoeur, *Hermeneutics and the Human Sciences*, trans. J. B. Thompson (Cambridge: Cambridge University Press, 1981), Gaye Tuchman, *Making News: A Study in the Construction of Reality* (New York: Free Press, 1978), Andrew Edgar, 'Objectivity, bias and truth', in A. Belsey and R. Chadwick (eds) *Ethical Issues in Journalism and the Media* (London: Routledge, 1992), pp. 112–29, and John Fiske, *Media Matters* (Minneapolis, MN: University of Minnesota Press, 1994), pp. 125–90.

6 For arguments against the ideological construal of this claim see Matthew Kieran, 'News reporting and the ideological presumption', *Journal of Communication*, 47/2 (1997), pp. 79–96.

7 Rorty, *Contingency, Irony and Solidarity*, pp. 6–7.

8 ibid., p. 73.

9 ibid.

10 See Brian McNair, *Glasnost, Perestroika and the Soviet Media* (London: Routledge, 1991).
11 John Rawls, *A Theory of Justice* (Oxford: Oxford University Press, 1972), pp. 48–51.
12 See Stanley Karnow, *Vietnam: A History* (New York: Viking Press, 1983).
13 'KGB: Michael Foot was our agent', *Sunday Times*, 19 February 1995, for which Foot was eventually awarded substantial damages and received a printed apology from the paper.

4 The problem of humbug

Mary Midgley

The pleasures of denunciation

Cynicism has its own morality. Cynics are moralists as much as the rest of us, indeed they can often be heard being quite self-righteous. What cynics feel righteous about is the need to expose hypocrisy: to point out yawning gaps between our ideals and our practice. It is no trouble finding those gaps; they open up almost everywhere. Since most reformers are human beings, they can usually be convicted of inconsistency. Sooner or later, they can be caught tolerating things which should not really be tolerated, things which may be every bit as bad as the evils they are attacking.

Thus, in the early nineteenth century, people in Britain who campaigned to abolish black slavery in the USA were attacked as hypocrites for picking on this particular evil while ignoring others which might be worse. Defenders of slavery, such as Carlyle, asked why the abolitionists didn't occupy themselves with the evils of industrial slavery nearer home. In the same way, more recently, during the era of apartheid, spokesmen for the South African government used to point out that people in countries that criticised them were themselves allowing inhumane practices in their own territories. They asked why the critics did not attend to their own business and clean up their own backyards.

This kind of counter-attack has a real point. But some tricky principles are involved. The obvious conclusion is that outsiders who attack a bad practice are hypocrites unless they are above reproach themselves. This seems rather too simple. The objection to casting first stones is strong and genuine, but it is not quite right for this kind of case.

Jesus, when he made his point about stone-casting, was talking about the status that is needed if one is to *punish* people for past offences.[1] People prepared to do this need to be irreproachable and indeed properly authorised. But if we demanded the same kind of status before allowing people to make protests about ongoing evils such as slavery and apartheid we would make such protests impossible. In practice, hardly anybody has hands clean enough for completely satisfactory stone-casting.

The question is, how central do we want to make this issue of hypocrisy in our moral spectrum? It does not usually follow the simple pattern displayed by classic literary hypocrites like Tartuffe[2] and Mr Pecksniff.[3] These straightforward plotting villains exist but they are relatively rare. The pervasive problem of everyday hypocrisy is not exemplified in such extreme characters but, rather, arises from the appalling mixedness of our ordinary human nature.

One can see how tempting it is for journalists, and the media generally, to assume that hypocrisy really is a simple and straightforward matter which should always be exposed. The stereotypical picture of a hypocrite is one who professes to do something for an honourable, publicly declared motive while really doing it from a disreputable hidden one. So any possible extra motive can be pounced on for exposure. Thus, as Raymond Snoddy points out, the suspicion of such a motive led the *Mail on Sunday* to feel justified in publishing a quite irrelevant story about Peter Bottomley's sexual inclinations after he had tried to help a social worker.[4]

Much of the news agenda, from political interviewing to investigative journalism, concentrates on suspicions of this kind. It is supposed to be motivated by a stern drive to expose hypocrisy. By a curious coincidence, however, it seldom explores the whole range of possible outside motives, which might really be quite interesting. Instead, it focuses pretty steadily on a few exciting private motives, chiefly sex. In the last few years, for instance, much of this kind of attention has been directed against Prince Charles's marriage. His critics have contrasted the shortcomings of his private life with the (often impressive) views that he expresses on public matters. Wasn't this barrage of accusation itself somewhat hypocritical?

The obvious way to test this would be to ask the journalists involved – and still more the proprietors of their papers – whether they would be willing to have the details of their own private life exposed to the public over many years with the same thoroughness and the same venom. And would they (incidentally) expect a marriage to survive well in such circumstances? The usual reply to this query is that people in powerful positions must expect to endure more public scrutiny than the rest of us. But newspaper proprietors certainly wield more real power today than the heir to a constitutional monarchy. And clearly, the kind of scrutiny that is appropriate for power should concern, not private life, but matters directly relevant to public affairs on which that power is deployed.

The mixedness of motives

The interesting thing about this whole argument is that the defenders of intrusive journalism evidently see the exposure of this supposed kind of hypocrisy as a general justification for all their activities. They take it that all our actions, from the best to the worst, have multiple sources. We never act from one motive alone. That is why such charges can never be disproved. If we did insist on having rulers who were moved only by patriotic motives, we would need to wait a long time to find them. And if we ever did find them, they might well be so unlike the people whom they govern that they would find their job unintelligible.

As things are, then, we know that practically nobody manages to summon up the perseverance needed for success in any profession – let alone one as bruising as politics – without the help of outside motives which don't appear on its work-specification. The commonest and most obvious of these motives are ambition, pugnacity and sociability of particular kinds, such as a fancy for drinking in particular bars. But there are always a heap of others as well. Non-political motives are bound to direct people's interests, playing some part in the choice of particular policies to support. There is absolutely nothing wrong with this so long as their owner keeps checking these motives steadily to see that they correspond with duty to the public. All this, naturally, applies in journalism too.

It surely is true, then, that in politics practically no individual, however idealistic, is faultless and certainly no country is so. All nations and all groups either tolerate some injustice and oppression within them or at least draw advantages from the practices abroad, advantages such as cheap food and cheap labour – 'guest-workers' and so on. Even when reformers do confine themselves to their own backyards, trying to improve things within their own nation, they still meet the same sort of difficulty. If they want to get anything done they have to find someone to work with. They can hardly ever choose their allies. They also have to concentrate their fire, selecting certain causes and turning their backs on others. They cannot deal with all ongoing needs at once. So they must turn a blind eye to some of the evils around them and accept some colleagues of whom they bitterly disapprove. Biographies of even the most thorny and scrupulous reformers, such as Mill and Gandhi, illustrate this painful necessity.

Strachey's crusade

Does this mean that, since we are all miserable sinners, none of us is ever in a position to express outrage and shout that things ought to be made better? This is surely not a sensible proposition. But there is a genuine conflict here. We need both to be honest about admitting how bad things actually are and also to give due credit to the efforts that are being made to make them better. This often means praising imperfect people and denouncing people who are by no means wholly odious. Indeed it can sometimes mean denouncing and praising the very same people.

This conflict is a real problem for journalists, and there are lots of forces at present pushing them towards simplifying things by sneering at everybody. This is not just because scandals sell better than eulogies. On top of that, we all have a tendency to feel that portraits *ought* really to be as dark as possible, with plenty of warts. There is a sense that there's something wrong and embarrassing about a wart-free nose, about praising anything or anyone at all strongly. This fashion set in when Lytton Strachey reversed the conventions of biography, ruling that discreditable facts about public figures should normally take precedence over creditable ones. Putting it crudely, Strachey's idea – much influenced by his reading of Freud – was that disreputable qualities always underlie good ones and represent a deeper truth. In general, therefore, the more enlightened and intelligent one is, the worse one's opinion will be of one's fellow human beings – however admirable their actual conduct may be.

In theory, Strachey's innovation was meant chiefly as a counter-balance to its opposite. It was meant to complete the picture, balancing whole shelves-full of biographies that had been straightforward eulogies by putting in the shadow-side. But, like many projects that aim at balance, it didn't work out that way. Post-Stracheyan biographies and biographical articles in magazines have tended *not* to form a balanced picture. Instead they substitute one kind of simplification for another. They concentrate attention on people's faults and weaknesses to the point where their exhausted readers sometimes begin to wonder why these particular people's lives were ever worth writing about.

More generally, our whole journalistic culture has been skewed this way, focusing on people's failures and weaknesses of character without the concomitant drive to understand why they have these faults, what the context is, and how they link up with their strengths and virtues. Sometimes a whole profession is guyed in this way. For instance, the genuinely absurd remarks that stupid judges sometimes make get generalised into a dismissive stereotype for the whole profession.

The immediate reaction to these particular remarks is appropriate enough. But the phenomenon is limited. We must have judges, and if we write them off wholesale because of such scandals we deprive them of the respect which is necessary to make their difficult work possible at all. Clearly, the kind of pedantry and narrowness which causes these scandals are the sorts of faults which, in human beings, do tend to go with the sort of quiet care, persistence and learning which judges need. And, so far at least, all our judges are human beings. Of course this kind of expectedness does not excuse the faults. But it means that they don't call for the astonished denunciations of the whole profession.

Pioneers, projects and personalities

This over-personal, melodramatic writing may well be useful in making us more aware of bad motives, which is a genuinely important topic. But the price of this insight has surely been a difficulty in being realistic about good ones. It imposes a narrowness, a distorted emphasis which blocks a wider understanding of how human projects work. Of course everybody is grossly imperfect, but some of these imperfect people – both past and present – manage to think up projects that are hugely valuable to the rest of us. In the case of biography, if we want to know about these people at all, we do so primarily because we want to know how they managed to do these surprising things, what was the thinking behind the feats that roused our curiosity in the first place. Initially, we need to see them simply as part of that project, in a role to which their faults and weaknesses are irrelevant for much of the time.

In relation to today's press and media, this need is especially strong when the project is still continuing. People who want to understand a new and honourable movement need to see it personified, crystallised in the figures of those who lead it. This is not a demand for a lie but for relevant selection. The natural human tendency to look for examples to follow is not hypocritical. It is just a simplification, a concentration on crucial achievements which leaves other, less relevant details in the background.

Concentration of that kind certainly can easily result in the build-up of mythical, heroic figures such as those whom Strachey debunked, figures such as Florence Nightingale and Gladstone, or more recently Gandhi, Einstein, Albert Schweitzer, Freud himself. Strachey hoped that, by smashing these icons, he could dispel the myth that surrounded them, revealing the naked truth behind it. But naked truths are harder to find than that. This approach surely displayed an extraordinary short-sightedness about both the power and the usefulness of myths. What it actually managed to do was simply generate a new myth centring on a new set of stereotyped figures, an imaginary bunch of naïve Victorian hypocrites.

By stressing the faults of the reformers Strachey made it look as if these people had been quite exceptionally crude and obtuse, bizarrely short of self-knowledge. He made it seem that they had belonged to an inferior tribe morally, an extinct species of alien pre-Freudian moralists who were really of no interest to enlightened thinkers in the Modern Scientific Age, because modern thinkers no longer go in for self-deception. Thus Strachey's story gave great force to the wider myth that the twentieth century itself was an entirely fresh start, the cannibalistic myth of 'modernity' which so grossly distorted thought early in that century, the myth which is now finally being castigated under the name of modernism.

This simplified, monolithic, debunking approach is a part of that self-consciously 'modern' tradition, a part which still persists to a surprising extent today. Many people still have a quite disproportionate terror that they will be guilty of hypocrisy if they are caught out approving of anything or anybody. They feel that their prime business ought always to be to look for the faults in any public person or enterprise and, when they have found them, to denounce the whole as a sham.

A striking example of this was the bizarre front-page story that the *Sunday Times* ran in 1995 accusing Michael Foot of having worked for the KGB.[5] Not surprisingly, this had to be hastily and completely retracted when he at once made it clear that he had only met a KGB operative in Moscow, something that had happened to virtually every prominent politician who visited the city at that time. More generally, however, almost all political interviewers fall into a ludicrous habit of interviewing people as if they were detectives grilling suspects at the scene of a crime, instead of trying to find out what these people actually mean and think. Readers and listeners have to endure constant repetitions of familiar charges and equally familiar rebuttals while the interviewer desperately tries to winkle out some secret crime.

The place of idealisation

This attitude surely operates with a quite unreal notion of the moral scene. It assumes that public figures must be black if they are not pure white, whereas we know very well that most people and most movements are parti-coloured, brownish or piebald. If we treat people who are leading a movement with respect, that does not have to mean that we are taken in and believe them to be perfect. We know that the picture which shows these people as idealised figures is selective. It is a symbolic simplification. But we still stick with it when we can because it saves us from wasting time on personal criticisms which are simply not relevant to the main project.

At the end of the last century, Parnell lost his career, and Ireland lost a precious chance of relief from its oppressions, because of an adultery that had absolutely nothing to do with the political issues that he stood for. Would we be able to avoid this mistake today? Suppose that, when the negotiations for the new South Africa hung in the balance, Mandela or de Klerk had been subjected to this sort of allegation, could it have been put aside and ignored? Surely it should have been, yet it is not clear that it could. Today's journalistic conventions make such ignoring very hard. Yet these conventions do change. Lloyd George's sex life enjoyed remarkable immunity. At the other end of the scale, Greek and Roman statesmen used to accuse each other of every possible sexual abomination so loudly and habitually that the public presumably took no notice of such charges at all. Our present difficulty is that we combine an unbridled interest in these personal matters with a determined pretence that public figures live lives far purer than the rest of us are ever expected to.

Where do we want to place ourselves on this wide spectrum? Morally speaking, people are always mixed. But – to mention a truism – since the officially acknowledged good side of them which involves their declared ideals, aims and projects is often of special importance for the rest of us, there is always a reason for taking those good intentions seriously for a start, a reason to give them credit for genuineness initially, before starting to suspect their faults. This is even more obviously true of societies and nations than it is of individuals, because societies are even more obviously bound to be morally mixed and full of conflicts.

When a whole society is accused of hypocrisy – like nineteenth-century Britain in the case of slavery or prostitution – the main point usually is that some of its members are still committing the crime while others are denouncing it. In that case there is not much point in personifying the whole nation as one enormous hypocrite, an outsize Tartuffe or Pecksniff. Personification encourages fantasies of a personal vendetta that can only be satisfied by total destruction. It generates indulgence in self-righteousness of a kind which blinds one to the relevant details.

It is also possible, of course, that the rest of the citizens are in a confused, self-deceiving state which they need to clear up. It can then be quite useful for outsiders to point out this unevenness and to demand more consistency. They can indeed sometimes do this by accusing them of hypocrisy, or of some more general form of humbug. In the case of slavery it was certainly also reasonable to tell people who were campaigning against it abroad to do something about the form of it that they were countenancing at home.

How far is consistency possible?

The kind of consistency which involves a realistic sense of priorities in matters like these is indeed important. Sometimes, relatively trivial moral issues do seem to absorb a quite disproportionate amount of public attention. For instance, it is surely reasonable to ask the people who now campaign against abortion as the most serious moral problem of the age whether they really consider it a worse evil than the deliberate manufacture and sale of land-mines, which not only kill far more innocent people at a more crucial stage of their lives but also mutilate many and make great areas of land useless to survivors. If, then, one is 'pro-life', should one not treat it as the worse evil of the two? Similarly, the kind of intense indignation that is felt against the use of drugs is usually not extended to the over-prescribing of tranquillisers and anti-depressants, nor to alcohol and tobacco.

In such cases, the temptation is always to confine one's indignation to exciting things done by groups other than one's own, without asking how these activities rank in the whole range of evils which one might be able to object to. And because, in a fast-changing age, the shape of this larger range is inclined to shift, sticking to these established targets does make moralising much easier. Undoubtedly we ought to resist this seductive kind of inconsistency. We should struggle to get our priorities clear. Yet it is surely not to be expected that we could ever reach complete consistency here.

What would it be like to have a policy which followed completely consistent and defensible priorities? Could we find one which never left us open to the charge of fiddling while Rome burns or of Pharisaically picking on our neighbours while ignoring our own crimes? In order to do this we would need a carefully researched chart of all the currently pressing evils with their relative urgency and closeness to our own responsibilities duly assessed and placed in order. Presumably we would then work steadily outwards from the nearest and most urgent ones towards those further off, making sure at each stage that our own hands were clean on each point before we dared to criticise our neighbours.

No doubt there would be a lot to be said for this kind of self-discipline and it would certainly provide a living for plenty of hungry researchers. But it would surely mean that it was a long time before we got round to shouting about Tibet or Nigeria. By contrast, what we actually do is to respond simultaneously and somewhat unpredictably to certain ongoing scandals which happen to strike us as being horrible beyond what we are prepared to tolerate. This kind of selective response is now expressed in the idea of *human rights* – the idea that, never mind the enormous differences between the various earthly cultures, there are some things which should not be done anywhere to anybody.[6]

Though some academics worry about the use of the civic, legalistic word 'rights' here, I think that, at the everyday level, most people today accept it, not only in the Enlightenment-driven West but all over the world. Oppressed peoples appeal to it, not, I think, merely using it as a foreign language but as a kind of genuinely universal moral concept. This is surely good. But the need to select such cases lays on journalists a great responsibility, which many of them feel profoundly, for telling us about these things so that we may have the chance of exploding constructively.

What, me?

When we do explode, the governments accused always feel injured and say that we don't understand their circumstances. And, as many cases that have come before the European Court have shown, British governments are no exception. Nobody likes being accused by outsiders, and if the outsiders were perfect they wouldn't actually like it any better than they do today when (as they often complain) their accusers are not perfect at all. At present, of course, Europhobia intensifies this habitual prickliness in Britain to an absurd degree, as is evident over the BSE (bovine spongiform encephalitis) scandal of 1996. (It is indeed increasingly clear that BSE might as well have meant Blame Someone Else.) Yet this kind of accusation is absolutely necessary. Between nations as between individuals, there do have to be charges brought and the local conscience cannot possibly be trusted to bring them. In the case of nations it is specially vital that outsiders – however imperfect – should sometimes take up this role because culpable governments can so easily suppress their internal critics.

Clean hands among these accusers do indeed make the charge far more telling, and dirty ones beyond a certain point can destroy its political force. But, strictly speaking, counter-accusations about the state of accusers' hands are never a defence against the original charge. The validity of an accusation does not depend on the accusers' merits, and is certainly not destroyed by suspicion about their motives. The only proper reply to accusations is to answer them directly. This is what makes the constant nagging exchange of counter-accusations between political parties so inexcusably irrelevant and exasperating. There is, moreover, no reason why the press and other news media should let themselves become involved in these games. They are there to examine the actual issues, the policies and the nature of their impact on ordinary members of the public. If they discuss any new proposal without reference to this kind of impact, treating it simply as a ploy used by one party to attack the other, they are neglecting this primary duty completely.

Priority trouble

What, however, about the matter of fiddling while Rome burns? We cannot, of course, dismiss complaints about relatively minor abuses as humbug on the ground that these things are trivial compared with worse ones. The fact that an abortion is not a land-mine does not show that it does not matter at all. The difficulty is to get one's priorities right in each kind of case. It is interesting that the charge of triviality is often made against those who campaign on behalf of animals. How (their critics ask) can you devote time and money to this matter while so many human beings are suffering?

Thus people often cite the mid-nineteenth-century case where an American mother was prosecuted for grave cruelty to her child, but the prosecution had to be brought under a recently passed law forbidding cruelty to animals, since the child was being treated in a way that this act made illegal for an animal. What a scandal (people say) that animals were protected before children! In fact the situation here was rather different. The position was that children had indeed had plenty of legal protection before that time, but there was a loophole in it. The existing law had not licensed the prosecution of *parents* for cruelty, since it mistakenly regarded them wholly as their children's protectors. After this case, that loophole was of course closed. Animals, however, had had no protection at all before the law in question had been passed and continued to have very little after it.

This is one of many cases in which people tend to exaggerate what is actually done for animals because they have not quite decided whether they are prepared to attend to them at all. There are, for instance, quite often complaints about the collection of money by animal charities. At present these charities take around 2 per cent of the total subscribed to charitable causes in Britain. Is that total too high? If so, what ought it to be? Point seven? One point three? Can anybody give a reasoned answer? Here again, objectors seem to operate with the idea of an ideal chart which would list the causes we could subscribe to in strict order of priority.

Sometimes, when I contemplate the bewildering flood of appeals that I receive from various causes, I wish there was indeed such a list. Would I do better if I picked out one – Oxfam, Amnesty or Greenpeace – and threw all the rest away? Doing this does save time and stamps, but it doesn't solve the problem. Unfortunately, the idea of a single order of urgency is not workable. There are a thousand *kinds* of things that need doing. And if we all picked out one of them as the most urgent this week and worked to support it, we might make it less urgent. Should we all then turn over to something different?

Here again, what we actually do is somewhat idiosyncratic and arbitrary, but not unworkable. We tend to specialise. Some of us devote ourselves thoroughly to particular causes, usually not because we have checked that nothing else is more urgent, but simply on the positive grounds that we can see the importance of this one. And as supporters we similarly attach ourselves more or less lastingly to particular projects.

That kind of attachment has the crucial advantage of giving these organisations the kind of continuity without which they cannot work at all. A more spasmodic, chronically critical approach would make effective campaigning impossible. Without covenants and bankers' orders, charities would have to spend their entire time trying to raise funds for the next day's work. This network of habits does have the disadvantage of making it hard for new causes to get started and for existing ones to change direction, which is a serious nuisance in a fast-changing world. It can also sometimes lock people into obsessions with things that are genuinely trivial. But the idea of replacing it by a scientifically-calculated table of priorities is a non-starter.

Consistency and shame

The point here is that we should be wary of assuming that the press and news media ought to conform to a single scale of news values, as if one could lexically order stories according to their significance. Some philosophers, such as Rawls and the Utilitarians, have tried to formalise significance by this kind of calculus, but after a very rough beginning their formulae always run into the sand. There really are many kinds of things that we are and ought to be interested in and know about. Perhaps one of the troubles with the news media is its excessive concentration on narrowly political matters. As most of us recognise, many issues and events are of central importance to people in ways that are not directly related to politics at all.

Altogether then, it does not make much sense to dismiss pronouncements as humbug either on the grounds that they are not consistent with that ideal priority system or that they are being made by people whose own lives don't fully live up to them. There is surely something particularly odd about the suggestion that mere inconsistency between the accusers' theory and practice could invalidate accusations. If consistency here were all that mattered, they could easily produce it by simply dropping their attempt at reform. It is not difficult to be a consistent scoundrel or a whole-hearted lump of apathy.

People who are attacking hypocrisy sometimes do talk as though this kind of consistency were indeed all that they were after, as though they would be satisfied if (for instance) the slave-owners or other oppressors simply dropped their pretensions to be morally respectable. This would, as moralists sometimes say, make them 'at least honest'. But this kind of honesty scarcely seems to be worth much. The attackers' real target in these cases is of course not that kind of honesty but its opposite. They want to close the yawning gap between theory and practice upwards, not downwards. Their cry is not really 'Why don't you profess what you are doing?' but 'Why don't you do what you profess?'

The interesting thing here is what gives protest its foothold in this inconsistency between theory and practice, that is, humbug, which is therefore, in a strange way, a necessary stage in the process of reform. This is what people mean by saying that hypocrisy is the tribute which vice pays to virtue.[7] If we try to imagine what a society would be like that was totally unpretentious morally – a society which really had no ideals that were any higher than its actual practice – we shall probably find it hard to make any sense of the possibility. Even the Mafia, for instance, has quite demanding standards. Similarly immoralism, as Nietzsche conceived it, is a most exacting way of life.[8] Because human impulses continually conflict, any sort of workable existence has to involve priorities among its standards and aims which lie far beyond its present practice.

Ideals and practice are, in fact, always some way apart, even among people whose ideals are quite unpretentious. They are linked by a longish piece of elastic on which we can pull in either direction, upwards or downwards. The tension is usually quite strong because there is a genuine wish not to be totally inconsistent. People who pull downwards, trying to lower the ideals, are not necessarily cynics. They may still be idealists themselves. (Nietzsche did a good deal of it.) As we have just seen, these down-pullers may be aiming at honesty, though they don't always make it clear why honesty should be thought so important when other, larger ideals are dropped. Or these people may think that some of the current ideals really are misconceived. But very often the pull is intended to work upwards by shaming the majority into greater efforts towards aims that it already acknowledges, and into acknowledging further ones which it hasn't yet admitted.

This process of progressive shaming can be clearly seen at present over our concern for and reporting of environmental issues. Since the 1960s or 1970s we have reached an extreme stage of rampant hypocrisy about this, a stage where even the crustiest of unrepentant sinners has to give the matter lip-service, and where the gap between this talk and practice sometimes seems to be immeasurable. All the same, there is some strength in the elastic. Some things do get done; how effectively, we shall see in the next few decades. Meanwhile the smell of humbug sometimes does become almost intolerable. But if we had skipped this hypocritical stage, it's not clear how we would ever have got started at all.

Conclusion

I have been trying to understand a bit more fully the respectable motives that can bring people near to cynicism. Because cynicism itself is paralysing, I think it may be important to sort out the sensible parts of these motives from the unworkable bits. I have suggested that Strachey's revolution in biography has taught us a habit of rather mindless denigration, which current conventions in our news media tend to pander to and encourage. This habit did have a point, but it has become so habitual as to be fairly meaningless. I want to counter the still-persisting sense that there is something hypocritical in straightforward praise – the embarrassment about articulating ideals – the fear of seeming naïve if one says the morally obvious.

I am sometimes struck by the situation in which someone British is too embarrassed to make what is plainly the right and appropriate moral comment on a particular situation while someone American does it directly and without self-consciousness. Journalism is always open to these temptations, because anyone who has to write something in a hurry, from a school-child to an overworked leader-writer, always finds it easier to grouse than to grasp the real problem. But the moral fashion that made this approach seem positively laudable is surely about due for retirement.

Notes

1 John 8: 7.
2 In Molière's play of that name.
3 In Charles Dickens's *Martin Chuzzlewit*.
4 Raymond Snoddy, *The Good, the Bad and the Unacceptable* (London: Faber, 1992), pp. 1–8.
5 *Sunday Times*, 19 February 1995.
6 On this crucial and difficult subject see Timothy Dunne and Nicholas Wheeler (eds), *Human Rights, Human Wrongs* (Cambridge: Cambridge University Press, 1997) and Ken Booth, 'Human wrongs and international relations', *International Affairs* 71/1 (1995), pp. 103–26.
7 Duc de La Rochefoucauld, *Maxims and Moral Reflections* (Letchworth: Arden Press, 1910), p. 233.
8 See, for instance, Nietzsche's *Beyond Good and Evil*, p. 226: 'We immoralists! . . . we are spun into a strict network and hairshirt of duties; we cannot get out. In this we are men of duty, even we.' Compare p. 228, 'Isn't moralizing . . . immoral?' and his *Ecce Homo*, ch. 6, on the fierce difficulties that face Zarathustra.

5 Journalism, politics and public relations
An ethical appraisal

Brian McNair

Introduction

At the end of the twentieth century the citizens of western democracies have access to more information about politics than at any previous time in human history. Journalistic media proliferate, and politics is high on their agenda. Politicians are acutely aware of this, and work hard to influence public opinion through those media. A supporting network of professional communicators strives to ensure that political messages are accurately and widely disseminated, in the face of a journalistic profession which becomes more aware of, and resistant to, such efforts by the year.

Through print, television and radio, with mass access to digital broadcasting and the Internet now imminent, we – the electorate, to whom all this communicative activity is ultimately directed – have access to a continuous flow of political information in all its forms – news, current affairs, debate shows, phone-ins, commentaries, satirical comedy – from early in the morning until late at night.

Are we then, as a consequence, more knowledgeable about politics, and thus more powerful as citizens (assuming that Francis Bacon was right and knowledge is still power) than ever before? Or are we merely passive witnesses of a media spectacle beyond our control, in which the quantity of information communicated is high, but its quality as a resource in opinion-forming and political decision-making is low?

In posing the question in these terms we enter a debate which is not new, but which has acquired new urgency as the sheer quantity of political communication in circulation increases, and the debate about its effects on the democratic process intensifies. In both Britain and the United States in recent years the role of political communication in electoral victory and defeat has been crucial. Quantifying that role is difficult, but it is beyond dispute that effective political communication played a large part in saving Bill Clinton's second term, and that it greatly helped the British Labour Party to its first government in eighteen years.

If few would challenge the underlying truth of these observations, many are concerned about their implications for the conduct of democratic politics. Three general concerns are voiced:

- first, that the style and content of political journalism is not, as it should be, supplying the citizenry with useful information, but on the contrary is actually obstructing the communication of political messages;
- second, that political actors no longer formulate their policies on grounds of principle and rational argument, but do so in consideration of the perceived need to 'play well' in the media, and to please 'public opinion', itself often argued to be largely a media creation;
- and third, that the communicative work of both journalists and politicians has become distorted by the influence of what Edward Bernays in 1923 called 'press counsellors', and who are better known today as 'spindoctors', 'communications advisers', 'media consultants' or 'PR gurus'.

Taken together, it is argued, these developments have undermined the integrity of the public sphere, and rendered the late twentieth century's apparent participation of the masses in the democratic process illusory. Worse, they have encouraged mass apathy and growing non-participation in politics, as exemplified by the American case[1]. Such criticisms identify three groups of actors whose communicative ethics we should be concerned with:

- the politicians, in and out of government, for whom information flows are important power resources;
- the journalists who monitor, report, scrutinise and analyse the politicians' actions and rhetoric;
- and the group occupying a place in the communicative process somewhere between the first two: the aforementioned public relations advisers and spin-doctors.

Political communication is, to a large extent, both the process and the result of interaction and negotiation between these groups, each of which has its own ethical codes, defined in relation to the normative principles of liberal democracy. Politicians in a democracy are supposed to communicate (professionally, at least) for the purpose of ensuring good government, presenting citizens with political choices, laying claim to political power, and informing citizens honestly and openly about the administration of government.

The public relations practitioner (whether in the guise of lobbyist, spin-doctor, or Whitehall press officer) aspires to facilitate the effective communication of a message from a political actor to a wider public, in most cases through the media, since these are the channels through which the vast majority of people receive their political information. He or she also communicates in the other direction, lobbying politicians on behalf of organisational clients such as companies, trade unions and single-issue pressure groups. Because the public relations industry (including its political wing) is young (very much a twentieth-century phenomenon) it has developed ethical codes and practices which are designed to enhance its status and prestige as a *profession*, and thus to legitimise its existence as a necessary and worthwhile element of the contemporary media environment. The deliberate telling of lies on behalf of a client, for example, is not regarded as ethical.

Journalists, finally, are considered a key source of the information on which the integrity of the public sphere depends. But they are also expected to monitor the political environment on the citizens' behalf, and keep a watchful eye out for the abuse of power. This has been their 'fourth estate' role since the time of Edmund Burke.

These roles and functions are, of course, ideals. They describe things as they should be, and not necessarily as they are. But they are ideals taken seriously by all three professional groups, and reflected in standards of communicative behaviour which we as citizens are entitled to see applied, even if imperfectly. When they are not, then the democratic condition of an authentic public sphere, supported by rational information flows, through channels open and accessible to all, is called into question. This essay assesses the form and content of contemporary political communication from the perspective of the politician, the public relations professional, and the journalist respectively, in the context of the ethical standards which they have set themselves, and of the ongoing debate about these issues which so occupies academic and professional observers at the present time.[2]

Communicating politics

We begin with the politicians, since it is they who stand at the apex of the communicative pyramid, and compete most aggressively for the prizes awarded in the game of democratic politics. They do so, at this point in capitalism's evolution, in a uniquely public way, subject to the approval of a genuinely mass electorate. It is, after all, only eighty or so years since women were excluded from this electorate, and not too long before that, that men without the approved wealth and education qualifications were also deprived of the vote. Now, regardless of class, sex, ethnic or religious background, all are equal in the privacy of the polling booth. Politicians must compete for our support, using the channels of mass communication at the centre of our cultural lives to project their ideas, values and policies. To the extent that politicians require public support political communication is largely about publicity. Where feudal lords (and their contemporary counterparts in China, Iraq and elsewhere) imposed their will on powerless subjects, politicians who claim to be democratic leaders must win popular consent, and be seen to have won it. They must have *legitimacy*, or they cannot govern.

There are two stages to winning legitimacy. One is to be seen and heard in the public sphere, by securing a requisite *quantity* of media coverage. As one observer notes, 'the struggle for visibility is at the centre of all politics'.[3] Civil servants and party functionaries prefer anonymity and secrecy, but the ambitious politician must be seen and heard, if the highest reaches of office are to be his or hers.

As many politicians know to their cost, however, not all publicity is good publicity. A second stage in winning democratic legitimacy in today's political environment is to secure *qualitatively* favourable coverage, which accentuates the positive and downplays negative features of a politician's or a party's public identity. This fact has led politicians to develop increasingly sophisticated means of managing the media so as to secure such coverage. In the process, argue the critics, the communication activity of politicians has become artificial, manipulative, even deceitful. The rational content of political discourse has been subordinated to the needs of public opinion management.

Jurgen Habermas's framing of the argument continues to be influential. For Habermas, 'publicity' as we understand the term today is the harmful by-product of democratic politicians' perceived need for favourable media visibility. Because *favourable* publicity is desired, the presentation of information tends to be selective and dishonest. As he puts it, 'publicity work is aimed at strengthening the prestige of one's own position without making the matter on which a compromise is to be achieved itself a topic of public discussion' (1988, p. 200). Publicity seeks to divert the attentions of the public from critical debate about the real business of politics (the issues), and towards passive consumption of symbols (personality and style). If publicity is, in normative terms, the process of informing the public on important matters, in current conditions of mass mediatised politics it has lost its educative and critical functions. Through publicity 'arguments are transmuted into symbols to which one does not respond by arguing but only by identifying with them' (p. 206). Political decisions are made 'for manipulative purposes and are introduced with consummate propagandistic skill as publicity vehicles into a public sphere manufactured for show' (p. 221).

Habermas wrote these words in the 1960s, but recent events lend support to his central argument. Bill Clinton's political resurrrection and eventual victory in the presidential election of November 1996 was the result not least of his highly public, highly visible abandoning of some hitherto cherished policies, and the adoption of others previously associated with the US right. As Clinton's communications adviser Dick Morris (1996) boasts in his account of the Clinton first term, this 'positioning' of the president in a place somewhere between traditional notions of left and right was done deliberately to attract voters, a strategy which – despite Whitewater, Hillarygate, 'Slick Willie' and all the other personal scandals which afflicted his first-term administration –

was successful, if measured by the proportion of votes cast. Clinton's ideological principles and instincts were sacrificed to the greater goal of retaining political power, much to the anger of ordinary Democratic party members who, despite their pleasure at the prospect of a second Clinton term, accused him of betrayal of the causes on which he had first been elected in 1992.

In Britain, similar accusations have been made of the Labour Party since the election of Tony Blair as leader in 1994. Here, too, it is alleged that political principles have been sacrificed in the pursuit of power; that policy has been formulated and communicated with an eye on public opinion rather than what is right for the country; that 'New Labour' is all style and no substance, masking what amounts to a historic betrayal of British socialism and of the British working classes. The fact that New Labour won a General Election in 1997 does not invalidate the criticisms of those who hold such views, nor mollify their feelings of betrayal since, they would argue, a left-of-centre party in power without a principled approach to government is hardly a better prospect than another Conservative term of office.

Elsewhere I have argued that criticisms of this type are naïve, betraying a romanticised, patronising view of both the social democratic left (which has by definition never been 'socialist' in any theoretically rigorous sense) and the working classes, who have consistently rejected 'authentic' socialist policies and who, on the contrary, have sustained right-wing governments in Britain for most of the century (McNair 1995, 1996). Intepretations of policy aside, however, can the politicians who have led these 'betrayals' be fairly accused of unethical behaviour in their ever more managed and calculated approach to the communication of their messages?

An answer to this question can only be given on the basis of specific circumstances. If politicians, in the content of their communication, knowingly deceive the electorate, then we are certainly entitled to criticise their ethical standards. When politicians, in government or opposition, lie about their motives, ambitions and decisions; when they suppress information which the public has a right to receive; when they 'leak' aggressively and unfairly against opponents and colleagues, they are behaving unethically, and there have been instances of all three in recent British history, on all parts of the party political spectrum. If, on the other hand, they are simply using the available repertoire of communicative techniques and instruments to project ideas which may deviate from traditional norms, but which are a sincere response to changed political and socio-economic circumstances, then the charge of ethical violation seems excessive. No individual politician, or party, can be blamed for the fact that considerations of image and style are today as important to political success as the detail of policy, and none can be blamed for participating enthusiastically in 'the game' as it is now played. On the contrary, failure to do so, in the manner of the Labour Party before the arrival of Peter Mandelson as communications director in the mid-1980s, might be viewed as a greater evil, since it deprives the electorate of meaningful choice and makes minority government more sustainable. Commentator Anna Coote, para-phrasing the French sociologist Pierre Bourdieu, points out that

> as traditional differences between left and right break down, so the notion of faith [in politicians] becomes increasingly important: what matters to voters is not what politicians promise, or even what they stand for, but whether they can be trusted. That, in turn, depends on the personality of the politician and the character of the relationship with the voter. These are expressed largely by means of image and style.[4]

Greater emphasis on 'image and style' is, in short, the price of mass democracy in a late capitalist, post-Cold-War environment, whether one likes it or not.

Managing political communication: the ethics of political public relations

Whether politicians are ethical or not, the design and execution of their media performances are increasingly delegated to professional advisers and consultants: specialists in political public relations, marketing, lob-bying and advertising who are employed, usually behind the scenes, to advise on and manage the communication process. The names of the best-known members of this profession – George Stephanopoulos, James Carville, Dick Wirthlin and Dick Morris in the United States; Brendan Bruce, Tim Bell, Peter Mandelson, Alistair Campbell in Britain – have become, for their critics, emblems of the ethical decline in political life, and generated a major sub-genre of political journalism devoted to the discussion of their alleged crimes. These include manip-ulation and intimidation of the media to advance the politicians' pub-licity goals, pressurising politicians to denude themselves of principle and integrity in deference to presentational gloss and, in the worst cases, of usurping the place of the politician and becoming major political players in themselves. The worst offenders in this regard are said to be the 'spin-doctors', a new breed of communicator who does not facilitate the flow of political information (a long-standing and respected function ideally carried out in a disinterested manner by civil service functionaries and other 'apolitical' staff) so much as 'doctor' it for media, and then public consumption. Journalist Simon Heffer contrasts the more traditional function of press officer with that of the spin-doctor in the following terms:

> The press officer, even if he was a party rather than a government employee, would mainly concern himself with the provision of facts and background information . . . The spin doctor is concerned mainly

with spin. His role goes beyond the facts; it is to outline to journalists exactly what he feels the thrust of their story should be; it is to persuade them to accentuate the positive and ignore or at least play down the negative.[5]

The term was imported from the United States in the 1980s, and has since come to be used as a form of mild abuse, surrounding those to whom it is applied with a slightly sinister air of magic and mystery. Spin-doctors seek to manipulate press coverage by controlling access to senior politicians and, in particular, denying it to journalists who do not seem amenable to the 'persuasion' mentioned by Heffer. Their main weapon is aggressive lobbying, accompanied by punitive action against dissenting journalists. They are often accused of being arrogant and overbearing. Columnist Iain MacWhirter complains that the 'media minders cruise the lobbies these days like celebrities. No longer are they the servants of the press, whose function it is to get the party message across as clearly and as widely as possible. They now regard themselves as players in their own right'.[6] Labour's Peter Mandelson and Alistair Campbell have been the most frequently attacked in these terms, most famously in relation to the fax sent to the BBC newsroom when the verdict of the O. J. Simpson trial was announced. They were concerned about the possibility of having a Tony Blair speech driven down the BBC's running order by the news from Los Angeles, and the fax was a blatant attempt to influence editorial policy.

The attempt failed, in so far as the fax became a news story in itself, making more transparent and newsworthy the process of political news management. In October 1996 the *Panorama* current affairs magazine marked the Labour conference by devoting an entire edition to the work of spin-doctors, much to the anger of Campbell and Mandelson. The fax incident, and others like it, thus led to a new policy of increased vigilance on the part of BBC producers, reducing the ability of political news managers of all parties to influence journalistic agendas.

In his defence, Alistair Campbell has repeatedly maintained that the notoriety of the Simpson fax shows how rare is conflict of this kind between journalists and party news managers and that, in any event, the activity of 'spinning' is not a qualitatively new or unethical feature of democratic politics. 'Spinning' may have grown in importance and visibility alongside the growth of the political media, but it dates back at least as far as the reign of Charles II, who employed Samuel Pepys to act as his 'press handler'. Responding to the *Panorama* programme in which he featured prominently as one of Clare Short's 'people who live in the dark' Campbell pointed out that:

> We live in the media age. There are more newspapers, magazines, television and radio stations than ever before. They all have space to fill, and they look to politics to fill a good deal of it. The political party

that does not understand the needs of the media is doomed. Much of the work involves ensuring all outlets are spoken to, a consistent line is taken, and our central points communicated. None of that stifles debate.[7]

This seems reasonable, provided that it is communication rather than intimidation to which journalists are exposed. If Campbell, Mandelson and their colleagues can be blamed for a bullying and over-zealous approach to ensuring 'consistency' of policy presentation – and even they admit that they *have* been guilty of this on occasion[8] – then they should also be given the credit for instilling professionalism and coherence in their employer's communication management, with all that has subsequently flowed from this in terms of electoral success. Whether the price of this success has been too high will perhaps be clearer at the end of Labour's first term.

Lobbying

One branch of the political public relations industry whose ethical standards have been most directly and deservedly challenged in recent years are the lobbyists. Such organisations as Westminster Strategy, the Communication Group, Government Policy Consultants, and the now infamous Ian Greer Associates, exist to advance the interests of extra-parliamentary clients in the House of Commons. They 'lobby' for some acts of legislation and against others, by using a variety of formal and informal communicative tactics. In the case of Ian Greer Associates and certain Conservative MPs, as was revealed by the press in 1995 and 1996, this involved passing brown envelopes full of money in exchange for said MPs asking official questions of ministers. The 'cash for questions' scandal, and other examples of 'sleaze' documented in the early 1990s were clear violations of the ethical standards of the professions involved.

On the other hand, most political lobbying companies do not seek to bribe politicians, and most politicians would not accept bribes if they were offered. That some do, have then been exposed by the press, and have seen their careers damaged by the resulting waves of criticism, might be interpreted to mean that the British political system is not yet in the same league of corruptibility and criminality as those of many other comparable countries. Nevertheless, this dimension of the political communication process requires continued monitoring, not just by the various parliamentary committees and watchdogs which have been set up in the wake of the 'sleaze' scandals of the 1990s, but by the political media. In this respect the *Guardian* and the *Sunday Times*, which led the investigative reportage of the Hamilton affair, have played an exemplary role, and one which should be viewed as a model for the role of the 'fourth estate'.

The ethics of political journalism

Unfortunately, the praise which legitimately accrues to some newspapers for their exposure of unethical practices in the political arena is more than matched by persistent criticism of the media's role in degrading and trivialising the democratic process. Some of these criticisms raise the issue of ethical standards, since they concern features of political journalism that are deliberate and intentional. Others highlight trends which are the product of factors beyond individual journalistic control but which, intentionally or not, are alleged to damage the quality of public political discourse.

The press and political bias

In relation to the press, two ethical criticisms are made most frequently. The first concerns the long-standing issue of bias, and the tendency of so many newspapers to act as propagandists for right-of-centre political masters. This bias results, it is argued, not only in editorial support for the ideas and values of the right, and against those of the left, but dishonest and inaccurate reportage. Well-known examples include the 1980s coverage of the activities of the 'loony left' in London, the *Daily Mirror*'s false accusations of Arthur Scargill's 'links' with Libya in its coverage of the 1984–5 miners' strike, and a succession of British General Elections in which the Labour Party was unable to secure a fair hearing from the vast majority of the press. Although empirical evidence for a pro-Tory effect of this coverage is difficult to assemble, many commentators have argued that the seventeen-year hold of the Conservative Party on government was not unrelated to the degree of unquestioning support which it enjoyed from all but a few broadsheet and tabloid newspapers over this period.[9]

Former Conservative minister Lord Wakeham is among those in his party who frankly concede that the role of the press was crucial in securing electoral victory in 1992. In his view, 'the sharpness of the pro-Conservative newspapers' comments and the depth and breadth of their reporting undoubtedly helped to ensure some of the movement towards us in the last weeks of the campaign' (1995, p. 5). The 'sharpness' and 'depth' referred to by Wakeham included such stories as the *Daily Mail*'s 'tax bombshell' coverage, and the *Sun*'s day-of-poll headline, 'If Kinnock wins today, will the last person to leave Britain turn out the lights'.

Anti-Labour press bias was not new in 1992, but it reached unprecedented heights and may, in the view of many observers, have made a crucial difference to the result. For leading Tory fundraiser Lord McAlpine, writing in the *Sunday Telegraph* a few days after John Major was returned to office, the press were 'the heroes of [the 1992] campaign'.

> Never has the attack on the Labour Party been so comprehensive. They exposed, ridiculed and humiliated that party, doing each day in their

pages the job that the politicians failed to do from their bright new platforms. This is how the election was won.[10]

The press in a democracy has, of course, the right to say what it likes within the law, but the self-proclaimed ethical standards of the journalistic profession may be thought to preclude efforts to 'fix' elections by the deliberate distortion and misreporting of political information. There is, as Noam Chomsky and others have persuasively argued, little difference between the Soviet-era propaganda sheets and those newspapers of the 'free press' which volunteer themselves as cheerleaders of one political party over another, irrespective of 'the truth'. The fact that the period between 1992 and 1997 saw a decline of pro-Conservative press bias, attributable in large part to sustained and skilful courting of the Murdoch titles by the Labour Party, does not alter the underlying argument: that journalists in a democracy – even those working on tabloids – have a responsibility to pluralism and diversity of political debate, and to refrain from peddling myths and lies about groups who may be viewed in certain quarters as 'subversive'. The fortunes of the Labour Party in government will be significantly shaped by how seriously the British press take this responsibility in the coming years.

The tabloidisation of political journalism

If the period between 1992 and 1997 was one in which the press became less like the collective house organ of the Conservative Party, it was also one of unprecedented reportage of political scandal, much of it affecting the Conservative Party itself. It may be that the two phenomena are related, and that Messrs Murdoch, Black, Montgomery *et al.* found it increasingly difficult to give unbending support to a party so apparently prone to moral lapses. In vigorously reporting the numerous cases of alleged ethical misconduct amongst politicians which have been revealed in recent years, however, the press has been accused of undermining faith in the political system itself, and of itself behaving unethically.

I referred above to the 'cash for questions' scandal, and the widely welcomed reportage of those newspapers which exposed it. Less welcome, for many observers, have been the many exposures of alleged sexual and 'lifestyle' misconduct amongst MPs. These have included serial philandering (Steven Norris), bizarre sex practices (the tragic death of Stephen Milligan), closet homosexuality (Jerry Hayes), alcoholism and drunk driving (Nicholas Scott). Almost all of these accusations involved the Conservative Party, and many required ministerial resignations, contributing much to the decline of the government's poll ratings after 1992. In reporting these stories, newspapers have been accused of masking the pursuit of commercial advantage (in an extremely competitive press market) behind pious concern for the nation's morals. Politicians, it is argued, have a right to privacy in so far as their private activities do not interfere with their public duties. What, for example, has Jerry Hayes's sexual preference got to do with his parliamentary life, given that he has been a liberal on gay rights in any case?

The royal family, too, has seen its private problems and difficulties relentlessly exposed in the press, leading to a climate in which its future as the pillar of the British constitution is under serious threat.

The ethical defence of such expository journalism is usually presented as follows. Regardless of the motivations behind it (and there can be little doubt that commercial rather than public interest considerations have been prominent in the thinking of tabloid editors) the press has a right, indeed a responsibility, to expose hypocrisy in public life. When politicians who on conference platforms preach about the social evils presented by single motherhood, or who choose to campaign around 'back to basics' moral values, turn out to be unfaithful to their wives, or neglecting their illegitimate children, the voters have a right to know. The conduct of private life in such cases has a clear relevance to public policy, and contradictions between the two are the proper subject of political journalism.

Revelatory coverage of the royals also has a public interest defence. Andrew Neil justified the *Sunday Times* serialisation of Andrew Morton's biography of the late Princess of Wales by arguing, firstly, that it was the product of Diana's own desire to have her side of the story reported, and furthermore, that the public has a right to know of matters which have serious constitutional significance, even if these are painfully private. He favourably contrasted the media visibility of the Charles–Diana marital split with the secrecy and widespread public ignorance which surrounded the abdication of Edward VIII in 1936.

The above justifications for a political journalism which is, whatever else it may be, undeniably titillatory, voyeuristic, and commercially successful, are indeed consistent with the ethical standards of a profession which since its emergence from the ruins of feudalism in early modern Europe has aspired to watch over the powerful. If the public's estimation of the political class suffers as a result, we might argue, then whose fault is it but their own?

Some media sociologists complain that the resulting coverage is 'part of a tendency to distract the public from matters of principle by offering voyeuristic pseudo-insights into individual matters' (Gripsund, 1992, p. 94). Others positively welcome the (unintentionally) subversive effect of such material appearing on our breakfast tables each morning, creating as it does an 'informed popular scepticism' (Fiske, 1992, p. 61) towards the powerful.

Readers of this book will have their own views on the impact of 'sleaze' journalism on our political culture. There are, clearly, some cases where the revelatory reportage of élite misbehaviour is consistent with the ethical codes of liberal journalism, and others where it is not. Distinguishing between the two is the task, firstly, of the journalists themselves, if they do not wish their already low reputation as a professional group to sink even further; of those who buy the newspapers concerned, and who give such coverage commercial value; and of the industry regulators, the Press Complaints Commission, whose judgements on these matters have not always been consistent or effective, prompting demands for legal measures to prohibit the worst excesses. Most journalists, including those who would not touch a toe-sucking royal story if it were handed to them on a plate, agree that it would be a pity if these demands led to legislation, since the law would be used most aggressively by the powerful to censor the legitimate, wholly ethical exposure of élite corruption and abuse.

Broadcasting

Broadcast political journalism has, until relatively recently, avoided the ethical challenges confronted by the print media. In Britain and many other countries, broadcast journalism has been strictly regulated to ensure that it is not biased towards one political party or another, and serves the public as a whole with political information and analysis of the quality demanded by modern democratic procedures. As a consequence, even in countries with almost entirely commercial systems, such as the United States, broadcast news has an image of neutrality and non-partisanship – a reputation for standing above and back from the party political fray – which gives it a distinctive role in the public sphere. Increasingly in the 1990s, however, broadcast journalists have been accused of abusing this role, and of damaging the political communication environment in the process.

Referring back to an earlier stage of the discussion, the growth of broadcast media, and television in particular, has been held responsible by many for the ascendancy of political style as an element in voter decision-making. Broadcast journalism, because of its space limitations and the brevity it imposes on political discourse, has produced what the senior BBC correspondent Nicholas Jones describes as 'a media environment habituated to the relentless pursuit of the soundbite' (1995, p. 51). The American James Fallows, editor of *The Nation*, accuses his colleagues in broadcast news of 'a relentless emphasis on the cynical game of politics' (1996, p. 31) which 'threatens public life itself'. Although individual broadcasters can hardly be blamed for an environment which they confront as a pre-given of their work, broadcasters as a group are the third essential strand of the politician–spin-doctor–journalist web, and as such implicated in the transformation of political communication into the deployment and manipulation of neat catchphrases (soundbites) and pleasing images (photo-opportunities).

Many variants of these criticisms exist in the literature, but they can perhaps be summarised in the claim that, for reasons of commerce, technology and professional vanity, the style of political journalism has gradually come to take precedence over substance. As the quantity of broadcast political communication available to viewers and listeners has grown exponentially, its quality has declined.

The ethics of broadcast style

Walter Cronkite, for example, has attacked what he sees as 'the trend towards trivialising "infotainment"'.[11] The increasingly revelatory and voyeuristic content of press journalism about politics was discussed earlier. Now, the argument goes, as broadcasting systems become more commercialised and competitive, similar features are becoming apparent in television and radio journalism.

Cronkite's reference was to America, but it applies also to Britain where, with cable, satellite and digital technologies quickly coming on stream, broadcasting is undergoing rapid change. Will this be accompanied by a 'tabloidisation' of broadcast journalism? If so, for Jon Snow of Channel 4 News, 'the whole fabric of democracy is threatened. In a world in which debate is replaced by exchanged seven second soundbites, the content of politics falls victim to the more easily communicated evidence of human frailty'.[12]

Criticism is focused not only on the familiar evil of 'tabloidisation'. Broadcast political journalism also stands accused of developing a repertoire of stylistic traits which, though intended to connote authority, balance, neutrality, and so on, actually inhibit the communication of substantive information. The media analyst Bryan Appleyard observes of television news that 'the cult of seriousness has become a style in itself . . . there has been an extraordinary blooming of technical and representational style, driven by a highly competitive market that demands the maximum impression of significance and sensation'.[13]

Nowhere is this more apparent than in the 'cult' of the 'star' presenter, exemplified in Britain most notably by Jeremy Paxman and John Humphrys and, on occasion, Sue MacGregor, James Naughtie and others who have acquired reputations for increasingly aggressive adversarial interviewing styles. At regular intervals in recent years these individuals have been accused of being excessively confrontational in their dealings with politicians, and of turning political interviews into sterile exchanges of accusation and counter-accusation which may entertain, but do not inform. The interview, it has been argued by politicians and broadcasters alike, becomes a test of a politician's ability to engage in verbal jousting rather than the articulation of policy.

The subject of political journalism becomes the *game* of politics, rather than the issues; the *process*, rather than the policies. As James Fallows observes, the 'context that gives meaning to information' (1996, p. 130) is sacrificed to make way for ratings-friendly drama.

For the 'stars' themselves, on the other hand, hostile interviewing is wholly consistent with their ethical responsibilities to the audience. John Humphrys, in rejecting politicians' criticisms of his style, has argued that broadcasters like himself play a key role in exposing the gap between what politicians say and what they do. In an increasingly managed communication environment, the in-depth political interview allows an element of unpredictability and challenge to be reintroduced, to the benefit of the citizen. The results may often lack rationality and coherence, but 'interviewing politicians is an important bridge between the electorate and their political leaders. We have to distil the national argument, to represent the voters' concerns'.[14] Michael Cockerell agrees that while Humphrys (and the other 'star' interviewers) 'may sometimes deploy a terrier-like persistence in his interviews that can sometimes be counter-productive . . . his aim is to strip away the public relations gloss and use his own sharp teeth to counter pre-rehearsed soundbites'.[15]

The ethics of political interviewing is a subject which, perhaps understandably, has mainly preoccupied the politicians who are most regularly subjected to the techniques developed by Humphrys and his colleagues. For that reason alone, we should be cautious before endorsing calls for a journalistic retreat from the confrontational style. Occasional examples of presenter-vanity and 'hyperadversarialism' (as James Fallows calls it) are a small price to pay for a journalism which is not intimidated by the powerful.

Conclusion

Each of the three groups whose communicative behaviour we have examined in this essay is participating in a competition – a game, to use the metaphor frequently applied in this context. The politicians and the journalists compete to set the news agenda, and to have their perspectives on events reported. The spin-doctors act as coaches and managers on behalf of the politicians, and as technical assistants in realising the desired communicative effects. We, the voters, are positioned as spectators, with occasional walk-on parts. At the end of each electoral cycle we are asked to choose whom we think has performed best during the preceding period, and who is likely to perform best in the forthcoming one.

The politicians ask us to make that decision on the basis of the policy options which they lay out before us. Their spin-doctors and communication advisers operate on the assumption that we will also be influenced by the presentation, as well as the policy content of the message, a consideration which places great emphasis on the political performers' style and image. The journalists, meanwhile, probe this confection of policy-substance and image-surface, exposing and widening the gap between rhetoric and reality, laying bare the contradictions, drawing our attention to the existence of the game and the artifice employed by its participants.

None of this is incompatible with the respective ethical standards of each group. Politicians advocate, media consultants advise, journalists scrutinise. They are all, in that sense, merely doing their jobs. The difference between now and earlier times – and what has made this such a burning issue – is principally that the game is, from the viewpoint of the players, more competitive and managed. For us as spectators it is more omnipresent, even intrusive, than ever before. At times we come to feel that we have overdosed on politics. We grow weary with the politicians' posturings, the journalists' probings, and the spin-doctors' efforts to pull the wool over our collective eyes. Yet the luxury of excess is not one which we should take for granted. Less than one hundred years ago, as was noted above, women did not have the vote in Britain. Free from the gaze of electronic media, politicians and other élite groups could pursue their business relatively free from journalistic intrusion. As recently as the 1950s the journalistic norm in dealing with politicians was (as seen from this distance in hilarious black and white newsreel footage) embarrassing, laughable deference. As for the world beyond the countries of advanced capitalism, many populations still live under criminally corrupt or authoritarian regimes, where a Jeremy Paxman, a James Naughtie, and even a Kelvin Mackenzie would not last ten minutes.

Of course there are excesses, and none of what has been said thus far is intended to lessen the significance of ethical lapses when they occur. Politicians lie. Journalists pursue confrontation for confrontation's sake, and expose the private failings of public figures for no more noble cause than the commercial advantage of their proprietor. Spin-doctors overdo it with threatening faxes and bullying phone calls.

The encouraging thing in all this, however, is how often we come to know about these abuses of the political communication machinery, how often they are exposed and themselves become part of the evidence and information on which we make our political judgements. This essay on the ethics of political communication could not have been written without reference to the vast quantity of media debate about – the ethics of political communication. We exist – largely thanks to the media – in a state of informed 'knowingness' which does much to protect us from the politicians' tendency, assisted by their professional media advisers, to dissemble, deceive and manipulate. And, of course, we have our own reservoirs of experience against which to compare everything that the political communicators say and do. The media supply a large part of the information on which we base our political behaviour, but by no means all.

We cannot reverse the communicative trends discussed in this essay, nor, I would argue, should we wish to. We inhabit the most media-literate, information-rich society in human history, where it is ever more difficult for élites to keep secrets, and to suppress debate, should ethical failings predispose them to do so. We *are* probably overloaded with political information, much of it trashy and superficial, but better that than the inhibited, boot-licking media of a few short decades ago.

As we enter the era of digital television and the Internet, we face another expansion of the political media, as hundreds of new channels come on air or on-line with space to fill. In meeting that challenge we as citizens should be vigilant, and ensure that our journalists are vigilant on our behalf, maintaining their own ethical standards, those of the politicians on whom they report, and the spin-doctors who seek to influence their coverage. We should encourage media education in schools and universities, so that the citizens of the twenty-first century learn the skills of critical reading and viewing as part of their preparation for civic responsibility. We should demand freedom of information and governmental openness. We should support appropriate restrictions on media ownership, so that the means of political communication are not open to monopolisation by wealthy individuals, and the potential for one-sided press bias is minimised. We should defend public service broadcasting, while accepting that it must adapt to meet the demands of new technologies and new viewing and listening patterns. And if all of that is not enough, we will simply have to exercise our right not to play the game: to switch off, withdraw our support, and call it to a halt.

Notes

1 The French philosopher Jean Baudrillard says, for example, that 'for some time now, the electoral game has been akin to TV game shows in the consciousness of the people. The people enjoy, day to day, like a home movie, the fluctuations of their own opinions in the daily opinion polls. Nothing in all this engages any responsibility. At no time are the masses politically engaged in a conscious manner', in *In the Shadow of the Silent Majorities . . . or the End of the Social* (New York: Semiotext, 1983), p. 38.

2 Although the opinions expressed are entirely my own, the argument draws on work funded by the Economic and Social Research Council on political communication and democracy currently being undertaken by the author in collaboration with colleagues at the Stirling Media Research Institute of Stirling University, Scotland.

3 M. Woollacott, 'When invisibility means death', *Guardian*, 27 April 1996.

4 A. Coote, 'Labour puts its neck on the line', *Sunday Times*, 29 September 1996.

5 S. Heffer, 'Spinning for a living . . . who cares?', *British Journalism Review* 6/4 (1995).

6 I. MacWhirter, 'Not what the spin doctor ordered', *The Scotsman*, 9 August 1996.

7 A. Campbell, 'Auntie's spinners', *Sunday Times*, 22 September 1996.

8 In an interview given to the *Guardian* in February 1997 Campbell conceded that his and his colleagues' response to Clare Short's 1995 statements on tax had been inappropriate and unfair (J. Mulholland, 'Labour's Mr Media', *Guardian*, 17 February 1997).

9 See Martin Linton's *Guardian* lecture, 'The battle for Jennifer's ear', given at Nuffield College, Oxford, on 30 October 1994. In it he asserts that 'Labour has never won an election when it was more than 18 per cent behind the Tories in

press share' (reported in M. Linton, 'Sun-powered politics', *Guardian*, 30 October 1995).

10 Quoted in D. McKie, 'Fact is free but comment is sacred', in I. Crewe and B. Gosschalk (eds) *Political Communications: The General Election Campaign of 1992* (Cambridge: Cambridge University Press, 1995), p. 128.

11 W. Cronkite, 'More bad news', *Guardian*, 27 January 1997.

12 J. Snow, 'More bad news', *Guardian*, 27 January 1997.

13 B. Appleyard, 'Please adjust your mind set', *The Independent*, 9 February 1994.

14 J. Humphrys, 'In the firing line', *Guardian*, 24 May 1995.

15 M. Cockerell, 'Whose fingers on the mike?', *Guardian*, 27 March 1995.

6 The myth of Saddam Hussein
New militarism and the propaganda function of the human interest story

Richard Keeble

The making of the Gulf War myth

It could be argued there was no Gulf War of 1991. In the way in which the term is generally used and understood, what took place in the Persian Gulf in January to February 1991 was not a 'war' at all. It was nothing less than a series of massacres. This is not a mere semantic quibble. The distinction (and the accompanying notion of the 'war' myth) has profound theoretical and analytical implications for any study of the press coverage. There was no credible enemy. The Iraqi army was constantly represented in the British and American press in the run-up to the conflict as 1 million strong, the fourth largest in the world, 'battle-hardened'[1] after the eight-year war with Iran, led by monster madman Saddam Hussein. When, in January and February 1991, Iraqi soldiers were deserting in droves and succumbing to one slaughter after another, Fleet Street still predicted the largest ground battle since the Second World War. Stories of enormous Iraqi defensive structures with massive berms and a highly sophisticated system of underground trenches filled the media. In the end there was nothing more than a walk-over, a rout, a barbaric slaughter buried beneath the fiction of heroic warfare.

The nature and significance of the war sprang out of the realms of myth, rhetoric and media spectacle. Focusing on the conflict as a construction in this way can draw attention to the broad political and economic factors, the nature of the militarism of the states involved and the propaganda role of the mainstream media within those states. More particularly, it can highlight the propaganda function of the sensationalist, human interest story.[2]

Major, high-profile wars are no longer fought as merely military events. People are slaughtered, children and soldiers are traumatised, buildings, hospitals, radio stations, tanks are destroyed. But major wars are now fought as media spectacles for largely non-strategic purposes. The Gulf War had little to do with getting Iraqi soldiers out of Kuwait. It had little to do with protecting Saudi Arabia from an Iraqi invasion. It had little to do with protecting the oil supplies. The conflict had little to do with getting rid of Saddam Hussein. He was supported by the international élites of the East and West in the decade leading up to August 1990, he was supported by the CIA even after August 1990[3] and no doubt a powerful faction in the allied élite still supports his regime.[4]

Kicking the Vietnam syndrome, constructing the Saddam myth

A major war needed to be constructed – to be seen to be fought and won – in large part so that the US élites could eradicate the trauma of the Vietnam defeat from their collective memory.[5] A hastily constructed, mythical Saddam Hussein suddenly appeared as the perfect enemy against whom the perfect war could be waged. Since the collapse of the Soviet Union the massively resourced military industrial complex was facing a potential crisis and desperate to find a new enemy. Britain's Falklands adventure in 1982 over an insignificant group of islands populated largely by penguins set the precedent for the transformation of militarism into spectator sport.[6]

Then, following the Falklands precedent, Grenada (1983), Libya (1986) and Panama (1989) were dabbled in as enemies by the United States. But none could compare to Saddam Hussein. Moreover, the myth of the war was to prove all the more potent since it also served the interests of the Iraqi élite by resolving some of the contradictions of their old-style militarism. Since the ceasefire in the Iran–Iraq war of 1988, thousands of men were returning to cities from the front, ending up dissatisfied and jobless.[7] Many of them were engaged in revolts against the regime, especially Kurds and Shi'as.[8] A 'war' could eliminate large groups of them. As Faleh Abd al-Jabbar comments, 'The rout relieved Saddam of the most troublesome part of his army and preserved the most loyal divisions.'[9]

The media spectacle of the mythical war

The Gulf simulated war ended up like a motion picture spectacular[10] with the coalition forces acting each day as if according to a pre-arranged script. As Fuad Nahdi, one of the three *Los Angeles Times* reporters in Riyadh, commented, 'The first press conference of the day would be at 7.30 a.m. From then on you knew exactly what the line for the day was going to be. The script had been written beforehand and I felt like the reviewer of a good play or film.'[11]

So the censorship regime (the pooling arrangements, the denial of access to the front to journalists, the intimidation of reporters by the military) served essentially symbolic purposes. It was an expression of the arbitrary, monopoly power of the military over the conduct of war. Similarly the almost total monopoly of the pools by American and British media representatives symbolised these countries' dominance over the global communications networks.[12] The military, according to the dominant myth, went into the Vietnam War with their hands tied behind their back (by traitorous media and peace-freaks). Vietnam was a war that 'got out of control'. Desert Storm was the US military's attempt to wage the perfect war: to control and give it a contrived, happy ending. Censorship was used not so much to preserve military security as to promote a positive image of the massacres.

New militarism and the propaganda function of the press

The Gulf War can usefully be seen as a manifestation of a distinctly new kind of militarism. As James Combs argues over the Falklands adventure and the US invasion of Grenada:

> It is a new kind of war, war as performance. It is a war in which the attention of its *auteurs* is not only on the conduct of the war but also the communication of the war. With their political and military power to command, coerce and co-opt the mass media, the national security élite can make the military event go according to the script, omit bad scenes and discouraging words and bring about a military performance that is both spectacular and satisfying.[13]

Military strategy becomes essentially a media event, an entertainment, a spectacle. Warfare, moreover, is transmuted into a symbolic assertion of United States and to a lesser degree British global media (and military) power. Media manipulation becomes a central military strategy. This 'mediacentrism' is a pivotal element of new militarist societies.[14]

Instead of mass active participation in militarist wars (such as 1914–18; 1939–45 and Vietnam), people are mobilised through their consumption of censored media (the censorship largely imposed by journalists themselves) whose job is to manufacture the spectacle of 'warfare'. People respond to the propaganda offensive with a mixture of enthusiasm, contempt, apathy and scepticism. Yet, most crucially, media consumption and public opinion polling provide the illusion of participation just as satellite technology provides the illusion of 'real live' coverage of the war.

MacKenzie has described the 'spectacular theatre' of nineteenth-century British militarism, when press representations of heroic imperialist adventures in distant colonies had a considerable entertainment element.[15] Featherstone, too, has identified the way in which the Victorian 'small' wars of imperial expansion in Africa and India were glorified for a doting public by war correspondents such as William Russell, G. A. Henty, Archibald Forbes and H. M. Stanley.[16]

But Victorian newspapers and magazines did not have the social penetration of the mass media of today. And Victorian militarism was reinforced through a wide range of institutions and social activities: the Salvation Army, Church Army, and uniformed youth organisations, rifle clubs, ceremonial and drill units in factories. MacKenzie comments, 'In all these ways, a very large proportion of the population came to have some connection with military and paramilitary organisations.'[17] By the 1970s this institutional and social militarism had given way to a new media-centric, consumerist, entertainment militarism in which the mass media, ideologically aligned to a strong and increasingly secretive state, had assumed a dominant ideological and propaganda role. Indeed, the manu-factured new militarist wars of the 1980s deliberately served to reinforce the power of the political and economic élites within the national security state and the marginalisation of the mass of the public.

Unlike militarist wars which lasted years, new militarist wars are over quickly. As Benjamin Bradlee, former executive editor of the *Washington Post* commented bluntly of the events of January–February 1991, 'The trouble with this war was it was so fucking fast.'[18] But the 42-day Gulf conflict was a long war in new militarist terms. The military become, then, the primary definers of the fast-moving event while journalists, kept far from any action, are in no position to challenge their inventions.

Moreover, the strategic imperatives of new militarism mean that wars become inherently difficult to report. They are fought by planes (to which journalists have no access), at high altitude and often at night. New weapons incinerate their victims, making calculations of casualties even more difficult. The emphasis on computer games in military planning means the distinction between 'real' and Nintendo-style wars becomes blurred.

The media myth of defence

The dominant view reproduced in the mainstream media represents the state as having fought defensively only in exceptional cases since 1945. The Gulf War, accordingly, was represented as a legitimate, defensive response to an unprovoked attack by Saddam Hussein on innocent, vulnerable, tiny Kuwait (and, by implication, on vulnerable western civilisation). Such an interpretation significantly obscures the offensive (and often covert) ele-ments of the UK and US state systems and military strategies.

In fact, since 1945 the UK and the USA have deployed troops somewhere in the globe at least once every year, usually away from the media's glare. Rose argues that since 1945 British troops have been involved in more wars in more places across the globe than those of any other country.[19] And Steve Peak identified the Falklands War as the 88th deployment of British troops since 1945.[20] In the case of the USA, Cecil Currey finds that since 1950 America has used either force or its threat about 500 times.[21] Former CIA agent John Stockwell suggests that the agency has been involved in 3,000 major operations and 10,000 minor operations which have led to the death of 6 million people worldwide.[22] Pentagon adviser John M. Collins, in his seminal analysis of strategy in these largely secret wars, known as low intensity conflicts (LICs), isolates just 60 examples this century.[23]

The dominant media view fails to acknowledge the inherent aggression of the state, representing the short, sharp attacks (or defensive actions as argued by the administration of the day) of the USA on Grenada, Libya and Panama in the 1980s as the typical form of warfare. In fact, the reverse is nearer the truth. Some 57 per cent of Collins's sample lasted under five years but 33 per cent exceeded 10 years. For instance, he points out that the LIC against Libya has been going on since 1970. The eleven-minute attack on Libyan targets in April 1986 (a manufactured crisis staged as a media event and co-ordinated to coincide with the beginning of the 7 p.m. news in the USA, according to Kellner[24]) was just a tiny feature of this multi-pronged conflict.

Most warfare of new militarist societies clearly avoids the use of massive armies of the size the coalition forces assembled in Saudi Arabia, during the lead-up to the 1991 conflict. Instead permanent warfare (driven by the demands of the military industrial complex to which the media are closely aligned) is conducted through special force intervention, the support of proxy forces and leaders, through diplomatic, trade and other economic sanctions, through secret service destabilisation and assassination.[25]

The making of the Saddam myth

Central to the construction of the Gulf War myth, then, was the sensationalist demonisation of Saddam Hussein. Yet the press construction of the myth of Saddam Hussein first began in the months leading up to August 1990 and only then completely dominated the coverage throughout all the British media. Before the Kuwait invasion, the principal bogeyman in the Middle East for the mainstream press was Iran. Searle demonstrates how the *Sun*'s racist venom was directed at this country throughout the 1980s. On 18 October 1987, after the USA destroyed two Iranian ex-oil rigs in the Gulf, it commented, 'The Americans have enough firepower in the Gulf to render the country a wasteland. Maybe that would not be a bad thing for the rest of humanity.'[26]

During the Iran–Iraq war (1980–8) Iraq was, in general, referred to simply as Iraq or Baghdad. As significant sections of the West tilted towards Iraq so Saddam Hussein was covered by the media in favourable terms. Robert Freedman highlights stories in the western press which spoke approvingly of Saddam's moves to privatise the economy in the mid-1980s and he was even compared to Thatcher in this context.[27]

The myth of Halabja

Even the press coverage of the chemical bombing of Kurds in Halabja on 16 March 1988 was notable for its comparative restraint.[28] Yet more than 5,000 civilians were killed and another 7,000 maimed for life. Timmerman suggests the gas was a hydrogen cyanide compound the Iraqis had developed with the help of a German company.[29] Made in the Samarra gas works, it was similar to the poison gas the Nazis had used to exterminate the Jews more than 40 years earlier. Survivors interviewed by Human Rights Watch, Middle East confirmed that the bombs were dropped from Iraqi and not Iranian planes, since they flew low enough for their markings to be legible.[30] Human Rights Watch also lists 60 Kurdish villages attacked with mustard gas, nerve gas and a combination of the two over the previous two years.[31]

Little blame was levelled personally at Saddam Hussein in the press for the Halabja atrocity. No Hitler or Nazi jibes emerged. The *Guardian* of 17 March 1988 was typical: 'It is hard to conceive of any explanation for the chemical bombardment of Halabja other than one which Iranians and Kurds offer – revenge.' The madness of Saddam Hussein, his lust for power was nowhere identified as the cause of the outrage. While a 24 March editorial defined the atrocity as 'Iraq's latest and greatest war crime' it mirrored the government's position on the war, taking no side and calling for a ceasefire.

At the same time the press gave considerable prominence to US government claims that Iranians were also responsible for the chemical attacks. *The Times* carried prominently the report headlined 'US evidence suggests Iran also use chemicals', while the *Guardian* quoted a Reuters report of US State Department spokesman Charles Redman claiming, 'There are indications that Iran may have also used chemical artillery shells in the fighting.'

Six weeks after the attack, a UN report, made by a Spanish military doctor, Col. Manuel Dominguez Carmona, concluded it was impossible to say whether Iraq or Iran or both were to blame.[32] In February 1990, a US Army War College report concluded that Iraq was not responsible for the Halabja massacre and that 'it was the Iranian bombardment that had actually killed the Kurds'.[33] Was this mere US government-inspired misinformation because Iraq was then a close ally? Certainly the media at the time of Halabja raised serious questions about the supposed guilt of Iraq. These doubts were completely absent in the coverage of the 1990 crisis and later massacres. The Halabja bombing, rather, featured prominently in all the demonisation propaganda directed at the Iraqi leader.

Bazoft ambivalences

The ambivalence of the élite's approach to Saddam Hussein at this time was most apparent in the coverage of the hanging of the *Observer* journalist Farzad Bazoft on 15 March 1990. An explosion had destroyed the al-Hillah plant north of Baghdad on 17 August 1989 and Bazoft had travelled there with an English nurse, Daphne Parish, taking photographs and even soil samples.[34] After being arrested by Iraqi security police he had 'confessed' to being an Israeli spy. Immediately after the hanging British intelligence leaked information that Bazoft had stolen £500 from a building society ten years earlier. According to John Pilger, MI5 was acting on behalf of the Thatcher government 'desperate for any excuse not to suspend its lucrative business and arms deals with Saddam Hussein'.[35]

The *Sun*'s 'exclusive' headline went: 'Hanged man was a robber'; the *Mail*'s: 'Bazoft a perfect spy for Israel'; *Today*'s: 'Bazoft was an Israeli agent'. A *Sunday Telegraph* editorial condemned Bazoft as a spy, likening investigative journalism to an offence against the state. The investigative journalist Simon Henderson also argued that Bazoft was a spy. He concluded, 'At no time did the British admit that Bazoft had been spying, nor did Iraq flesh out its allegations. The reason was clear: if Britain admitted to the spying the two countries would have had to break off diplomatic relations.' Neither country wanted this. 'So the Bazoft incident was left to die down.'[36]

The propaganda function of the human interest story

After the Iraqi invasion of Kuwait of August 1990, the personality of a mythical Saddam Hussein became the prime focus of sensationalist press coverage. Hussein, in effect, became Iraq. In this way, the human interest bias, which is deeply embedded in journalists' culture, served a crucial propaganda function, simplifying an enormously complex history, seriously distorting the representation of the conflict and drawing attention away from other important social, political, geostrategic, religious and economic factors.

As Curran, Douglas and Whannel argue, human interest is not simply a neutral window on the world but embodies a particular way of seeing.[37] Accordingly, the possibility of basic structural inequalities is rejected while non-historical forces of 'luck, fate and chance' are represented as dominant within a given, naturalised world. Paul Kennedy sees the human interest bias as an indication of the potency of the conservative historical ideology which prioritises human interest factors above deeper underlying, contextualising factors.[38]

This view is reinforced by Sparks who says, 'The popular conception of the personal becomes the explanatory framework within which the social order is presented as transparent.' The media fail to convey the 'social totality' comprising 'complex mediations of institutional structures, economic relations and so on'.[39]

Ultimately, the hyper-personalising of the crisis served the crucial propaganda function of directing all blame on to the one man: Saddam. Thus, when during the 1991 conflict the allies bombed the Almeriyya shelter in Baghdad or the retreating conscripts on the road to Basra, causing hundreds of deaths, there was one simple, predictable response: it was all Saddam's fault. The allies in the massacre-speak were always 'kicking

Saddam's arse', his conscripts were always reduced to non-people, animals; Iraqi civilian deaths were either 'inevitable' or 'mistakes'.

Hitler Hussein

Another central feature of the demonisation strategy and the construction of the mythical Saddam was the representation of him as the new Hitler. The *Telegraph*, of 3 August, was typical. It wrote, 'President Hussein's decision to invade Kuwait is proof of his Hitlerian determination to get his own way.' Robert Harvey, in a leader page feature, contributed, 'For once the overworked comparison with Hitler is apposite.' The *Mail* editorial of the same day commented, 'Like a rerun of Hitler's invasion of Czechoslovakia in the 1930s, the Iraqi dictatorship has flouted international opinion and grabbed a small but wealthy neighbour. Nothing justifies this outrage.' In the *Sun* of 4 August, Dr John Laffing, described as an expert on Arab affairs, wrote that 'power-crazed tyrant Saddam Hussein was exposed yesterday as a Führer freak who models himself on Adolf Hitler' and had set up a shrine to Hitler.

On 5 August, the *Sunday Times* said of the Iraqi invasion, 'It was a strategy on Hitlerian lines: the annexation by *blitzkrieg* of a weak neighbour.' The *Observer* editorial of the same day commented, under the heading 'Why this Hitler of the Gulf has to go', 'It is going to be desperately difficult to get out of this one without the exchange of rocket fire. If the comparison with Hitler holds good, it may prove impossible.' And the editorial continued, 'Comparing people to Hitler can be counterproductive as Sir Anthony Eden (over Nasser) and Nicholas Ridley (over Chancellor Kohl) both found to their cost. But in Saddam Hussein the world is facing another Hitler . . . He has the same kind of expansionist ambitions and brutal lack of humanity. Like the German Führer he has an underlying vision of an all-powerful Iraq funded by oil and backed by force.'

The Independent of 3 August editorialised, 'The appetites of dictators grow with what they feed upon as Europe learnt to its cost when dealing with Hitler.' And its profile of 11 August began, 'In the overworn comparison with Hitler and Stalin there is a kernel of truth. For he shares the secret of great dictators – he understands the psychotic relationship between fear and love.' The *Mirror* intoned, 'Saddam Hussein is the Adolf Hitler of the Arab world. If he isn't stopped now the West will pay a heavy price.'

A similar focus occurred in American press coverage. The Gannett Foundation study found 1,035 mentions of Saddam Hussein as Hitler from 1 August to 28 February 1991 in the print media.[40] On both sides of the Atlantic the analogy was reinforced in cartoon representations. Macarthur comments, 'Hardly any reporters were heard challenging the President in his Hitler comparisons at press conferences.'[41]

Yet the Hitler angle did not appear to politicians and the press 'naturally'; it served a number of important ideological, propaganda purposes. With the collapse of the Soviet Union, the spectre of the 'communist threat' could no longer be raised as a justification for US military action. As a propaganda tool the Hitler threat was remarkably efficient: it was simple and seemingly unproblematic. In popular rhetoric, Hitler has been transformed into an enormous symbol of evil and danger. Focusing on the enemy as a Hitler could only serve to direct massive emotional negativity to that single person, and at the same time elevate the moral purity of the forces lined up against him. As *The Independent* leader of 3 August commented with commendable clarity, 'Since the changes in Russia some people have been lamenting the lack of a convincing enemy. Here he is.' Saddam Hussein was and remains a brutal dictator. The paper's profile of 11 August remarked, 'President Saddam has achieved the apotheosis of the totalitarian ideal.' Yet for ten years the superpowers were happy to cultivate Iraq as a 'friend'. During those years there were many opportunities for the press to put the Hitler label on Saddam. The Ba'ath party, indeed, had Fascist origins, being formed in Damascus in 1941 out of an aid committee set up by Alflaq and Bitar to assist Rashid Ali's Nazi-backed revolt in Iraq.[42] One of the first mentions of Saddam Hussein as Hitler appeared on 16 September 1988. Hazhir Temourian wrote, 'Saddam Hussein, the little psychopath who clearly believes he will get away with emulating his hero, Hitler, must be punished with the powers of the civilised world.' But this was in the leftist *New Statesman and Society* (pp. 20–2).

All the post-August 1990 Hitler hype sought to say implicitly, 'There have been many horrible dictators since 1945 but Saddam Hussein is the worst of all.' By no sensible historical criteria could the validity of that assertion be assessed; it was merely serving rhetorical, ideological and ultimately political/military purposes.

The endlessly repeated Hitler analogy represented a highly selective, ideologically motivated use of history by the USA and its prominent allies. For its essential purpose was to draw on pre-Cold War rhetoric to silence many histories, in particular the imperial roles of the USA and UK in the Middle East and more globally. As Bennett comments, 'The vivid, personalised framing of Saddam Hussein as Hitler made a clean historic break with past administration policies toward Iraq and established a new historical and emotional reference from which opinion formation could begin anew.'[43]

The Hitler analogy also served a critical role in the complex, multi-faceted propaganda project to highlight the military option above the diplomatic one; after all Hitler was removed only by force.[44] As Christopher Layne says, 'The 1930s analogy rests on the assumption that 'aggression' must be resisted, not appeased whenever it occurs because it will snowball unless firmly stopped.' It was a sort of variation of the Cold War/

old order domino theory which drove the USA into the débâcle of Vietnam.[45] Those who questioned the Bush agenda were thus labelled 'appeasers' (returning again to pre-1939 rhetoric) and saddled with all the negative connotations of that word. It served to highlight Saddam Hussein and the country he was supposed to run as a powerful, global threat which needed to be tamed or destroyed if President Bush's 'new world order' was to be established.

After the Kurdish massacres, with Saddam still in power (and with the USA maintaining its pre-invasion policy of ambivalence towards the Iraqi regime) the Hitler analogies suddenly disappeared from the media. The analogy was exposed as an ideological device to legitimise the US and allied stance.

Madman Saddam

Along with 'Saddam' as Hitler, the other dominant aspect of the coverage of Iraq after the Kuwait invasion was to represent Saddam as mad and evil. On 7 August, John Kay wrote in the *Sun*, 'Britain's élite SAS regiment could assassinate crazed Iraqi President – and defuse the growing Gulf crisis in one blow.' The *Guardian* editorial commented, 'In the two years since the Gulf War ended it has been at times hard to decide which of the two damaged regimes that staggered out of that bloody conflict was the more deranged or the more dangerous.' The *Mail* of 3 August, in a centre-spread headlined 'A new Hitler plots his empire', described Saddam Hussein as a megalomaniac. The *Express* headlined, 'Mad despot who wants to rule the Arab world'. The story beneath gave prominence to a piece of Mossad misinformation which was to feature regularly in the press in the lead-up to the massacres. It reported, 'This week an Israeli graphologist who examined his handwriting at the request of the secret service Mossad – without knowing the identity of the author – ruled that he is in urgent need of psychiatric treatment.'

Linked to this representation was the emphasis on Saddam (and by association those who supported him) as being barbarous and brutal. In effect, the press was portraying him as a monster, non-human, uncivilised and thus worthy of any treatment dealt him.

The *Mirror* profiled him on 3 August: 'Already he is a mass murderer, a man guilty of genocide, a monster who has used gas and chemical weapons on civilians and enemy troops and whose war with Iran cost half a million lives.' On 7 August, the *Sun* evoked the animal metaphor in this disreputable way: 'A stone lifted at the Iraqi embassy in London yesterday and a reptile crawled out.' It was referring to ambassador Shafiq Al-Salih who supposedly shrugged when asked the fate of British hostages in Iraq. The paper continued, 'We hope an American B-52 wipes the crooked smile from his lips.' In much of the coverage Saddam is presented as the embodiment of evil. The *Mail* of 3 August: 'Hussein is known to approve 30 types of torture. They include mutilation, gouging out of eyes, cutting off the nose, sex organs and limbs, hammering nails into the body, burning with hot irons and roasting victims over flames.'

What is striking about this dominant genre of Saddam profiling is the way in which he is represented as existing in a natural state of bloodthirsty anarchy where none of the normal human factors operate. The history of British and American imperialism, political, religious, environmental dynamics play no part in this biography. It is completely untouched by history. There is little concept of Saddam Hussein as a diplomat. Thus the dominant representation remains extraordinarily two-dimensional and consistent throughout the crisis and massacres.

As Prince argues on these anti-historical projections and images, 'Iraq was thereby exiled from the modern world and the 20th century, banished to a nameless, pre-civilised period, effectively distanced in spatial, temporal and moral terms from the West.'[46]

Saddam trapped within the frame of popular culture

The crisis, with all its immense complexities, was from the outset represented within the dominant frames of popular culture which represent reality as a simple fight between good and evil. As Gilbert Adair said, 'Saddam Hussein himself has become a concentration of pure malevolence, of a type instantly, irresistibly, reminiscent of the villains in James Bond movies.'[47] And Roy Greenslade, editor of the *Mirror* during the massacres of the Kurds, later commented, 'We covered the war in a fairly mainstream, tabloid way. Here was a recognisable enemy. Saddam was an evil man. That was the great assumption.'[48]

John Schostak develops this theme. He writes,

> By evoking the experiences now overlaid with the mythology of the Second World War, Hussein's actions and the West's counter actions could be explained simply and simplistically to the public. The complex history of involvement by the West in Middle Eastern affairs, which had allowed tyrants to arise and be supported was largely glossed over. The invasions and subversions carried out by Western powers all over the world could be ignored in this simplistic drama echoing the fight of good over evil.[49]

According to William F. Fore, the mass media are the devices used by the controllers of our culture to keep it simple.[50] In this they reproduce the rhetoric of the political élite. For instance, President Bush told Congress, 'I have resolved all moral questions in my mind: this is a black versus white, good versus evil.' This moralistic, anti-historical rhetoric, reproduced in the press, helped portray the Kuwait invasion as an inexplicable and irrational undertaking.

Press construction of the Kurdish myth

Press representations of Saddam Hussein since the war have shown significant fluctuations. The 1991 Kurdish revolt served to portray a nation, previously marginalised in the media, as suddenly heroic in their liberation struggle, while the suppression of this revolt and that of the Shi'as in the south reinforced the image of Saddam as ruthlessly oppressive.

Yet the romantic presentation of the Kurdish plight (which fitted so neatly into dominant simplistic goodie versus baddie representational frames) shrouded the CIA's covert involvement in the Kurd's history, past and present, which was always marginalised in the media.[51] As Heikal commented on the Kurds and Shi'as, 'If the two uprisings had been truly motivated by the desire for radical changes in the structure of Iraq, they might have succeeded; as it was, many of those involved were merely trying to exploit a chaotic situation for reasons of greed and revenge.'[52]

Moreover, while the press represented Prime Minister John Major as being forced by the pressure of public opinion and media coverage to dream up the enclave idea to protect the Kurds from the marauding Saddam, other political factors had far more impact.[53] In particular, the Turkish leadership feared that the mass of Kurds fleeing over their borders would add support to the growing revolt of Turkish Kurds, spearheaded by the Marxist-oriented Partia Karkaris Kurdistan (PKK), so coverage of this group was either non-existent or marginalised in the media.

Given their support during the war, the Turkish leaders probably felt that they had reason to expect some favours from the USA. In fact, the Turkish President Turgut Ozal first suggested the Kurdish haven on 7 April.[54] Major's proposal came only the following day. In the south, Saudi concern over Iranian, Shi'ite advances into Iraq probably doomed the Shi'ite revolt to defeat.

How Saddam is transformed into a naughty schoolboy

For long stretches since March 1991 Saddam has disappeared from sight in the press. One section of the western élite is clearly happy that he remains in power (countering Iranian expansion and serving as an easy 'enemy' to bomb at appropriate times). Another section wants him out and uses exclusion zones, covert action and the occasional symbolic bombing raid to put pressure on his regime. But Saddam is no longer represented as a global threat worth the trouble of fighting heroic wars to dislodge.

Significantly, during the January and June 1993 risk-free air attacks on Iraq by the USA, all blame was again levelled at Saddam.[55] But from being 'worse than Hitler' he was transformed into a naughty little schoolboy worth a 'spanking'.[56]

Conclusion

The 1991 Gulf conflict was America's manufactured 'big' war in which it supposedly finally kicked the Vietnam syndrome. Saddam was always the monstrous global threat the allies were fighting. Around his personality a crucial narrative was manufactured to help legitimise the allied stance. In this way the human interest bias of the press, rooted in journalists' everyday routines but located in this study in its historical and political context, came to serve a crucial propaganda role.

As Reese and Buckalew conclude, 'The most pervasive, powerful and difficult to counter illusion [of real warfare] emerged from the routine, structural workings of the media system.' And they add, 'The interlocking and reinforcing triangle of government, news media and corporate needs works together to further a culture supportive of military adventures such as those in the Gulf.'[57]

Significantly, US military interventions since 1991 have not been hyped as acts of heroic warfare in the press. New militarist warfare, as identified here, is a very specific, mediacentric, spectacular phenomenon. When the conditions are not right for major, overt conflict, then this style of warfare is pursued in secret (as in Bosnia), or given low-key coverage and called 'peacekeeping' (as in Somalia and Haiti) or 'punishing Saddam' (as during the US bombing of Iraq in September 1996).

Indeed, as western élite rhetoric about Saddam Hussein fluctuates, so the consensual voice of the press follows meekly in its wake.

Notes

1 Iraqi troops were known to have performed badly in the 1980–8 war with Iran when thousands had deserted. See A. Abbas, *The Iraqi Armed Forces, Past and Present in Saddam's Iraq: Revolution or Reaction?* (London, CADRI/Zed Books, 1986), p. 220 and Norman Friedman, *Desert Victory: The War for Kuwait* (Annapolis, MD: Naval Institute Press, 1991).
2 See, for example, Noam Chomsky and Edward Hermann, *Manufacturing Consent* (London, Vintage, 1994).
3 Alan Friedman, *Spider's Web: Bush, Saddam, Thatcher and the Decade of Deceit* (London, Faber, 1993), p. 172.
4 Helga Graham, 'How America saved Saddam', *New Statesman and Society* (20 September 1996), pp. 24–6 and Richard Keeble, 'How the West pulls punches against its favourite demon', Gemini News Service (London, 14 January 1997).
5 There were many other factors driving the USA (and its allies) towards the construction of a mythical war. For example: it could serve to bring some sense of unity to deeply fractured societies and legitimise the media, military and industrial élites in the eyes of the public; it was needed by the USA to assert militarily its primacy in the 'new world order' against the growing economic strength of Germany and Japan; it could destroy the social and economic infrastructure of Iraq which, while posing no threat to the West, was seen as a threat by the Israeli élite; it could serve as an obscenely macabre testing ground for new weapons with humans and a society's infrastructure as targets;

it could help President Bush banish his 'wimp' image for good and help his re-election prospects.

6 See Robin Luckham, 'Of arms and culture', *Current Research on Peace and Violence* (Tampere, Finland) iv/1 (1983), p. 18 and Michael Mann, *States, Wars and Capitalism* (Oxford: Blackwell Publishers, 1988).

7 Efraim Karsh and Inari Rautsi, 'Why Saddam Hussein invaded Kuwait', *Survival* (January/February 1991), pp. 18–30.

8 John Pilger, 'Who killed the Kurds?', *New Statesman and Society* (12 April 1991), pp. 6–7.

9 Faleh Abd al-Jabbar, 'Why the uprisings failed', *Merip* (Washington DC; May/June 1992), pp. 2–14.

10 George Gerbner, 'Persian Gulf War: the movie' in Hamid Mowlana, George Gerbner and Herbert Schiller (eds), *Triumph of the Image: The Media's War in the Persian Gulf – a global perspective* (Boulder, CO: Westview Press, 1992), pp. 243–65.

11 Interviewed London, June 1992.

12 For example, only three places in the pools went to reporters from countries other than the USA or UK.

13 James Combs, 'From the Great War to the Gulf War: popular entertainment and the legitimation of warfare', in Robert Denton (ed.) *The Media and the Persian Gulf War* (Westport, CT: Praeger, 1993), pp. 257–84. See particularly p. 227.

14 This definition of mediacentrism differs from that promoted by Philip Schlesinger and Howard Tumber, *Reporting Crime: The Media Politics of Criminal Justice* (Oxford: Clarendon Press, 1994). They apply it to studies of the media which focus on media content and journalists' relationships with sources. For this approach they substitute a 'source-media analysis' model.

15 John MacKenzie, *Propaganda and Empire: The Manipulation of British Public Opinion 1880–1960* (Manchester: Manchester University Press, 1984).

16 Donald Featherstone, *Victorian Colonial Warfare: Africa* (London: Blandford, 1993) and *Victorian Colonial Warfare: India* (London: Blandford, 1993). See also Raymond Sibbald, *The Boer War: The War Correspondents* (Stroud, Glos.: Alan Sutton, 1993).

17 MacKenzie, *Propaganda and Empire*, pp. 5–6.

18 John R. Macarthur, *Second Front: Censorship and Propaganda in the Gulf War*, 2nd edn (Berkeley and Los Angeles, CA: University of California Press, 1993), p. 147.

19 Stephen Rose, 'Spend, spend, spend – on military only', *New Statesman* (3 January 1986).

20 Steve Peak, 'Britain's military adventures', *The Pacifist* 20/10 (1982).

21 Cecil Currey, 'Vietnam: lessons learned', in Phil Helling and Jon Roper (eds) *America, France and Vietnam: Cultural History and Ideas of Conflict* (Aldershot: Avebury, 1991), pp. 71–90.

22 John Stockwell, *The Praetorian Guard: The US Role in the New World Order* (Boston: South End Press, 1991), pp. 70–3.

23 John M. Collins, *America's Small Wars* (Washington and London: Brassey, 1991).

24 Douglas Kellner, *Television and the Crisis of Democracy* (Boulder, CO, San Francisco, Oxford: Westview Press, 1990), p. 138.

25 See also Asaf Hussain, *Political Terrorism and the State in the Middle East* (London and New York: Mansell Publishing, 1988), p. 45.

26 Chris Searle, *Your Daily Dose: Racism and the* Sun (London: Campaign for Press and Broadcasting Freedom, 1989), p. 36.

27 Robert Freedman, *Middle East from the Iran–Contra Affair to the Intifada* (Syracuse, NY: Syracuse University Press, 1991).

28 Steven Rose and Abraham Baravi, 'The meaning of Halabja: chemical warfare in Kurdistan', *Race and Class* 30/1 (1988), pp. 74–7.

29 Kenneth R. Timmerman, *The Death Lobby: How the West Armed Iraq* (London, Fourth Estate, 1991), p. 293.

30 Human Rights Watch, Middle East, *Iraq's Crime of Genocide: The Anfal Campaign against the Kurds* (New Haven, CT and London: Yale University Press, 1995), p. 70.

31 Ibid., pp. 262–5.

32 John Bulloch and Harvey Morris, *No Friends but the Mountains: The Tragic History of the Kurds* (London: Viking, 1992), p. 144.

33 Stephen Pelletierre, Douglas Johnson and Leif Rosenberger, *Iraqi Power and US Security in the Middle East* (Washington, DC: US Army War College, Strategic Studies Institute, US Government Printing Office, 1990). See also Martin Yant, *Desert Mirage: The True Story of the Gulf War* (Buffalo, NY: Prometheus, 1991), p. 109.

34 Daphne Parrish gives her version of events in *Prisoner in Baghdad* (London: Chapmans Publishers, 1992).

35 John Pilger, 'Shedding crocodile tears', *New Statesman and Society*, 20 March 1992, p. 10.

36 Simon Henderson, *Instant Empire: Saddam Hussein's Ambition for Iraq* (San Francisco: Mercury, 1991), pp. 214–16.

37 James Curran, Angus Douglas and Gary Whannel, 'The political economy of the human interest story', in Anthony Smith (ed.) *Newspapers and Democracy: International Essays on a Changing Medium* (Cambridge, MA: MIT Press, 1980) pp. 288–316.

38 Paul Kennedy, 'A. J. P. Taylor and profound causes in history', in Chris Wrigley (ed.) *Warfare, Diplomacy and Politics: Essays in Honour of A. J. P. Taylor* (London: Hamish Hamilton, 1986), pp. 14–29.

39 Colin Sparks, 'Popular journalism: theories and practice', in Peter Dahlgren and Colin Sparks (eds) *Journalism and Popular Culture* (London, Newbury Park, CA, New Delhi: Sage, 1992), pp. 24–44.

40 Gannett Foundation, *The Media at War: The Press and the Persian Gulf Conflict* (New York: Columbia University, The Freedom Forum, 1991), p. 42.

41 Macarthur, *Second Front*, p. 72.

42 John Bulloch and Harvey Morris, *Saddam's War* (London: Faber, 1991), pp. 53–4.

43 Lance Bennett, 'The news about foreign policy', in W. Lance Bennett and David L. Paletz (eds) *Taken by Storm: The Media, Public Opinion and US Foreign Policy in the Gulf War* (Chicago: University of Chicago Press, 1994), pp. 12–40. See particularly p. 32.

44 Glasgow University Media Group, 'The British media and the Gulf War', research working paper (Glasgow, 1991), p. 3.

45 Christopher Layne, 'Why the Gulf War was not in the national interest', *Atlantic Monthly* (July 1991), pp. 615–81.

46 Stephen Prince, 'Celluloid heroes and smart bombs: Hollywood at war in the Middle East', in Robert Denton (ed.) *The Media and the Persian Gulf War*, pp. 235–56. See particularly p. 244.

47 Gilbert Adair, 'Saddam meets Dr Strangelove', *Guardian* (29 January 1991).

48 Roy Greenslade interviewed in London, May 1994.

49 John Schostak, *Dirty Marks: The Education of Self, Media and Popular Culture* (London: Pluto, 1993), p. 85.

50 William Fore, 'The shadow war in the Gulf', *Media Development* (October 1991), pp. 51–3. See particularly p. 52.

51 See Phil Agee, *Covert Action: What Next?* (London, Agee Hosenball Defence Committee, 1976); Bulloch and Morris, *Saddam's War*, p. 31, and William Blum, *The CIA: A Forgotten History – US Intervention since World War Two* (London: Zed Books, 1986), p. 278.

52 Mohamed Heikal, *Illusions of Triumph: An Arab View of the Gulf War* (London: HarperCollins, 1992), p. 320.

53 For example, Martin Shaw, *Civil Society and Media in Global Crises: Representing Distant Violence* (London: Pinter, 1996), pp. 79–96, argues that the British media, in particular television, played the dominant role in persuading John Major to promote the Kurdish 'safe havens' proposal.

54 Eddie Abrahams (ed.) *The New Warlords: From the Gulf War to the Recolonisation of the Middle East* (London: Larkin Publications, 1994), p. 40 and David McDowall, *The Modern History of the Kurds* (London and New York: I. B. Tauris, 1996), p. 375.

55 Douglas Kellner, 'Gulf War II, the media offensive', *Lies of our Times*, May 1993, pp. 17–19 and Douglas Kellner, 'The US media and the 1993 war against Iraq', in Yahya R. Kamalipour (ed.) *The US media and the Middle East* (Westport, CT: Praeger, 1997), pp. 105–18.

56 Norman Fairclough, *Media Discourse* (London and New York: Edward Arnold, 1995), p. 95 and Richard Keeble, 'From butcher to bad boy' (London: Gemini News Service, 19 January 1994).

57 Stephen D. Reese and Bob Buckalew 'The militarisation of local television: the routine framing of the Persian Gulf War', *Critical Studies in Mass Communication* (Annendale, VA, 1995), vol. 12/1, pp. 40–59. See particularly p. 41.

7 Privacy, the public interest and a prurient public

David Archard

Going public: what is an invasion of privacy?

A mass circulation newspaper publishes the photograph it has obtained of a prominent public person engaged in what is evidently an intimate sexual encounter with another identifiable individual. The photograph, which is explicit but not offensively pornographic, is accompanied by a news report which spells out the significance of the image. Let us suppose that the newspaper can offer some plausible reason for publishing this story; what kinds of reason they might offer will be considered in due course. The paper does not publish it simply because it is a titillating image. Indeed let us allow that *only* the publication of the image would serve as sufficient support for the report it accompanies.[1] In short, publication of the photograph is not gratuitous. What is wrong with publishing the image and report?

First it might be wrong if the manner in which the photograph had been obtained was clearly impermissible. This would be the case if, for instance, the photographer had trespassed on private property to take the picture or a photograph lawfully taken (say by friends of the couple) had been stolen by the newspaper.[2] There might be a worry about permissibility if the photograph had been obtained clandestinely, that is, without its subjects knowing that it was being taken. 'Clandestine' also means 'underhand' and 'surreptitious', suggesting that the secrecy involved was somehow wrong or unfair. The wrongness, we will assume, is not of a kind already discussed. It could be that the subjects of the photograph not only did not know they were being photographed but might reasonably expect not to have been photographed. No one bathing on a deserted private beach of an uninhabited island miles from any other territory can expect that photographers lie undetected off shore with long-lens cameras. But a person's reasonable expectation not to be photographed is not necessarily a rightful expectation that she should not be. The press cannot, for obvious reasons, always advertise to those it is investigating when, where and whether they are conducting the investigation.

Publication of the photograph might be thought wrong if taking it formed part of a pattern of clear, persistent and intrusive harassment of its subject. A photographer who follows his quarry day and night wherever she goes, never letting her out of his sight, and photographing her every move, behaves unreasonably. It is proper that such behaviour should be the subject of a legal injunction to desist. The taking of the published photograph is not of itself wrong. After all, it might have been the one and only shot taken at a single opportune moment. It is the pattern of harassment which led to the taking of the photograph which is unacceptable.

The taking and publishing of the photograph would arguably be wrong if it breached confidentiality. If someone enters into a confidential relationship with another person, who reveals to others information which is obtained only through that relationship, then that person is in breach of an obligation of confidentiality. That obligation can arise through either an express or tacit contract. Princess Diana sued for breach of confidence when in 1993 a tabloid newspaper published photographs of her working out in a gymnasium which had been obtained without her knowledge or consent and with the connivance of the owner of the gym. This law was not used, but might have been, in the similar case of the publication by the *Sunday Sport* in 1990 of photographs of the actor Gorden Kaye while he lay injured and barely conscious in a hospital bed. Some have argued that the law of confidentiality might be used in Britain to cover invasions of privacy.[3] However, it is not plausible to think that every photograph whose publication gives rise to worries about invasion of privacy need have been obtained in a manner which breached confidence.

Finally, the photograph's publication might give cause for moral concern if the choice of image or the language accompanying it were clearly intended to humiliate, ridicule, belittle, or unfairly stigmatise the subject, or if the story's publication formed part of a pattern of reporting with such an intention. Here it is reasonable to think that a story goes beyond the reporting of a newsworthy event and fair comment upon it. There is a point at which *Schadenfreude* at another's failings, which may be regretted if not condemned, passes into unacceptably vindictive persecution. Many had the feeling that this occurred with the tabloids' reporting of Sarah Ferguson's long fall from grace in 1996.

Let us assume that the photograph of our example does not fall foul of any of these kinds of worry. If there is still felt to be something wrong with publishing it then that worry will most likely be expressed along the lines of its being no business of the press what this person freely does in private with another consenting individual. It is this worry which is captured by the notion of a wrongful invasion of privacy. What follows is an attempt to make sense of that worry when it is set against arguments which purport to justify such an invasion.

Privacy has to do with keeping personal information non-public or undisclosed. Personal information is that set of facts about oneself that a person does not wish to see disclosed or made public. The facts need not take the form of written statements. Personal information is contained within or can be inferred from a photograph or sound recording. Obviously what one person strives to keep private another may be happy to see as common knowledge. Some of us are shy about revealing our age, others unembarrassed. Most of us would probably think of our sexual and financial affairs as properly private.

This understanding of privacy is not the only one possible.[4] Privacy has been defined in terms of being let alone, control of access to one's body and personal space, autonomy in personal matters, and solitude. No one of these definitions enjoys universal acceptance and each is subject to familiar criticisms and counter-examples. The most obvious, and frequently defended, alternative to the definition offered here is that which speaks of privacy in terms of a person's control over access to herself and to her personal information.[5] A newspaperman who obtained personal information about me, perhaps in an entirely licit fashion, but who did not make it public would on this definition, but not on mine, be breaching my privacy.

There are at least three reasons for preferring my definition in the present context.[6] The first is that it is reasonable to prefer a 'non-reductionist' definition of privacy, that is, one which cannot be fully rendered in terms of other concepts.[7] If privacy is to be accounted a distinct interest (and its invasion a distinct wrong) then it should not be defined in terms of more fundamental interests. Defining privacy in terms of control over access to oneself is defining it in terms of the more fundamental interest of autonomy. If I am wronged in losing control of access to my personal information this is so inasmuch as my desire to keep control of this information is overridden.

The second reason is simply that an unexploited loss of control over one's personal information just does not seem to amount to an obvious violation of my privacy. If I no longer have exclusive access to my personal information but that information is undisclosed, not made public, then it does not appear as if my privacy has been invaded. Of course it is true that safeguarding control of personal information increases, and loss of that control diminishes, the extent to which one's privacy is protected. But it would be a mistake to confuse what may serve an interest with the interest itself.

Third, in the present context of discussing the putative wrongness of the press publishing certain stories or photographs it is my definition that best captures what it is that is invaded when it is said that a person's privacy has been invaded by publication.[8]

A disclosure of personal information may follow upon an invasion of privacy according to the non-standard definitions. If, for instance, my telephone is bugged or my private behaviour filmed by a secret camera, then I am likely to have suffered trespass and a loss of control over access to my personal space. Yet it would be the publication of the taped phone calls or film that would constitute the invasion of my privacy.

What I take to be a paradigmatic invasion of privacy in my sense is the publication of the details of someone's personal circumstances: that someone is gay, is HIV positive, is having an extramarital affair, engages in a certain kind of sexual activity, has an illegitimate child, and so on. These constitute just the sorts of revelations that constitute the stories beloved of the tabloid press and that give rise to moral concern about the privacy of individuals. I do not propose to tackle the question of what legal or official regulative procedures might be appropriate, whether for instance there should be a law of privacy. Nor shall I even presume that there is a right to privacy. I shall, for the moment, assume only that each individual has a strong interest in her privacy and that any breach of a person's privacy must be shown to be justified by the display of good reasons for the breach. Such good reasons must meet the proviso that making public something that is private should not merely serve a valued end but be the only thing that does and can serve that end. Revealing a Cabinet Minister's sexual peccadilloes can effectively display his hypocrisy and unsuitability for high office. But if drawing attention to his public acts does as good a job of discrediting him then the disclosure of his private affairs is gratuitous.

No one is naïve enough to deny that journalists may rationalise their behaviour. The disclosure of a politician's sexual affairs may indeed serve a useful purpose, such as revealing him to be a liar or untrustworthy, but such a disclosure also pleases a paying public who are titillated by learning the details of another's sexual behaviour. Claiming that a noble end warrants a disclosure which is intended to satisfy the ignoble tastes of the readership is hypocritical but hardly surprising or rare. Such rationalisation reflects poorly on the character of editors and reporters but it does not, of itself, show the publication of a story to be illicit.

I shall also assume that we can distinguish between what may be wrong with breaching privacy and what may wrong in the manner in which that breach is achieved. To publish what should be private is one kind of possible wrong; to find out what is private by illicit means is another kind of wrong. Thus, the wrong of bugging a telephone to tape the conversations between David Mellor and his mistress or of stealing a letter from Paddy Ashdown's solicitor detailing his extramarital affair can be separated from the putative wrong simply of revealing the details of the affair in either instance.[9]

Finally, I take for granted a background presumption in favour of the freedom of the press to report what it deems appropriate. The relevant freedom is one to publish what the press deems to be sufficiently attested facts. The freedom to publish opinions is one that is famously defended by J. S. Mill in chapter 2 of his *On Liberty*. That defence invokes considerations of the truth and the role that an unconstrained plurality of expressed views may play in securing the truth. One could of course argue similarly that the truth of any matter can only be reached if all relevant information bearing on its determination is made public.

Whereas the Millian argument might seem to presume that the truth is valuable for its own sake, it could be urged that making all known pertinent facts available to the public serves a valued political purpose. This is that the citizens of a democracy are the better able to make sound judgements – both of what is for their own good and what is for the common good – the more informed they are about all relevant facts. The ability to make sound judgements on these matters is what ensures that democratic procedures yield desirable political outcomes.

Whatever the arguments for such a presumption in favour of a freedom of the press, the point is that such a general presumption exists. It works in favour of the press's activity, even before a newspaper has need to invoke a ground for the publication of a story charged with an invasion of privacy. Thus a newspaper might claim that spiking such a story not only violated the freedom of the press but ignored the particular ends served by this one story.

If there is a countervailing presumption in favour of respecting a person's privacy it will be, I assume, a fairly strong one. But it need not be, I also take for granted, an overwhelmingly strong one. Those who defend a right to privacy do not defend it as an absolute right. What sorts of reasons are offered in justification of breaching an individual's privacy? I shall consider three: (1) when somebody is or becomes a public person she, by that very fact, loses her privacy; (2) where a proven public interest can be shown to be served by the disclosure of the private; (3) where the public is interested in knowing what is private. The first two are familiar and often cited as good reasons. The last is cited only to be contrasted with the second and dismissed as an evidently bad reason. I want to offer critical comments about the first two and then suggest some grounds for thinking the third reason has been too quickly rejected.

The public figure as not entitled to privacy

Consider this extract from the famous, influential article on the right to privacy by Samuel Warren and Louis Brandeis: 'to publish of a modest and retiring individual that he suffers from an impediment of his speech or that he cannot spell correctly is an unwarranted, if not unexampled, infringement upon his privacy, while to state and comment on the same characteristic found in a would-be congressman would not be regarded as beyond the pale of propriety.'[10] Assuming that both individuals have an interest in keeping these disabilities private there are two ways of understanding the claim that the aspirant politician has less reason to complain if his defect is publicised. The first lies in arguing that a speech impediment or inability to spell bears on his suitability to serve in a public office. He would be the worse congressman for having these failings and an electorate is entitled to know any material facts that would influence their preferences for one candidate for office over another. The second way of understanding the claim of Warren and Brandeis is to think that someone who enters public life thereby rightly suffers a loss of privacy. To become a public person is to undergo a change in one's status, associated with which is a lesser degree of privacy. On the first understanding of the claim it is said that whatever bears on your public role ceases to be properly private; on the second understanding it is said that a public person is less private simply in virtue of his or her public status.

Let me now consider this second understanding. Many who achieve fame speak – some in protest, others in grudging acceptance – of the loss of privacy that comes with the territory of fame. Clearly it is harder to keep your life private if you are a public person. Others, and not just the press, have an interest in knowing more about you and your life, an interest which is not displayed towards the ordinary citizen. However, the question is whether what a public person can keep private should be so kept.

One set of considerations that appears to speak in favour of the non-privacy of public persons has to do with fairness. The idea is that it is somehow only fit and proper that public persons should not have privacy. There is a general version of this thought and one specifically having to do with the role of publicity. Let me consider the particular version first. In a 1977 case where the Court of Appeal dismissed an injunction against a former press agent revealing secrets about his charges, a ground for the decision was 'that those who seek and welcome publicity, so long as it shows them in a good light, cannot complain about invasions of privacy which show them in an unfavourable light'.[11] If the bad publicity followed accidentally from the effort to secure good publicity – one sought to look one way and ended up appearing another – the claim would hardly be contentious. Equally there might be merit in it if the good publicity was secured fraudulently, by means, for instance, of a significant lie about the person or the false disparagement of another.

But a wrong has been done by the invasion of privacy. It is not enough simply to say that doing such a wrong is warranted by its resulting in an evil (the bad publicity) cancelling out the good (the favourable publicity) which has been sought and secured. Consider the argument: someone who chooses to wear clothes that show her in a good light cannot complain if she is made to wear clothes that show her in an unfavourable light. Or, those who choose to play a sport which shows their talents in a good light cannot complain if they are forced to play a sport which shows their talents in an unfavourable light. They are not compelling arguments. Neither is that which says good publicity somehow deserves bad.

The general argument is that a loss of privacy is the fair price a famous person pays for her fame. The rewards of fame are large – wealth, social status, public recognition, power and influence, and so on – so why, it might be suggested, should there not have to be a cost exacted in return, that cost being a lesser degree of privacy than the ordinary person? This is unconvincing. A plausible principle of fairness might reasonably allow that a person's public status is simply earned outright and does not morally require a compensating cost. A public status, unlike a job, university place or election victory, need not be thought of as something which can be unfairly acquired at a cost to specific others who lose out. That the general public choose to make the untalented famous is the good luck of the latter; such celebrity is not somehow undeserved. A principle of rectification is inappropriate in this context. Consider how the lucky lottery winner might respond to the suggestion that her good fortune in gaining so much demanded a compensating repayment of a significant part of her winnings.

Imagine that the relevant principles of fairness are grounded in some shared understanding as to what fame should entail, an understanding which could be reached without knowledge by the parties to it of who in fact will be or become famous.[12] Where would be the agreement that public status comes at the price of a loss of privacy? Such a 'contract' would be refused by all who aspire to that status and it would be grossly burdensome to those who have no choice in the matter, those who are born to fame or have it thrust upon them. Imagine that you become a public person despite yourself: you are a relative of the Prime Minister, witness a major crime, survive a disaster. You endure unchosen costs due both to what it is that made you famous and that very public status. You are now told that society understands this status further to require that you lose your privacy. Who, it will be asked, shares in *that* understanding?

A loss of privacy as serving the public interest

The idea that, in fairness or by agreement, public status comes with a loss of privacy is unpersuasive. Far more persuasive is the thought that a person's privacy may be breached if the information disclosed serves a proven public interest. A code of press practice may specify the various conditions that could count as involving a genuine public interest in publication, such as detecting or exposing crime, protecting public health, preventing the public from being misled. Showing public officials to be corrupt, grossly inefficient, criminally negligent, or dishonest is certainly in the public interest, provided that these failings bear directly on their performance of their public duties. Thus, for example, revealing that a minister is a highly paid non-executive director of a company which regularly seeks contracts with the government is a matter for public concern. However, the majority of cases where privacy is breached touch on matters of sexual morality and it is that much harder to see how the public interest is served by their disclosure.[13] Let me rehearse a number of distinct arguments in respect of the publication of the details of a minister's sexual misconduct – all of which, in one form or another, should be fairly familiar.

Before doing so it is important to be clear what role is played by any sexual impropriety as such. In some cases what may be decisive in discrediting a politician is that his sexual misbehaviour is illegal, such as sex with persons below the age of consent. Or such misbehaviour may compound other and perhaps more serious failings. David Mellor was probably forced to resign in 1992 less on account of his extramarital affair with Antonia de Sancha than because of the subsequent revelation that he had enjoyed a holiday at the expense of Mona Bauwens, whose father was a funder of the Palestine Liberation Organisation. What reasons might then be given for thinking that the disclosure of a person's sexual misconduct serves the public interest?

There is, first, the view that any kind of private immorality disqualifies a person from public office. An adulterer is not fit to be a Minister of the Crown for no other reason than that adultery is wrong and fitness for public office requires a morally untarnished character. The view has a charming Victorian resonance to it and is as utterly removed from reality as that period is from our own. We should set the standards of public office high but not so high as to require of our officers that they be angels.

Second, we might argue that the adulterer is a hypocrite. He may be. Posing in public as a family man and defending the values of the family as an electoral gambit, whilst entertaining a mistress in private, is hypocritical. But how important is it to learn that our minister is a hypocrite? There may be little or no reason to believe he is a hypocrite in all matters, especially those that are central to the discharge of his duties. Further, the significance of his hypocrisy in this particular matter is diminished by the thought, surely shared by most of us, that few live up to their proclaimed ideals in this area of their life.

There is a dangerous kind of hypocrisy. Imagine that Smith is in a position to influence policy in some area where the private consensual behaviour of citizens is at issue. Imagine further that the way in which he publicly chooses to influence policy is directly at odds with his own private preferences and behaviour. Then it can be argued that his public actions penalise those with whom he in fact shares a common interest. Those who share that interest may, with justice, view his hypocrisy as harmful and deserving of exposure. The most obvious instance of this kind of reasoning is to be find in the statements of Outrage, whose members seek to bring out from the closet those politicians and clergy whose public words and deeds gainsay (and betray) their private homosexual identity.[14]

A third claim is that a man who lies to his wife will also deceive his country; a man who breaks his marriage vows will break the oath of office. David Mellor's father-in-law publicly attacked him in the media with the claim, 'If he'll cheat on our girl he'll cheat on the country.'[15] If he is a liar and a cheat in all matters let this be shown. Nothing in the pattern of human dissembling reveals the adulterer, simply in virtue of his adultery, to be any less trustworthy or reliable in general. Most people can recognise the difference – in moral significance and motivation – between a personal betrayal and public treachery. Of course someone may be exposed as untrustworthy for the manner in which he has conducted an affair, or has sought to conceal it. Cecil Parkinson, in October 1983 for instance, was probably fatally damaged by the fact of his broken promise to divorce his wife and marry his mistress, Sarah Keays. He might have survived the disclosure of his adultery, but his failure to honour the pledge did supply grounds for resignation.[16] Even so, a man may be dishonourable in business, friendship, and many other matters beside love alone.

The fourth thought is that an adulterous minister is distracted by his adultery from his duties or is less capable, in consequence of his affair, of performing them. That may be so. But so he may be also in virtue of being a conscientious family man,[17] or because of playing golf, reading books or a hundred and one other private pursuits. Claiming this kind of reason[18] as a ground for publicising private immorality has the desperate air of self-serving rationalisation.

Gossip and the interest of the public

There may be personal information which, if disclosed, serves the public interest but most of the reasons given for thinking that the private sexual behaviour of public figures is that kind of information seem tendentious. This brings us to the third reason that might be given for breaching an individual's privacy. This is simply that the public is interested in knowing – not that there is a public interest in knowing, but just that most people would like to know and would derive some pleasure from knowing.

Normally a clear distinction is made between a story being in the public interest and a story being one that interests the public, and the latter is quickly dismissed as a good reason for publication. In my view this distinction and dismissal is too hasty. I do not intend to suggest that there is no distinction and that the public's interest in knowing something does constitute a public interest in knowing that thing. It is rather that society's interest in knowing about the private lives of its public figures may have value and thus, in a way hitherto ignored, help to define the moral space in which the press operates. It is not that a presumption in favour of individual privacy can only be defeated by showing in some specific case that invasion of this person's privacy serves a particular public interest. It is that a general norm of privacy is shaped and constrained, in the first instance and at a prior level, by an opposing general norm of social interest in knowledge. The best way to appreciate this is by thinking of journalism as print gossip.

The differences between leaning across the garden fence to whisper the details of a neighbour's improprieties and publishing them on the front page of a popular newspaper are several. One, apparently trivial but important to the American courts, is that print gossip is written whereas neighbourhood gossip is oral.[19] Another is the scale of subsequent knowledge. Neighbourhood gossip, like a secret, is normally characterised as being told to only one person, but one person at a time and in the confident expectation that the information disclosed will be passed on seriatim. The front-page story spreads its information instantaneously and over a much larger population. It follows that the subject of print gossip is incapable of avoiding the knowledge that his private business is public knowledge. In the case of neighbourhood gossip everyone may also know but he need not know that they do. Yet another difference is that neighbours are understandably far less cautious about the laws of slander and defamation. Newspaper gossip is, normally, better researched, more likely to be true, even if no less malicious in intent. Finally, there is the difference that the newspapers do our gossiping for us. In the neighbourhood we are the agents of its transmission. This difference is moderated by the thought that newspapers sell on the basis of those stories it judges its public want to hear. As readers we may not actually start the gossip but we play our role in ensuring that it is started.

These differences are not so great as to obscure the fact that the journalistic exposure of private lives is a kind of gossip – and is thought distasteful for that reason. Yet closer scrutiny of gossip sheds a different light on its morality. Consider, first, two kinds of reason one might find gossip distasteful: the motives of those who gossip and its effects on those who are the victims. Gossip proper is 'idle', it is aimless and effortless, done with no purpose other than its own enjoyment.[20] Of course, it can be gloating, full of *Schadenfreude*, or vicious; it can serve manipulative purposes such as the blackmailing or stigmatisation of its victim. But so can any kind of talk which concerns other people, and it is these contingent features of the gossip that make gossip objectionable not the mere fact that it is gossip. Gossip may harm those whose private deeds it exposes to public scrutiny. But note that gossip, like any talk about others, can be condemned for falsely defaming those it speaks of. To say that we have an interest in keeping our private lives private and are harmed when this is not so is just to say we have an interest in privacy. It does not follow – and indeed it is just this which is in question – that society does not also have a distinct interest in knowing what individuals would like to keep private. Finally it should be obvious that some general practice may have bad effects for some within it and be motivated (always, sometimes) by viciousness but nevertheless be a good thing on the whole.[21]

Gossip should not then be condemned out of hand for the wrong reasons. It would also be a mistake to ignore the possibly valuable social purposes served by gossip. Let me sketch three such purposes – bearing obvious relationships to one another – which have been noted in anthropological studies of gossip.[22] The first is that gossip plays a role in defining a community and maintaining its unity. Whom one gossips about and with whom is one of the ways in which the insiders of a group differentiate themselves from outsiders. Learning the rules of gossip, acquiring the substance of previous gossip, are how someone may be inducted into a group.[23]

The second and probably most important purpose gossip can serve has to do with the shared values of the community in which it is conducted. There are a number of ways in which this is so. Gossip bears on conduct which is evaluable by these values and it bears on such conduct *because* it is evaluable.[24] Gossip is a way of testing out or rehearsing these values by exposing conduct that they would seem to proscribe.[25] In gossip these values, and thereby also the identity and unity of the group which professes them, may be reaffirmed.[26] Finally, gossip exposes the wrongdoer to public shame or ridicule and consequently functions as a deterrent to such wrongdoing.[27]

The third purpose gossip serves is an egalitarian one. Gossip demystifies the pretensions of public status; it can expose the ordinariness of the famous by showing them to be no more and no less capable of avoiding the failings we know ourselves to display all too often. There is a mystique that surrounds the rich and famous whereby the mundane – both in shortcoming and in achievement – seems beyond them. Gossip is a testing of that mystique. A frequently made observation is that the antics of the 'younger royals' faithfully recorded by the popular press finally stripped the British royal family of any remaining aura it might once have possessed. As sympathetic royalists have commented, that aura, if it is needed, can only now be sustained by the construction of an artificial wall around the activities of royalty.

It is also true that the intimate and personal aspects of people's lives are more revealing of their true character than their public behaviour.[28] Exposing such aspects – which gossip may alone be capable of doing – thus sheds light on the real nature of those whose fame and public status might represent them in other and misleading ways. It is not simply that the famous are just like us and that it is important to know this; it is that fame of itself would suggest otherwise, a suggestion which gossip can very effectively rebut.

In suggesting that gossip serves these social purposes I do not ignore the immediate response that these purposes in turn need to be shown and not just assumed to be valuable. Deference to the rich and famous may be thought an estimable feature of society; an egalitarian demystification of their true nature may be deemed socially destructive. One could object that the very moralism of gossip is what makes it unappealing and agree with Oscar Wilde that whereas 'gossip is charming . . . scandal is gossip made tedious by morality'.[29] One might argue that it is dangerous to assume that a community does share a single set of values; that anything which may be represented as enforcing or asserting such a set of values is to be, for that reason, deprecated as dangerously conservative. Such comments can and should be made.

However the following also needs to be said. First, that gossip might serve any valuable social purpose is too often ignored. The preceding was intended to show that, at the very least, it might. Second, the messenger should not be shot for communicating an unwelcome message. The problems which attach to the possession by a community of values – shared, disputed or absent – should not be attributed to the medium, gossip, in which these values can be publicly communicated. Indeed it is to the credit of gossip that it brings into the light of publicity the lights by which a society claims to live. An important consequence of doing this is that we can learn the true value of our values. Rightly or wrongly, for instance, we expect our public figures to exemplify in their own behaviour the standards of conduct which we think our community tries to live by. Realising that they can no more live by these ideals than we can may lead us to suspect that we have got these values wrong. We may, of course, think that standards in public life are declining (and be right to think so). However we may also think that the standards have been set so high that a falling short of them – even by public exemplars of virtue – is inevitable. Such thinking, fuelled by gossip, will play its part in an invaluable debate about what the values of our community ought to be.

However, it does seem unfortunately true that a particular obsession with the *sexual* behaviour of public figures reveals a characteristically British puritanical prurience, an unresolved unhealthy combination of fascination with and revulsion at sexual activity. Too much of the reporting of private sexual behaviour seems to indulge the vicarious tastes of a public who want to have their moralistic cake and to eat it as well. As many commentators have noted, the British obsession with the sexual behaviour of their public figures contrasts unfavourably with the comparative indifference of the Europeans.

Conclusion

So far nothing has shown that there is a specifiable set of circumstances in which it would be justified for the press to invade a person's privacy or what such circumstances might ever be. Nothing has been said about the value to us, and its foundations, of our privacy. The concern has been to review the sorts of reasons one might give for believing that privacy could justifiably be invaded. The conclusions have been as follows. There is no warrant for thinking that a person loses his privacy in virtue of becoming a public person. The public interest may be served by disclosing the private behaviour of a public person. But where the disclosure is of the sexual affairs of a public person the arguments to show that disclosure is useful are often unconvincing.

Most interestingly, the public's interest in knowing what public figures do in private – an interest which print gossip serves – should not be dismissed as morally valueless. Such an interest is not a legitimate public interest as that term is properly understood. Rather, gossip provides a forum wherein we affirm our identity as a community, assure ourselves that everyone can behave badly and explore the force of our moral conventions which determine what is and is not bad behaviour. That is not enough to show that the public's interest does warrant invasions of privacy. It shows only that there is a further dimension – one which has been unjustly neglected – to the moral space in which such invasions are evaluated.

The surprising thought, then, is that a public's interest in the private conduct of its public figures is a reason of sorts for disclosure. It is not that interest as such which justifies the disclosure. Rather it is that such an interest serves a socially regulative purpose – reminding us that we are all very much alike in our private affairs and informing collective reflection upon the standards we claim to share and live by. And this in turn prompts a final thought. The more confident a community is in the standards it expects its members – whether public persons or ordinary citizens – to live by and the more assured it is that everybody, famous or no, is as fallible as anybody else in trying to live by these standards, then the less likely it is that the community's media will feel pressed to meet a public need to learn what our public figures do in private. That, one suspects, may be a lesson to be learnt from comparing the British press with others.[30]

Notes

1 The photograph is not, in the words of guidance by Lord Wakeham to the press on privacy and the public interest, 'merely illustrative'. See Roy Greenslade, 'Privacy on parade', *Guardian*, 25 November 1996, G2 p. 17.

2 Raymond Snoddy, *The Good, the Bad and the Unacceptable* (London: Faber, 1992), p. 35, provides the example of 'snatchmen' who 'accompany reporters on interviews with relatives in tragedy stories and snatch – steal – pictures of the dead from the mantelpieces'. I am grateful to Matthew Kieran for pointing out this reference to me.

3 M. P. Thompson, 'Confidence in the press', *The Conveyancer and Property Lawyer* 57 (1993), pp. 347–58.

4 For a useful collection of pieces on the subject see Ferdinand David Schoeman (ed.), *Philosophical Dimensions of Privacy: An Anthology* (Cambridge: Cambridge University Press, 1984).

5 Sissela Bok, *Secrets: On the Ethics of Concealment and Revelation* (Oxford: Oxford University Press, 1982), pp. 5–6, defines privacy as the condition of being protected from unwanted access by others; I. Altman, 'Privacy: a conceptual analysis', *Environment and Behavior* 8 (1976), pp. 7–8, defines it as selective control over access to oneself or to one's group; and E. Van den Haag, 'On privacy', in J. R. Pennock and J. W. Chapman (eds) *Privacy: Nomos XIII* (New York: Atherton Press, 1979), p. 149, defines it as the exclusive access of a person to a realm of his own.

6 Perhaps not decisive reasons but a full defence of any preferred definition would require a separate chapter.

7 J. J. Thomson, 'The right to privacy', *Philosophy and Public Affairs* 4 (1975), pp. 295–314, is a justly celebrated exposition of a reductionist account of the

interest of privacy as an amalgam of the interests of property, the person and confidentiality.

8 For a defence of this definition in the context of journalism see W. A. Parent, 'Privacy, morality, and the law', in Elliot D. Cohen (ed.) *Philosophical Issues in Journalism* (Oxford: Oxford University Press, 1992), pp. 92–109.

9 The bugging was morally dubious, but it was legal becuase done with the consent of the landlord of the flat the couple were using; the theft of the letter was a crime and punished as such.

10 Samuel Warren and Louis Brandeis, 'The right to privacy', *Harvard Law Review* 4 (1890), p. 205.

11 Thompson, 'Confidence in the press', p. 350. The case was *Woodward* v. *Hutchins*.

12 This is a rough-and-ready version of John Rawls's derivation of principles of justice from behind a 'veil of ignorance'; see his *A Theory of Justice* (Oxford: Oxford University Press, 1972), Part I.

13 As Matthew Parris's entertaining book *Great Parliamentary Scandals, Four Centuries of Calumny, Smear and Innuendo* shows, politicians in Britain have regularly been brought low by sexual scandals, even if their financial improprieties have also regularly, if less often, done the same (assistant eds David Prosser and Andrew Pierce; London: Robson Books, 1996).

14 Consider, by contrast, the statement by Peter Tatchell of Outrage about the press exposure in January 1997 of the Conservative MP Jerry Hayes as a homosexual: 'Jerry voted to equalise the gay age of consent and scrap the ban on homosexuals in the armed forces. His private behaviour is consistent with his public pronouncements', *Guardian*, 9 January 1997, p. 2.

15 Quoted in Parris, *Great Parliamentary Scandals*, p. 304.

16 For the circumstances of his resignation see, for instance, Hugo Young, *One of Us: A Biography of Margaret Thatcher* (London: Macmillan, 1991), pp. 343–5.

17 'Spending more time with my family' has become the favoured recent public reason for resigning from high office, with the implication, whether intended or not, that a full domestic life is incompatible with the performance of one's official duties.

18 As was done in the case of David Mellor's affair with the actress, Antonia de Sancha.

19 For discussion of this and other differences see Robert Post, 'The legal regulation of gossip: backyard chatter and the mass media', in *Good Gossip*, ed. by Robert F. Goodman and Aaron Ben-Ze'ev (Lawrence, KS: University of Kansas Press, 1994), pp. 65–71.

20 See Gabriele Taylor, 'Gossip as moral talk', in *Good Gossip*, pp. 34–46.

21 Ronald de Sousa makes the explicit comparison with capitalism according to a familiar line of reasoning, 'In praise of gossip', in *Good Gossip*, p. 27.

22 I am grateful to Joanna Overing for making me aware of such material.

23 Max Gluckman, 'Gossip and scandal', *Current Anthropology* 4/3 (June 1963), pp. 307–16, esp. p. 313.

24 'gossip dwells on those features of behaviour which call cultural rules into play – those items of information that enable people to make evaluations', John Beard Haviland, *Gossip, Reputation and Knowledge in Zinacanton* (Chicago: Chicago University Press, 1977), p. 5.

25 'Zinacentecos, through gossip, continually test ordinary rules and evaluative words against actual behaviour', ibid., p. 55.

26 'gossip and scandal have important positive virtues. Clearly they maintain the unity, morals and values of social groups', Gluckman, 'Gossip and scandal', p. 308.

27 'By generating shame in those who violate social standards, [gossip] helps to enforce agreed-upon values', P. M. Spacks, *Gossip* (New York: Knopf, 1985), p. 141, quoted in Ronald de Sousa, 'In praise of gossip', p. 32.

28 Aaron Ben-Ze'ev, 'The vindication of gossip', in *Good Gossip*, p. 15.

29 Cecil Graham gives voice to this claim in Act III of Wilde's *Lady Windermere's Fan* (first performed 1892 and published 1893).

30 I am grateful for the comments and questions of participants at the Leeds University Media Ethics Conference, September 1996, where a first version of this chapter was delivered. I am also grateful to Matthew Kieran for his helpful editorial suggestions.

8 Beyond Calcutt
The legal and extra-legal protection of privacy interests in England and Wales

Ian Cram

Introduction

In April 1989, against a background of increasing parliamentary and public concern about unwarranted intrusions by the press (particularly some tabloid newspapers) into the private lives of individuals,[1] the Conservative government announced the setting up of an 'Inquiry into Privacy and Related Matters', to be chaired by David Calcutt QC. This inquiry was to be confined to an examination of intrusions by the print media and the adequacy of remedies for press intrusion. During its deliberations, the inquiry was presented with a clear example of the sort of conduct which had given rise to concern: it occurred when a journalist and a photographer from the *Sunday Sport* managed to obtain access to the hospital room in which Gorden Kaye – a well-known actor – was recuperating after receiving injuries to his brain as a result of a car crash. Mr Kaye apparently agreed to talk to the men and be photographed. Medical evidence subsequently showed that Mr Kaye could not have given fully informed consent to the interview and photographs. In the subsequent legal action to restrain the publication of statements made by the plaintiff or pictures of him, Lord Justice Bingham said that the newspaper's conduct towards Mr Kaye was

> a monstrous invasion of his privacy. . . . If ever a person has the right to be let alone by strangers with no public interest to pursue, it must surely be when he lies in hospital in no more than partial command of his faculties. It is this invasion of privacy which underlies the Plaintiff's complaint. Yet it alone, however gross, does not entitle him to relief in English law.[2]

Although Mr Kaye succeeded in preventing publication on other grounds,[3] Lord Justice Bingham expressed the hope that the inquiry then in progress might prove fruitful in establishing a more satisfactory means of privacy protection. The Report of the Committee on Privacy and Related Matters (hereafter *Calcutt I*)[4] which followed in June 1990 made a series of recommendations which, despite being largely ignored by the

Major government, have nevertheless, in that government's own words, 'served to set the framework for the debate on press regulation and privacy ever since.'[5] In January 1993 a review of the effectiveness of the print media's voluntary self-regulation conducted by (the newly-ennobled) Sir David Calcutt QC was published. The report, entitled *Review of Press Self-Regulation*[6] (*Calcutt II*) examined whether a key recommendation of *Calcutt I* – the creation of the Press Complaints Commission – had been effective. Other contributions to the privacy debate appeared shortly thereafter. A consultation paper from the Lord Chancellor's Department and the Scottish Office entitled *Infringement of Privacy*[7] was issued in July 1993. Two years later, the government's own response, *Privacy and Media Intrusion*,[8] was published.

This article takes as its starting-point the piecemeal nature of legal protection of privacy interests which *Calcutt I* found wanting. It then considers the recommendations in *Calcutt I* to rectify matters and the Major government's response. It will be argued that, given the apparent lack of political will to create a direct, court-enforceable right of privacy, attention should, in the short term at least, focus upon the utility or otherwise of non-legal forms of protection of the sort encountered in media codes of practice. By way of conclusion, the level of protection offered by the European Convention on Human Rights and Fundamental Freedoms will be considered. The commitment of the subsequent Labour government to incorporate the Convention into domestic law means that this may well prove to be the most likely avenue by which the protection of privacy is to be attained. To begin with however, something needs to be said about why privacy is important.

The importance of privacy

It is clear that within much liberal thinking, considerable importance is attached to safeguarding the autonomy of individuals. The notion that individuals be given the conditions within which to pursue their own particular version of the good life – the idea of privacy or a protected sphere of private life within which the individual is free from interference from others and can determine who has access (and in which circumstances) to personal information – seems a useful means of promoting autonomy and thereby the conditions needed for human flourishing. The converse position, in which the individual has little or no control over the disclosure of personal information may diminish the prospects for entering into meaningful relationships with others and playing a fuller part in community life. Of course, it would be wrong to conceive of privacy as an absolute value. It may, for example, as Feldman reminds us, be necessary to interfere with a parent's privacy rights in order to protect the rights of children to be free from abuse.[9]

Legal protection for privacy interests

That English law provides no general protection against the disclosure of personal information in the form of a right of privacy is well known. Anyone who wishes to prevent such a disclosure must bring his or her claim within another recognised remedy heading, such as defamation, nuisance, confidence, etc. These indirect forms of privacy protection may be divided into two broad categories: criminal and civil remedies. The scope of the principal remedies within each category will now be sketched.

Criminal remedies

At first glance, the range of remedies provided by the criminal law do not appear very useful in a privacy context, since they are concerned primarily with the punishment by the state of certain forms of conduct rather than with preventing the disclosure of information. One recent text on the subject[10] manages to avoid reference to the criminal law altogether, and so arguably misses the important role played by the subject in regulating the conduct of the media in trying to obtain information for publication. A brief glance at the criminal law reveals that the following conduct is subject to penal sanction: the intentional interception of communications by post or the public telecommunications system;[11] the 'watching or besetting' of a place (or approach to such a place) where a person resides or happens to be;[12] the pursuit of a course of conduct[13] which amounts to the harassment of another and ought reasonably to be recognised as such.[14] Those involved in 'media scrums' might equally in theory be charged with a number of offences revolving around the unreasonable use of the highway, such as the statutory offence of wilful obstruction of the highway[15] and public nuisance at common law.[16]

Civil remedies

From the perspective of the victim of media intrusion, this class of remedies is initially more attractive for two reasons. First, breach of any entitlement in civil law normally entitles the injured party to seek compensation from the injuring party (defendant). Second, the courts may, in appropriate circumstances, issue an interlocutory injunction before the trial of the main action against the defendant to prevent the publication of material which will feature in the main action. In what follows a bare outline of each of the principal civil law remedies that might afford a measure of protection for individual privacy is presented.

(1) *Trespass*: If a defendant enters or remains on land contrary to the wishes of the plaintiff who has exclusive possession of the land, an action for trespass will lie. The remedy offers no assistance, however, to cases such as Gorden Kaye's, where the person whose privacy is being interfered

with does not enjoy exclusive possession of the land.[17] Nor does it avail when, in the era of the telephoto lens, photographs of individuals are taken from a vantage point outside the property which that individual possesses. One ameliorating feature of the trespass action is that, unlike private nuisance which is discussed below, the plaintiff need not show that he or she has suffered any damage as a result of the trespass.

(2) *Private nuisance*: Where the conduct of the defendant interferes with plaintiff's enjoyment of his or her own land and the plaintiff can show that harm or discomfort was caused thereby, the plaintiff may sue in private nuisance. For the remedy to lie, the defendant's conduct must be of a continuous nature. Thus the taking of a single picture would not amount to nuisance whereas the constant aerial surveillance and photographing of the plaintiff's every activity would probably be actionable.[18]

(3) *Defamation and malicious falsehood*: A defamatory statement has been described as one which lowers the esteem in which the plaintiff is held by right-thinking members of the public or leads such people to shun, avoid or exclude him or her.[19] The defendant will however be able to resist the action if the statement was true, or made as a fair comment on a matter of public interest. A further defence exists where the statement attracts absolute privilege (thus allowing a statement to be made even where it is motivated by malice) or qualified privilege (the privilege is lost upon proof of malicious intent). Examples of absolute privilege include speeches and statements made in the course of parliamentary and judicial proceedings. Qualified privilege attaches to journalists' reports of parliamentary proceedings.

Aside from the fact that legal aid is not available in defamation cases, the major defect with this remedy is that it offers no protection from the publication (actual or threatened) of *true information* about the plaintiff. Moreover, it is unlikely that an interlocutory injunction will be granted to restrain publication in advance of the full trial when the defendant indicates that a plea of justification, fair comment or privilege will be entered in response.[20] However, if the plaintiff succeeds at the full trial, damages from a jury will be recoverable.

By contrast, the related action for malicious falsehood has been shown of late to possess several advantages over defamation although it should be said that it remains at best a marginal weapon against privacy infringements. The elements of this civil wrong are that the defendant has published maliciously false words about the plaintiff which have caused the latter special damage. Legal aid may be available to a litigant to pursue such a claim.[21] An interlocutory injunction may also be granted to restrain publication in the future where the plaintiff can show that the words which the defendant wishes to publish are clearly false. The value of malicious falsehood for persons in the public eye was demonstrated in the case of *Kaye* v. *Robertson*[22] which was noted earlier. There, Gorden Kaye was able to obtain an interlocutory injunction preventing the publication of material in the proposed article, which suggested falsely that he had given proper consent to being interviewed and photographed. No jury could reasonably have thought that such consent had been forthcoming. The court went on to consider what Mr Kaye's position would have been if, in the absence of an injunction, the *Sunday Sport* had published the story, representing that the plaintiff's informed consent was forthcoming. Such conduct would have constituted a malicious falsehood for which Mr Kaye would have been able to recover damages. The right to damages arose because of the special damage the plaintiff would have suffered in a financial sense if publication in the *Sunday Sport* occurred. After all, Mr Kaye's story was one which other newspapers would be willing to pay large sums of money for if exclusive rights were granted.

Calcutt I, which considered this ruling, deemed the action to be of little value for ordinary individuals since few persons would be able to point to the sort of special damage that Gorden Kaye was able to establish. There is the further and serious drawback that, like defamation, the action requires there to be a false statement.

(4) *Confidence*: Increasingly, lawyers in practice are looking to actions for breach of confidence to provide protection for privacy interests. Outside of situations where confidentiality is protected in a contract (as in a commercial context), the plaintiff, to establish a breach of confidence, must show first that the information or material has the necessary quality of confidence about it.[23] Thus in the context of personal information, it is held that information concerning a person's sexual life may be protected by the law of confidence.[24] Second, the information must be confided in circumstances importing an obligation of confidence. This may occur where a pre-existing relationship exists such as that between employers and employees, doctors and patients, and banks and customers. Alternatively, the obligation of confidence may arise in a wider category of case where information is disclosed to another person on the understanding that it will be kept secret. Where information disclosed to the confidant is passed on a third party, the latter too may be restrained from publishing the confidential information.[25] Finally, there has to be an unauthorised use of the information which adversely affects the plaintiff. The ready availability of interlocutory injunctions preventing publication in confidence actions is also worth noting.[26]

Where the elements of the confidence obligation outlined above are present, it may be open to the defendant to avail him- or herself of the public interest defence or claim that the information is already in the public domain.[27] The public interest defence operates to override an obligation of confidence where there is just cause or excuse for disclosing the information, such as the disclosure to the police of information concerning alleged criminal wrongdoing.[28]

As a surrogate for a law of privacy however, the action for breach of confidence is not without its difficulties. These have been more fully addressed elsewhere.[29] Chief among the problems is the uncertainty over whether the absence of a relationship of confidence between the party who wishes to keep certain information private and the journalist who surreptitiously (by means of surveillance device or eavesdropping) or even accidentally acquires it, is fatal to an action.[30] If such a relationship is not required and a duty of confidence attaches purely by virtue of the *nature* of information, then a considerable obstacle will have been circumvented, although, in that event, separate questions over the scope of the defences of public interest would continue to occupy the courts.[31] That the judges seem content to develop the law in this direction is apparent from the recent ruling of the High Court in *Hellewell* v. *Chief Constable of Derbyshire*. In that case, Mr Justice Laws held that where someone with a telephoto lens takes from a distance and with no authority a picture of another engaged in a private act, disclosure of the photograph would be actionable as a breach of confidence, subject to the usual defences.[32]

(5) *Court reporting*: English law recognises the potential harm to children and young persons which can be caused by the publication of details of court proceedings in which the child or young person is involved as a witness, victim or defendant. Several statutes regulate media reports of court proceedings involving children by creating exceptions to the general rule from *Scott* v. *Scott*[33] that justice be done in public. In the case of youth court proceedings, there is a bar on the publication of material (including pictorial images) which may lead to the identification of a child concerned in those proceedings.[34] This prohibition may be lifted for the sole purpose of avoiding injustice to a child or young person. By contrast, where a youth appears as a defendant or witness before an adult court, the court has a discretion over whether to prevent the identification of the youth concerned.[35] In the case of adults, indirect protection of a privacy interest has occurred through both automatic statutory bars on the identification of persons who allege that they have been victims of sexual offences[36] and the issuing by the judges of anonymity orders. The latter have been employed to encourage witnesses to assist in criminal prosecutions and have included cases where it is necessary to protect the identity of a police informer,[37] and female witnesses in a pornography and procuring trial.[38] In both sets of cases, it is important to realise that the real motivation behind the grant of anonymity is not considerations relating to the convenience of witnesses etc. but rather the longer-term interests of the effective prosecution of offenders.

Calcutt I and *II*: proposals for reform

Calcutt I concluded that protection of privacy in domestic law would be improved by a combination of a new set of criminal law offences and more effective self-regulation by the press. The introduction of a new civil law remedy for the infringement of privacy was postponed so that an improved system of self-regulation might be given a final chance.[39] Three new criminal offences were proposed in *Calcutt I* to prevent physical intrusion by the press. These were (1) entering private property without permission with intent to obtain personal information with a view to its publication; (2) placing a surveillance device on private property without permission with intent to obtain personal information with a view to its publication; (3) taking a photograph, or recording the voice of, an individual who is on private property without consent with a view to its publication and with intent that the individual be identifiable. A defence to any of these offences would exist where the intrusive act was done for the purpose of preventing, detecting or exposing the commission of any crime; or other seriously anti-social conduct; or for the protection of public health or safety.[40]

As to an improved system of self-regulation a new body – the Press Complaints Commission (PCC) – was proposed to consider *inter alia* whether newspapers or periodicals had committed unwarranted infringements of privacy through published material or the obtaining of such material. This and other norms of ethical journalism were to be laid down in a code of practice. Breach of the code would lead to censure and require publication of the PCC's adverse findings. The new body was to be financed by the press industry. If the PCC was subsequently deemed to have failed to provide effective regulation, Parliament should create in its place a statutory press tribunal with a power in law to enforce its findings.

Calcutt II which followed in January 1993,[41] concluded that the PCC which the press industry had set up in response to *Calcutt I* was in crucial respects a weaker body than that proposed in *Calcutt I*.[42] For example, *Calcutt I* had wanted the new body to be composed of persons who were appointed by a body which was independent of the press. Instead, the PCC was appointed by a body which was part of the press industry. *Calcutt I* had also wanted the new body to initiate inquiries rather than wait for a complaint to be made. Moreover, the period since *Calcutt I* had witnessed further examples of press intrusions into the lives of individuals.[43] There was evidence that some complainants in this period were dissatisfied with the length of time taken for investigation. Others argued that because the press controlled the appointment of members to the PCC, it could not appear truly independent. Accordingly, *Calcutt II* proposed that a statutory complaints tribunal be created. It further recommended that the government consider the case for a new civil wrong (or tort) for the infringement of privacy. As any new tort would not be restricted to the press, the recommendation clearly went beyond Sir David's terms of reference. Shortly afterwards, however, both the Lord Chancellor's Department[44] and the National Heritage Select Committee[45] produced reports endorsing the creation of such a new tort. The ball was now firmly in the Major government's court.

The Major government's response

The government published its response, *Privacy and Media Intrusion*, in July 1995,[46] by which time the press industry had already taken a number of measures to fend off the chorus of voices calling for statutory intervention. In June 1993 it instituted a helpline for members of the public concerned about whether the code of practice was being breached in a press investigation relating to the public. In November 1993 the PCC announced that, in future, disciplinary action could be taken against journalists and editors who breached the revised code of practice. Under this code, intrusions into an individual's private life, including the use of long-lens photography to obtain pictures of persons on private property, were not 'generally acceptable'.[47] Where the PCC deemed there to have been a breach of the code, the publication in question was 'duty bound' to print the adjudication with due prominence. Clause 5 further stated that material obtained by 'clandestine listening devices' or intercepted telephone conversations should not be published unless justified by the public interest. Further provisions of the code prohibit harassment[48] and the obtaining of information or pictures through misrepresentation.[49] Special guidance is given to the relevant privacy considerations in published material involving children.[50]

After the promolgation of the code, efforts to improve the system of self-regulation continued. In January 1994 a Privacy Commissioner was created, with powers to investigate urgent complaints about breaches of privacy under the code. The Commissioner was also to have powers to initiate investigations on his own[51] and to report to the PCC (now constituted with a non-press majority) with his recommendations.

Reviewing the industry's efforts to improve self-regulation, *Privacy and Media Intrusion* concluded that there was now no compelling case for statutory regulation.[52] Whilst further improvements to the press industry's system could still be made, neither criminal nor civil legislation ought to be brought forward. In the case of criminal sanctions, the government said it had been unable to construct workable legislation.[53] As for the introduction of a new civil law remedy, the consultation exercise carried out by the Lord Chancellor's Office had yielded no consensus about the need for such a reform.[54]

Extra-legal protection: media codes of practice

To date, the Labour administration led by Tony Blair has given little indication that it wishes to enact further statutory protection for privacy along the lines advocated by *Calcutt II* and others. It is clear therefore that non-legal forms of privacy protection will remain vitally important in practice. In this section, the privacy protections contained in the codes of practice found in broadcasting are analysed more closely.

Earlier, aspects of the code of practice for journalists and newspaper editors were noted. In the case of broadcasters, the Broadcasting Act 1996 established the Broadcasting Standards Commission (hereafter BSC) which took over the regulatory functions hitherto undertaken by the Broadcasting Complaints Commission (the Commission) and the Broadcasting Standards Council (the Council). The BSC is required by the Broadcasting Act 1996, s.107(1) to draw up a code of practice which will give guidance on the

> principles to be observed and the practices to be followed, in connection with the avoidance of . . . (b) unwarranted infringement of privacy in, or in connection with the obtaining of material included in such programmes.

The Commission was criticised for its failure to adopt a principled approach to privacy issues in its adjudications. Gibbons, for example, has written,

> In a field where there is a rich literature about freedom of speech and the desirability of giving it special protection in constitutional and legal adjudication, the Commission has avoided drawing upon it to guide its thinking.[55]

The consequence of this failure, Gibbons argues, was that the Commission was not accepted by broadcasters, some of whom believed that it acted 'merely a censor'.[56] Robertson and Nicol have claimed that a survey of the Commission's Annual Reports reveals inconsistent and irreconcilable adjudications.[57]

Gibbons too has noted that the Commission has adopted more than one approach to the question of whether an unwarranted invasion of privacy has occurred in instances of 'doorstepping', where the journalist attempts to obtain a comment or statement by waiting outside the home or workplace of the person whose views are sought and then confronting the latter when he or she makes an appearance.[58] One line of rulings suggests that doorstepping is justified (and thus a warranted invasion of privacy) only in cases when all other measures to obtain an interview have been tried and failed. Another line of cases suggests that, even where no alternative means of obtaining an interview exists, a lengthy period of encampment combined with persistent attempts to get an interview might be sufficient to sustain a finding of an unwarranted infringement of privacy. A third line of cases allows factors such as the degree of disquiet about the intended interviewee's alleged activities to affect considerations of whether the privacy intrusion was warranted. It is to be hoped that this unhappy state of affairs can be avoided by the BSC which, under the 1996 Act, is under a statutory duty to expound and justify the values and norms which underpin its code and adjudications.

The new regulatory body may also wish to reflect upon the separate code developed by the Council which, although primarily concerned with standards of taste and decency, reminded broadcasters of the privacy interests of those whose lives are caught up (usually in an involuntary way) in events which become newsworthy. The code continued,

> In some cases lives afterwards have to be reconstructed or new lives built. Television and radio should do nothing through a disregard for privacy which makes that process even more difficult once the spotlight has moved away.

The Council also spoke of the need for a public interest justification where an intrusion into privacy occurred and further required that specific consent be sought for filming inside hospitals, factories, schools and other 'closed' institutions.

Like its predecessors, the BSC cannot force a broadcaster found to have breached the BSC code to apologise or provide compensation for any injury or distress caused as a result of the breach. Unlike the PCC it has no power to initiate investigations of its own.[59]

In the case of commercial television services (terrestrial, satellite and cable) licensed by the Independent Television Commission (ITC), section 2 of the latter's Code of Practice lays down guidance about the circumstances in which an individual's privacy interests ought to be respected.[60]

Privacy and the European Convention on Human Rights and Fundamental Freedoms

The manifesto commitment of the present Labour administration to incorporate the above Convention requires us to consider the type of protection it offers privacy interests. Article 8 of the European Convention states:

1 Everyone has the right to respect for his private and family life, his home and his correspondence.
2 There shall be no interference by a public authority with the exercise of this right except such as is in accordance with the law and is necessary in a democratic society in the interests of national security, public safety or the economic well-being of the country, for the prevention of disorder or crime, for the protection of health or morals, or for the protection of the rights and freedoms of others.'

It follows then that to establish a violation of an Article 8 privacy right, a complainant would have to show three things:

1 that the concept of a 'private life' included control over access to personal information;
2 that the *state* had failed to *respect* the complainant's right to private life by allowing a private individual or organisation to obtain and publish personal information; and

3 that the resultant interference with the complainant's private life was either

    (a) not in accordance with the law, or

    (b) not for a legitimate aim, or

    (c) not necessary in a democratic society.

As the European Court has not doubted that the concept of a private life does embrace the notion of control over access to personal information, the question arises whether a state has failed to respect the right to private life when it allows others to obtain and publish personal information. *In X & Y v. Netherlands*[61] the Court stated that Article 8 is not merely concerned with the negative obligations on states not to interfere with individuals' private lives, but can in a more positive sense require the state to take measures designed to prevent interference by other individuals. The choice of means employed to secure compliance with Article 8 is however a matter which falls within a state's margin of appreciation.[62]

In assessing whether the right to private life in a specific instance does require the state to take steps to protect it, the Court has regard to the nature of the complainant's interest and the burden which would fall upon the state if the right was to be recognised. Where the interest of the complainant is deemed to be slight and the burden of reform upon the state great, this would militate against the conclusion that the right to respect had been violated. For the government it may be argued that the interplay of nuisance law, breach of confidence law and other miscellaneous statutory and common law provisions provides a degree of legal protection which the Strasbourg Court should be slow to deem inadequate.

On the remaining requirements that the interference be in accordance with the law, has a legitimate aim and is necessary in a democratic society, it is far from clear that the United Kingdom would be able to satisfy the Court. For example, there would appear to be no specific legal mandate for the intrusive conduct of the media.[63]

Despite such positive omens for privacy advocates, it should be remembered that when asked on a previous occasion to rule on what was in essence a free speech versus privacy dispute, the Commission in *Winer* v. *United Kingdom*[64] ruled that the absence of a privacy right actionable in domestic law did not demonstrate a lack of respect for the applicant's private life and home. Winer had complained that a book which revealed information about his married life (some of it true, some false) had violated Article 8. Winer's claim was rejected. His right to privacy was not wholly unprotected as he was able to (and indeed did) have recourse to defamation law in respect of the false allegations contained within the book. What of course *Winer*'s case does not tell us is what either the Commission or the Court would do when confronted with a case in which true information only was revealed and no domestic remedy existed to protect a complainant. One tendency of the Court in cases where Convention rights are in direct conflict is to concede a relatively wide margin of appreciation to a state, a stance which does little to advance the privacy interests of victims of media intrusions.

Conclusion

This article has considered the state of legal and extra-legal protection against media intrusion. Although the courts have tried to adapt existing legal remedies such as those provided by the law of confidence to the problem, successive governments have refused to countenance the intro- duction of a more general remedy for breach of privacy. For the time being, victims of intrusive media conduct will continue to be channelled along the improved, extra-legal remedy routes offered by the BSC, ITC and PCC. Whether these are sufficiently robust to handle further instances of intru- sive misconduct remains to be seen. In the final analysis, it is likely that the jurisprudence of the European Court of Human Rights will determine where the balance between individual privacy and media freedom lies.

Notes

1 The measure of parliamentary concern may be indicated by the frequency of Private Members' Bills in the 1980s which unsuccessfully sought to enshrine in law varying degrees of privacy protection. At the time of the announcement of the government's inquiry in April 1989, the Right to Reply bill sponsored by Tony Worthington MP had secured support from all sides of the House of Commons and had reached its report stage. Public concern over press intrusion was amply demonstrated in submissions to the inquiry. A poll carried out for the *News of the World* by MORI in 1989 showed that 73 per cent of the public agreed that the press intruded too much into the lives of public figures.
2 *Kaye* v. *Robertson* (1990). Reported as Appendix I to the *Report of the Committee on Privacy and Related Matters*, Cmnd. 1102 (1990), London: HMSO. ('Cmnd.' reflects that this paper is laid by command of the Crown for consideration before Parliament.)
3 These are examined below.
4 *Report of the Committee on Privacy and Related Matters*, Cmnd. 1102 (1990), London: HMSO.
5 *Privacy and Media Intrusion: The Government's Response*, Cmnd. 2918 (1995), London: HMSO, para. 1.5.
6 Cmnd. 2135 (1993), London: HMSO.
7 (1993) HMSO.
8 Cmnd. 2918 (1995), London: HMSO.
9 D. Feldman, *Civil Liberties and Human Rights* (Oxford: Clarendon Press, 1993) p. 356.
10 R. Wacks, *Privacy and Press Freedom* (London: Blackstone Press, 1995).
11 Interception of Communications Act 1985, s.1. This act does not, however, apply to technical surveillance devices.
12 The prohibition was originally contained in a statute from the last century, the Conspiracy and Protection of Property Act 1875, s. 7. For the current form of this offence see the Trade Union and Labour Relations Act 1992, s. 241. *Calcutt I* thought it was unlikely that this provision would be used against the press,

although it should be noted that despite its title, it has been invoked outside of industrial disputes to gatherings outside abortion clinics.

13 That is at least on two occasions – Protection from Harassment Act 1997, s. 7(2).

14 Section 1. For the purposes of the Act, 'harassment' includes alarming or distressing the person and 'conduct' includes speech, s. 7(1) and (3).

15 Highways Act 1980, s. 137.

16 *Hubbard* v. *Pitt* [1976] QB142.

17 It would of course have been open to the hospital management to rely on this form of action.

18 *Bernstein* v. *Skyviews Ltd* [1978] 1 QB 479.

19 *Tolley* v. *Fry* [1930] 1 KB 460.

20 *Bonnard* v. *Perryman* [1891] 2 ch. 269; *Fraser* v. *Evans* [1969] 1 QB 349.

21 *Joyce* v. *Sengupta* [1993] 1 WLR 337.

22 *Report of the Committee on Privacy and Related Matters.*

23 *Coco* v. *AN Clark (Engineers) Ltd* [1969] RPC 41, 47.

24 *Stephens* v. *Avery* [1988] 2 WLR 1280.

25 *AG* v. *Guardian Newspapers Ltd* (No. 2) [1990] 1 AC 109.

26 *Calcutt I* observed, 'In England and Wales, an interlocutory injunction will more readily be granted in a breach of confidence case than for defamation. In particular, whereas a defendant in a libel action need say no more than he intends to plead justification and an interlocutory injunction will be refused . . . by contrast in the case of breach of confidence he will need to make a strong case of public interest' (Cmnd. 1102 (1990), London: HMSO, at para. 8.10). The publication of photographs of the Princess of Wales (as she then was) exercising in the LA Fitness Centre, Isleworth Middlesex which appeared in the *Sunday Mirror* and *Daily Mirror* in November 1993 prompted lawyers acting for the Princess to obtain an interlocutory injunction, thus preventing further publication pending the outcome of her action for breach of confidence, contract and fiduciary duty. In the event the matter was settled out of court when the newspapers' owners paid the sum of £25,000 to a charity of Princess Diana's choice. One reason for the settlement may have been the fears of a consortium of newspaper owners that a victory for the Princess in the courts and the establishment of some form of privacy protection would seriously inhibit the newspapers' activities.

27 *AG* v. *Guardian Newspapers Ltd* (No. 2) [1990] 1 AC 109.

28 Although it should be noted that there is no need for any iniquitous conduct for the public interest defence to be available see *Lion Laboratories* v. *Evans* [1985] QB 526.

29 See Interception of Communications Act 1985 at pp. 55–6, 129–39.

30 For an assertion of the need for a prior relationship of confidence see the Law Commission, *Breach of Confidence*, Cmnd. 8388 (1981), London: HMSO. For the contrasting view that confidence can prevent disclosure upon the alternative principle of unconscionability see *Stephens* v. *Avery* [1988] 1 ch. 449, 456 *per* Browne-Wilkinson VC; and *AG* v. *Guardian Newspapers* (No. 2) [1990] 1 AC 109, 281 *per* Lord Goff. cf. *M & N* v. *Kelvin Mackenzie and News Group Newspapers Ltd*. (1988) (unreported). *Calcutt I* took the view that there had to be a prior relationship of confidence for the duty to attach (Cmnd. 1102 (1990) at para. 8.1).

31 *AG* v. *Jonathan Cape* [1976] 1 QB 752; *Woodward* v. *Hutchins* [1977] 1 WLR 760.

32 [1995] 1 WLR 804.

33 [1913] AC 417.

34 Children and Young Persons Act 1933, s. 49(1) as amended.

35 Children and Young Persons Act 1933, s. 39 as amended. There is an identifiable

trend in these cases towards allowing the identification of minors which has occurred mainly in cases involving extremely serious criminal conduct such as murder and rape. See for example, *R* v. *Lee (Anthony William) (A Minor)* [1993] 1 WLR 103.

36 Sexual Offences (Amendment) Act 1992. The bar is in force during the entirety of the alleged victim's lifetime regardless of whether the accused is subsequently convicted of the offence(s).

37 *R* v. *Reigate JJ ex parte Argus Newspapers* (1983) 147 JP 385.

38 *R* v. *Hove JJ ex parte Gibbons* (1981), *The Times* 19 June.

39 Hence the comment of the then Secretary of State for National Heritage (Rt. Hon. David Mellor QC MP) that the press was 'drinking at the last chance saloon'.

40 Where one or more of the new criminal offences had been committed, *Calcutt I* recommended that any person with 'sufficient interest' should be able to apply for an injunction to prevent the publication of information thereby obtained.

41 Cmnd. 2135 (1993), London: HMSO.

42 See further Cmnd. 2135 (1993), London: HMSO, at para. 3.94.

43 Ibid. at ch. 4.

44 Joint Report with the Scottish Office, *Infringement of Privacy* (1993), London HMSO.

45 *Fourth Report, Privacy and Media Intrusion* (1993), pp. 294–1.

46 Cmnd. 2918 (1995), London: HMSO.

47 Clause 4.

48 Clause 8.

49 Clause 7.

50 Clauses 12 and 13.

51 This had been recommended by *Calcutt I* in 1990 but had been rejected by the then chairman of the PCC, Lord McGregor of Durris.

52 Cmnd. 2918 (1995), London: HMSO, pp. 4–8. The PCC have since produced a Complainants' Charter, which commits the PCC to attaining specific standards of service in its dealings with the public.

53 Ibid. at para. 3.4.

54 Ibid. at paras 4.4–4.14.

55 E. Barendt, S. Bate, J. Dickens and J. Michael (eds), *The Yearbook of Media and Entertainment Law*, vol. 1 (Oxford: Oxford University Press, 1995), p. 134. One might add that a principled discussion of free speech must ask where the limits of this freedom lie.

56 Ibid.

57 Geoffrey Robertson and Andrew Nicol, *Media Law*, 3rd edn (Harmondsworth: Penguin Books, 1992) p. 554.

58 *Yearbook of Media and Entertainment Law*, p. 134.

59 In *R* v. *BCC ex parte Granada TV* (1994) *The Times*, 14 December, the Court of Appeal noted that the Commission had been given a wide latitude to determine what constituted 'privacy'. The courts would not, in other words, lightly interfere with the Commission's views on the matter.

60 The Broadcasting Act 1990, s. 7 states that the ITC must do 'all that it can to secure that the provisions of the code are observed in the provision of licensed services'.

61 (1986) 8 EHRR 235.

62 Within which the Court will not interfere.

63 See *Malone* v. *UK* (1985) 7 EHRR 14. A separate question – one not tackled here – is whether the interference is for a legitimate aim.

64 *No. 10871/84*, 48 DR 154 (1986).

9 Taming the tabloids
Market, moguls and media regulation

Bob Franklin and Rod Pilling

Self-congratulation and self-regulation

On 31 January 1996 Lord Wakeham, Chair of the Press Complaints Commission (PCC), hailed 1995 as 'a momentous year for the PCC' and for press self-regulation. 'We proved', said the carefully crafted press release, 'that the Commission is *independent* and that it can *bite* when necessary.' Few observers of the shaky progress of the Commission since its inception in January 1991 will have recognised Wakeham's description of the Commission as a forceful watchdog guarding against press misbehaviour; even fewer will have been moved to endorse Wakeham's self-congratulatory and bullish appraisal of the Commission's performance. Wakeham's confidence was undoubtedly boosted by a single high-profile case in 1995, which gave the PCC a considerable public fillip.

In April 1995 Britain's youngest tabloid editor Piers Morgan, then editor of the *News of the World*, ran a front-page story about the secret hospitalisation of Countess Spencer, under the splash headline 'Di's sister-in-law in booze and bulimia clinic'. This story must have promised, to Morgan, to be the latest in a line of royal and other scandals which had already won him and his paper three awards in his brief 16-months' tenure of the editorial chair. To Countess Spencer's husband, Earl Spencer, not surprisingly, it seemed very different. He complained to the PCC that it was an intrusion into his wife's privacy and a flagrant breach of the Commission's code of conduct. Given his celebrity and his fury, his complaint received media attention. Morgan tenaciously defended his decision to print, pointing out that the Spencers had sought favourable publicity in *Hello* magazine and that they must therefore be prepared for less favourable publicity. Morgan knew, of course, that the PCC's code of conduct provided a potential defence for such intrusions; he had used it in the past. It protected the publication of stories 'preventing the public from being misled by some statement or action of an individual or organisation'. His newspaper's defence had been forthright – a full-page article headed, 'Hypocrisy of the Earl Spencer . . . his privacy can be invaded for cash'. As the headline implies, his newspaper pointed out in no uncertain terms that the Spencers were very happy to receive – and even be paid for – certain types of publicity. It was therefore morally right for their public image to be investigated and exposed by the *News of the World*.

So far, this looked like a typical – if unusually heated – spat between a tabloid editor and a celebrity 'victim'. But then a significant exchange of letters elevated the débâcle to a new significance. Lord Wakeham took the unprecedented step of writing to the *News of the World*'s owner and publisher, Rupert Murdoch. The decision to involve the publisher was a new tactic in the PCC's limited armoury, although it had threatened such a strategy at the beginning of 1995. Murdoch, as so often, acted unpredictably. He astonished Morgan by giving him a ferocious dressing down and, on May 12, startled media commentators by making public his rebuke. He described Morgan as 'a young man' who had gone 'over the top'. Murdoch announced, 'I have reminded Mr Morgan forcefully of his responsibility to the code to which he as editor – and all our journalists – subscribe in their terms of employment.'[1] Morgan, evidently shocked by Murdoch's reprimand, publicly offered his 'sincere apologies' to Countess Spencer and accepted the PCC adjudication 'without reservation'. Lord Wakeham, well aware of his considerable public relations coup for the PCC and self-regulation, welcomed the intervention of the proprietor.

This incident, potentially a turning-point for the PCC, raises interesting questions about self-regulation. First, why is intrusion into privacy such an important issue and apparently so sensitive that it requires the intervention of a global media magnate? If the nature of PCC complaints can be considered as an indicator of public concerns, moreover, then newspaper accuracy – which accounted for 70 per cent of 1995's 2,508 complaints – is far more significant in public perceptions. Yet the PCC itself recognises the special importance of intrusion into privacy. It says in its 1995 annual report, 'Although only 12% of the complaints received by the Commission in 1995 related to intrusion into privacy, the task of ensuring that the provisions of the Code protecting the private lives of individuals are upheld is at the heart of the PCC's work';[2] this view is endorsed by the most powerful media figure in Britain, Rupert Murdoch. Why is this? One reason for this preoccupation is the PCC's sensitivity to the concerns of the Westminster establishment. There has been a succession of attempts to give some legal protection to privacy across the last decade, including unsuccessful bills introduced by back-bench MPs, the Calcutt inquiry of 1990, which recommended privacy legislation and the subsequent review of self-regulation in 1993 and, more recently, the revived proposal by the Lord Chancellor Lord Mackay for a civil tort of invasion of privacy.[3] The PCC is also responding to wider public concern about the role of the press. A MORI poll in 1992 echoed Westminster anxieties about press behaviour. Perhaps more significantly the PCC, and even Murdoch, recognises that issues of privacy are at the centre of widespread changes in journalism.

The old 'rumpy-pumpy': tabloid journalism and market pressures

It is widely argued that there has been a move toward a more tabloid
agenda in journalism. A focus on celebrities – and especially titillating
revelations about their private lives – has increasingly driven the news
values of the popular tabloid newspapers.[4] The *Sun* and its sister paper
the *News of the World* have been the undisputed market leaders in this
development although they have spawned a range of imitators. A range of
factors have triggered this development in news values. First, the key
players in Fleet Street – especially Kelvin Mackenzie, the editor of the
Sun during the 1980s – believed it was what readers wanted and that their
sales success proved this. Mass circulation tabloids, which characteristically gain most of their revenue from their cover price, are very much
driven by sales. Advertising success also rests principally on sales volume.
The kiss-and-tell formula is popular and popularity is a prerequisite for
the profitability of the tabloids. Second, the competition between tabloid
newspapers is intense. The Bingo wars of the 1980s gave way to the price
wars of the 1990s, especially marked by the *Sun*'s attack on the price front
on 12 July 1993.

But the search for circulation-boosting stories has been constant. That
search has often led journalists to explore people's private lives, those of
celebrities if possible, but of pseudo-celebrities or others if not. The
editors who were leading the field demonstrated this daily in their col-
umns. A tabloid veteran told ex-*Daily Mirror* editor Roy Greenslade about
the values that Piers Morgan was bringing from the *Sun* to *News of the
World*: 'I must say, Piers loves the old rumpy-pumpy. We can't get enough
to please him'.[5] This fierce competition between rival tabloids has developed in the context of the long-term decline in their sales in the post-war
period combined with growing competition from radio and television as
news sources. These latter media can deliver news more quickly than the
tabloids but, because of the regulatory regime to which they are subject,
are unable to compete on titillation. An important part of the tabloid
response to these broadcast rivals has been the constant quest for 'rumpy-
pumpy' or, expressed rather differently, a constant drive to intrude into
other people's privacy. Broadly speaking, people's private lives, especially
their sex lives, sell newspapers; such revelations always have. Some newspapers – notably the Sundays – have specialised in sex, crime and scandal
since the middle of the nineteenth century.[6] A new feature of this long-
standing obsession with the sexual habits of the famous and infamous is
its rampant spread across most parts of the media.

This tabloid agenda has not been limited to Sunday or daily mass-
circulation tabloid newspapers. Broadsheets have picked up many of the
tabloid stories and run with them, as they have fought their own battles to
retain and win a greater circulation in heated price wars. Lengthy features
have been run in the 1990s on the late Princess of Wales's relationships

with various men, while other stories have focused on film actor Hugh Grant's notorious liaison with Los Angeles prostitute Divine Brown; coverage of the latter story was greater in the *Guardian*, for example, than in any other paper.[7] The influence of the tabloids, moreover, does not seem to be limited to print media. Academics and regulators have criticised a shift in mainstream news programmes to a more tabloid agenda in which lighter stories about celebrities seem to be displacing coverage of serious foreign and other news stories.[8] Observers typically explain this preference for lighter stories by reference to the drive for ratings in a more competitive broadcasting environment and to lighter regulation. At the least-regulated end of broadcast news production – cable television – L!ve TV features the news bunny who signals approval or disapproval of news items by making thumbs up or thumbs down gestures; news bulletins are part of a schedule which includes topless (female) darts and 'lunchbox volleyball' which features young men in tight-fitting lycra shorts playing volleyball.

The gossip editor of the *National Enquirer*, Mike Walker, has noticed a different attitude towards gossip in the two years that his paper has been circulating in Britain and establishing an estimated 100,000 circulation. When invited on to television shows in 1996 he said he was no longer asked 'those questions about privacy, ethics and libel suits. Now they just introduce me as the *National Enquirer*'s "guru of gossip", and get right to the naughty bits: "Welcome back, Mike. So . . . who's doing Sharon Stone?"' If Walker is to be believed, the commodification of gossip is well advanced, and, unsurprisingly, he has a rationale for it: 'Gossip, after all, is just another word for news in a slinky red dress.'[9]

In defence of the indefensible

This move to a more tabloid agenda and the pressures it places on journalists to intrude into people's privacy explains the context in which issues of privacy became the most politically sensitive of public concerns about the press in the late 1980s and early 1990s.[10] The 'threat' of legislation to offer statutory protection of privacy undoubtedly underlies the importance and sensitivity which Wakeham and Murdoch attribute to the issue; both are eager to demonstrate that privacy is already adequately defended. In truth it is not. The limited protection of the press which prevails is contained in the PCC's *Code of Conduct*, a code agreed voluntarily by decision-makers in the newspaper industry, who also fund the PCC. The code specifically forbids intrusions 'into an individual's private life' except when it is in the 'public interest'. The 'public interest' can be established in three ways: by 'detecting a crime or a serious misdemeanour', by 'protecting public health and safety' or by 'preventing the public from being misled by some statement or action of an individual or organisation'.[11]

It was on the third of these criteria that Piers Morgan had largely based his defence for his intrusion into the life of the Spencers. He argued that they had voluntarily put their personal lives into the public arena and had made statements about it, so the *News of the World* report, which corrected their public image, was justified. The *News of the World* and other tabloids had cited the same defence in the discussion of a number of earlier stories that had involved intrusion. They were not alone in this. The notion that someone who seeks publicity is fair game for intrusive stories is bandied about on broadcast discussion programmes by journalists with enough regularity for an observer to conclude that it is an influential ethic in tabloid journalism. The *News of the World*, moreover, had received prizes rather than adverse adjudications for recent stories. Morgan and his colleagues had picked up awards from their fellow journalists for those efforts, which included several sexual scandals. To Morgan, Earl Spencer seemed to want to enjoy media attention on his own terms, only for positive self-promotion, and the code gave him the right to investigate and expose the 'hypocrisy' of that public image. To others, anxious about the right to privacy, this clause in the code seemed like a convenient loophole for almost every circulation-chasing story that invaded the private life of a celebrity or news-maker.

The PCC's rejection of Morgan's interpretation of the code clearly shocked him and some of his fellow journalists. This ruling seemed to throw some doubt over what had seemed clear-cut. Perhaps people who had enjoyed publicity, or had even been paid for it, were not necessarily fair game for intrusion. This conclusion is not inevitable; the PCC's ruling made clear it was distinguishing between Earl Spencer's rights to privacy and Countess Spencer's and that it was concerned by the intrusion into the latter's. However, 'ordinary' people may well conclude that the degree of protection from the code may depend on the complainant's connections and celebrity; not everyone has the high profile of Princess Diana's brother and sister-in-law. Geoffrey Robertson, the eminent media lawyer who chronicled the earlier failure of self-regulation in the Press Council, declared less than one month later that the PCC was a 'fraud and a con trick'.[12] But one point was inescapable: one of the most audacious of tabloid journalists – an opinion-leader – had been stopped in his tracks and the right to privacy had been publicly upheld.

Proprietorial pressures: the real regulatory power?

The way in which the right to privacy was defended, however, does raise a major issue concerning the role of the publisher in self-regulation. It was Murdoch's intervention which had proved crucial in securing Morgan's contrition and promised compliance with the PCC Code. This touches a nerve. Commentators on the generally unsuccessful Press Council have remarked that it only enjoyed a period of success when it had the support of two dominant publishers of that era, the so-called 'King–Thomson consensus'.[13] Conversely, accounts of the Press Council's least effective period, the mid- and late 1980s, show that more adjudications were registered against Rupert Murdoch's newspapers than against any other, without any apparent disapproval from the dominant Fleet Street proprietor. Indeed, at least one of these newspapers – the *Sun* under Kelvin Mackenzie's editorship – notoriously derided an adverse ruling of the Press Council and repeated the offending statements without any apparent reproof from Murdoch. It seems that self-regulation is not an independent system but depends on the support of those powerful individuals who are publishers and owners. This is a worrying form of accountability in a liberal democracy, one which is not expressed in constitutional form and is not a public process. It is also unreliable.

The support of a publisher is potentially fragile and fickle, as the highest profile PCC case of 1993, the so-called 'Di Spy' case, had shown. Mirror Group Newspapers (MGN) had withdrawn from the PCC after criticism from the then chairman, the late Lord McGregor, of the *Daily Mirror*'s decision to publish seven pages of photographs of the Princess of Wales wearing a leotard and cycling shorts and using an exercise machine. The photographs had been taken by a camera concealed in the gymnasium ceiling and had been sold to the *Daily Mirror* by the gymnasium owner. McGregor had decided to make an immediate personal statement in which he said that MGN was 'deliberately breaching the ethical boundaries which mark out an agreed competitive playing field for newspapers'.[14] The *Mirror*'s defence that the pictures illustrated a potential security risk for the Princess of Wales, that the gym was a public place and that the photographs had merely been purchased rather than taken by its own photographers, did little to placate McGregor or the *Mirror*'s competitor papers.[15] During the row, McGregor called for advertisers to boycott MGN newspapers, while the *Mirror* responded by describing McGregor as 'an arch buffoon'.

Within two days of initial publication, then *Mirror* editor David Banks announced that MGN were leaving the PCC. This would mean 25 per cent (by circulation) of Britain's national newspapers opting out of self-regulation, a loss to the PCC of MGN's contribution of over £100,000 and an end, effectively, to the credibility of self-regulation. The seriousness of the situation was marked by the importance of the peace negotiators. Interventions by Murdoch himself, and Sir David English, were crucial to the negotiation of a settlement between David Montgomery of MGN and Lord McGregor. Within 24 hours of leaving, the *Daily Mirror* returned to the PCC, which spent two hours discussing measures to enhance the credibility of self-regulation and prevent statutory regulation.[16] McGregor argued that the intervention of such senior figures was a demonstration of the strength of support for self-regulation but the incident also points to a worrying fragility. A system of regulation sustained and policed by the interventions of powerful individuals is potentially unsustainable, lacks any public accountability and seems to rest on arbitrary power rather than any legitimate authority. It also seemed, in this case, to be primarily determined by a desire to avoid the kind of regulation that was being threatened, a strategy to retain that power rather than submit it to authority.

Steering the blind goddess: directions for regulation reforms

If self-regulation is potentially unstable and if its success since the founding of the Press Council in 1953 has been at best patchy, what is the alternative? Is it further regulation? Journalists and editors have routinely mustered six arguments against statutory intervention. They believe: it is wrong in principle and constitutes censorship; it is impractical and unworkable; there are already too many statutory controls on press freedom; there is no evidence that it is necessary (for example, the PCC only found against newspapers 28 times in 1995); self-regulation is more flexible and allows a discourse, mediated by PCC, between readers and publishers; self-regulation offers the most effective sanction against potential offenders – namely peer review. British parliaments have also traditionally been wary of adding further legal restrictions on the press. Lord Wakeham, a veteran of Conservative regimes, said, on joining the PCC, 'As a Parliamentarian, I was *instinctively* in favour of self-regulation and opposed to statutory controls on the press.'[17]

Journalists are already subject to considerable regulation. William Waldegrave's 1992 White Paper *Open Government* listed 251 statutory instruments restricting disclosure of information which limit media competence to report government activity.[18] Newspapers are also subject to 46 legislative restrictions, including the various Official Secrets Acts 1911 to 1989 and the Prevention of Terrorism Act 1989.[19] This protection of information – and a readiness to impose injunctions preventing publication – is not balanced by statutory or constitutional rights to information. There is neither a general constitutional right of access to information in the public interest nor a Freedom of Information Act. The eminent media and civil rights lawyer, Geoffrey Robertson, has long believed that the general thrust of the law actually encourages kiss-and-tell intrusions into privacy and discourages public interest investigation: 'British law is the enemy of the British press. It circumscribes press virtues and comforts press vices. The blind Goddess of Justice raises her sword against the investigative journalist while her other hand fondles the Sunday muckraker.'[20]

Lawyers have notoriously been able to protect powerful people from disclosure by threatening litigation under various headings. Ironically, one of the most infamous of recent cases involves a media mogul. Robert Maxwell's small army of élite lawyers was successfully deployed to prevent publication by investigating journalists of allegations that he was abusing control of MGN pension funds. It was only after Maxwell's death that the long-suspected crimes came to light. Robertson would not have been surprised; he made this point about the 'blind goddess of British justice' more than ten years earlier: 'She suppresses the truth about crooked financiers, disreputable companies and hypocritical politicians on the pretexts of contempt of court, breach of confidence and infringement of copyright.'[21]

Robertson argued persuasively that the law made it easier to pursue kiss-and-tell stories than serious investigation. This adds a further powerful dynamic to that of the market in the shift toward a tabloid agenda, and a further pressure on privacy. The libel law has been a powerful and lucrative weapon for the wealthy; its high costs intimidate and counsel caution to even the bravest journalistic enquirer. Courts can punish inaccuracy with costly settlements, which most people cannot meet and yet the law of libel does not actually protect privacy. If a reporter can establish some aspect of a person's private life accurately, then it can be reported. There is, in effect, no legal protection for those aspects of the private lives of people that sell to newspapers. If a disgruntled lover, wife, husband or mistress wishes to retaliate by retailing accounts of a 'romance' to the tabloids, and they can provide adequate detail and substantiation, then there is little that the other parties can do to protect their own privacy. Conversely, an investigative journalist undertaking a serious enquiry into a matter of public concern has few rights of discovery of information and meets many obstacles to disclosure and publication.

Public and political concern with press behaviour in the late 1980s led to pressure for legislation to curb alleged intrusions. Regrettably, the effect of this legislation has been overwhelmingly to curb press behaviour and to give rights to people who were being written about, rather than to give journalists rights of enquiry and publication. Strong parliamentary support in 1989 for back-bench bills to give protection for privacy and a right of reply for victims of inaccuracy prompted the government to put the press on probation and to set up the Calcutt inquiry. The then Heritage Secretary, David Mellor, told the press that they were 'drinking at the last-chance saloon'. The Calcutt Report recommended closure of an ineffective Press Council, the introduction of a new self-regulatory body, which would itself be on probation for 18 months, and the introduction of civil laws to protect privacy.[22] The Press Council had few supporters and was closed at the end of 1990. The Press Complaints Commission replaced it but no privacy laws were introduced. The PCC was judged by Calcutt at the end of its probation to be 'ineffective' and he recommended a new statutory body with powers to fine and order corrections and apologies.[23] The government ignored his proposals. The PCC made changes, introducing some faster procedures, a new privacy ombudsman, more lay members and, after criticism of its chair, brought in Lord Wakeham, Mrs Thatcher's veteran political fixer, to revitalise the leadership of this regulatory body. But despite these piecemeal changes, many observers believed that the government should make a broader, more coherent, statement about regulation. A White Paper promised since early 1993 was repeatedly delayed. In March 1994, the Association of British Editors (ABE), undoubtedly exasperated by the government's unwillingness to express an opinion, published 'an alternative white paper' entitled *Media Freedom and Regulation*. It concluded that the British press was already unduly regulated and that it was unnecessary 'to create an entirely new wrong of infringement of privacy'.[24] In reaching this conclusion, the ABE rejected Lord Mackay's green paper suggestion that a new civil tort of privacy should be established with maximum fines of £1,000 for infringement. In July 1995, the government finally published its views on privacy and press freedom; it concluded that statutory regulation of the press was not desirable.[25]

Media attention throughout this flurry of reforming activity centred on the Calcutt Report and the official responses it engendered. Wider parliamentary concern to reform press behaviour, however, was illustrated by the report from the National Heritage Committee which favoured a statutory press ombudsman as well as by the proposal from back-bencher Clive Soley. His Freedom and Responsibility of the Press bill was a rare attempt to give public interest reporting rights to press journalists as well as an attempt to impose a statutory regulator on the press along the lines of the Independent Broadcasting Authority. By 1996, however, there was no prospect of statutory regulation; Wakeham, the PCC and the newspaper industry had persuaded politicians and public alike that self-regulation offered a sufficient guarantee of privacy.

The clamour of editors against curbing 'press freedom' and against censorship enjoys a long and honourable tradition. Bentham expressed it vigorously: 'The Liberty of the press has its inconveniences, but the evil which may result from it is not to be compared to the evil of censorship.'[26] This tradition, moreover, takes strength from Macaulay's concept of the press as the fourth estate of a liberal democracy, with a role to report on the powerful and make public their actions. In the light of this perception, few would wish to subscribe to legislation which would curb exposure of the corruption of a government or a media mogul; indeed, many might wish to see legislation which strengthened the hand of the fourth estate in this sort of enquiry. Public and political concerns, however, do not currently centre on the media as a fourth estate. There is a widely understood sense that we live in an age in which an individual's privacy has become a commodity which can be sold to a mass audience. A defence of tabloid journalism from the *News of the World* editor, Piers Morgan, illustrates the point: 'I'm not dictating to ordinary people, but say a married woman sleeps with the village policeman, her husband finds out, there's a fight and someone tells the *News of the World*. Then we'll run it. Is that wrong? Well, 4.9 million people thoroughly enjoyed the *News of the World* last week.'[27] In effect, says Morgan, the readers should have their titillation, unchecked apart from a voluntary code. The former *Daily Mirror* editor,

Roy Greenslade, writing about the very public media row over *Daily Mail* investigations into the private life of *The Independent* associate editor, Polly Toynbee, expressed concern about the consequences of this trade in private lives: 'intrusion into privacy is much less common than people believe. But when it happens it can have the most awful repercussions, ruining the victims' lives for ever.'[28] Greenslade points to a question central to the arguments about press regulation that have been occurring since the mid-1980s: 'Who is entitled to privacy?' The drive of market forces and the thrust of the law could well mean that very few – apart from media moguls – have this right. Journalism may be approaching a situation where news and gossip do become synonymous, and gossip editor Walker's view that 'Gossip, after all, is just another word for news in a slinky red dress' becomes widely accepted.[29]

Epilogue: the costs and rewards of self-regulation

What will be the cost to people's private lives of this trend towards tabloid reporting? And who will suffer? Clearly, celebrities will find themselves the subject of the greatest attention because their private lives are the most saleable. In 1996 television presenter Selina Scott complained to the PCC about a report headed 'My sex and smoked salmon with TV's Selina' which reported a relationship which allegedly happened 18 years earlier. But the most serious casualties of this journalistic trend will be ordinary people who, when their lives take some dramatic and often tragic turn, can find themselves at the centre of press interest. Lacking the financial and legal resources necessary to halt press intrusion, their everyday lives and experiences can be transformed into a commodity which can sell newspapers. Accounts of such ordinary 'tragedies' appear with increasing regularity in the tabloids; some 'survivors' argue that journalists' behaviour in reporting their story can be more distressing and damaging than the initial incident that triggered the media attention.[30] For ordinary people, self-regulation can prove a very costly business.

   Those people who find themselves politically at odds with the too-evident partisan commitments of the tabloids will also find themselves the subject of investigation. In 1996 *The Independent*'s Polly Toynbee wrote in favour of divorce law reforms, which the *Daily Mail* was campaigning against. She discovered that the *Daily Mail* was researching her relationship with a married journalist who had separated from his wife. She presumed its response was not going to be a thematic rebuttal of her own arguments, but a portrayal of her as a marriage-wrecker and she responded by writing her own attack on the *Daily Mail*.[31] In late 1995 Labour's deputy leader, John Prescott, discovered that his past was being researched by the *Daily Mail*. He began to receive telephone calls from former shipmates from the 1950s and 1960s to warn him that they had been grilled by a *Daily Mail* journalist about the young John Prescott. The line of questioning showed little interest in his political qualities. It centred on whether he had girlfriends, went drinking, was a bully and so on.[32] Prescott, like Toynbee, decided to attack before this was published. He used a guest column in the *News of the World* to denounce the *Mail*'s 'blatant attempt to drag my name into the gutter with slurs, smears and innuendo'. The *Mail* explained that a human interest feature had been misunderstood. Both Toynbee and Prescott were able to use rival media to defend themselves. In Prescott's case this seemed to put an end to any feature; in Toynbee's it provoked the *Daily Mail* into a response, with a feature on the 'wronged wife'. It also provoked much media comment in other quarters. Barbara Amiel, a regular *Daily Telegraph* columnist and wife of its proprietor, Conrad Black, the Canadian newspaper magnate, showed little sisterly sympathy for Toynbee's plight. After attacking Toynbee's journalistic record and perspective, she prescribed the following remedy: 'As for gutter journalism, I have turned it to profit. My husband has been the target of many poorly researched and actionable stories . . . We have a deal. I get part of his settlement to spend on frocks. Since he has never lost an action, this has been helpful to my clothes budget. It's a minor point in the debate, but a major one for me.'[33] Media lawyer Geoffrey Robertson might express little surprise at this sentiment. He argued almost twenty years ago that libel was a particular source of protection, and further wealth, for the already wealthy and powerful, 'a tax-free bonus to assuage the *amour propre* of wealthy libelled litigants'.[34] Ms Amiel clearly feels adequately protected, as well as gracefully clothed, by the current situation, but what about those people who are not married to press magnates? What protection can they expect as gossip increasingly mimics 'news in a slinky red dress'?

Notes

1 Joanna Coles, 'Murdoch blasts his young editor who went over the top after press body attacks NoW's countess coverage', *Guardian*, 15 May 1995.
2 Press Complaints Commission, *Annual Report 1995* (London: Press Complaints Commission), 1995.
3 For a discussion of the various proposals for reform of press regulation see Bob Franklin, *Packaging Politics: Political Communications in Britain's Media Democracy* (London: Edward Arnold, 1994), pp. 45–9.
4 For a discussion of changing news values see Bob Franklin, *Newszak and News Media* (London: Arnold, 1997) and James Fallows, *Breaking The News* (New York: Pantheon, 1995).
5 Quoted in Roy Greenslade, 'The nuts and bolts of the Screws', *Guardian*, 17 April 1995.
6 See Matthew Engel's *Tickle the Public: One Hundred Years of the Popular Press* (London: Gollancz, 1996).
7 Steve Peak and Paul Fisher, *The Media Guide* (London: Fourth Estate, 1996).
8 Rod Pilling, 'Changing news values in ITN's bulletins for ITV', unpublished MA thesis, University of Keele, 1995.

9 Mike Walker, 'Panting for gossip? Just enquire within', *Guardian*, 27 May 1996.

10 Ray Snoddy, *The Good, the Bad and the Unacceptable* (London: Faber, 1992).

11 Press Complaints Commission, *Code of Conduct* (London: Press Complaints Commission, 1994).

12 Geoffrey Robertson quoted in Peak and Fisher, *Media Guide*, p. 24.

13 See Jeremy Tunstall, *The Media in Britain* (London: Constable, 1983).

14 Andrew Culf, 'Press counts the cost of outrage by Mirror', *Guardian*, 8 November 1993.

15 See David Banks, 'Put up or shut up', *UK Press Gazette*, 14 February 1993, p. 1 and Hugo Young, 'Privacy curbs would only be the half of it', *Guardian*, 11 November 1993.

16 Andrew Culf, 'Rivals press Mirror to rejoin Commission', *Guardian*, 10 November 1993.

17 Press Complaints Commission, *Annual Report 1995* (London: Press Complaints Commission, 1995).

18 Cited in Hugh Stephenson, *Media Freedom and Media Regulation* (London: Association of British Editors, 1994).

19 See Andrew Belsey and Ruth Chadwick, *Ethical Issues in Journalism and the Media* (London: Routledge, 1992).

20 Geoffrey Robertson 'Law for the press', in James Curran (ed.) *The British Press: A Manifesto* (London: Routledge, 1978).

21 Robertson, ibid.

22 David Calcutt, *Report of the Committee on Privacy and Other Matters*, Cmnd. 1102 (London: HMSO, 1990).

23 David Calcutt, *Review of Press Self-Regulation*, Cmnd. 2135 (London: HMSO, 1993).

24 Stephenson, *Media Freedom*, p. 12.

25 *Privacy and Media Intrusion: The Government's Response*, Cmnd. 2918 (London: HMSO, July 1995), p. 16.

26 Quoted in Alan Lee, *The Origins of the Popular Press in England 1855–1914* (London: Croom Helm, 1976), p. 23.

27 Piers Morgan, quoted in the *Guardian*, 17 October 1994.

28 Roy Greenslade, 'The Polly and Paul show', in the *Guardian*, 17 June 1996.

29 Walker, 'Panting for gossip?'.

30 For an account of how those involved in tragedies cope with the subsequent media reporting of that involvement see Anne Shearer, *Survivors and the Media* (London: Broadcasting Standards Council and John Libbey, 1992).

31 For details of this case see Greenslade, 'The Polly and Paul show'.

32 Seumas Milne, 'Wary of the Press Gang', *Guardian*, 22 January 1996.

33 Barbara Amiel, 'Publish and be damned by your cant Polly Toynbee', *Daily Telegraph*, 13 June 1996.

34 Geoffrey Robertson, 'Law for the press'.

10 Ethical photojournalism in the age of the electronic darkroom

Nigel Warburton

In the sceptical phase of his *Meditations*, René Descartes entertains the possibility that all his experiences might have been caused by the artifice of an evil demon: 'I will suppose that the heavens, the air, the earth, colours, shapes, sounds and all external things that we see are only illusions and deceptions which he uses to take me in.'[1] This evil demon manipulates Descartes's sensory inputs to give a convincing illusion of direct engagement with reality. Descartes gets the same sort of experiences he would have had had they been caused by engagement with reality; but it is all the work of the demon.

The evil demon finds its modern equivalent in the cynical photojournalist or picture editor who uses new electronic technology to manipulate what the viewer of a news photograph sees. Sophisticated computer technology which converts an image to pixels, each of which can be electronically controlled, allows almost anyone to manipulate photographs convincingly.[2] In a matter of minutes two photographs can be combined seamlessly to give the illusion that, for instance, John Major was rubbing shoulders with Tony Blair, when in fact they were standing on opposite sides of the room. Or, as actually occurred, two pyramids can be shunted electronically closer together in order to fit the portrait cover format of *National Geographic*[3]. Inconvenient details can be extracted without leaving any indication that they were ever there, and new details can be added from other photographs. In fashion photography it is now common practice for the photographs of models to be electronically altered: the pupils of their eyes are often enlarged, or their legs lengthened. We can't trust what we see in photographs any more.

Perhaps the only rational strategy in such circumstances is the Cartesian one of treating as false any belief acquired from looking at photographs, unless we can be absolutely certain that it is true. We have plenty of evidence that the demon-like picture editor is likely, on occasion, to deceive us. This casts doubt on the whole assumption of veracity which has traditionally been the starting-point of reputable photojournalism.

In newspaper and magazine journalism photography has traditionally played a major role, providing visual and memorable evidence for what the accompanying text described. War photography, for instance, illustrated more immediately than print ever could commonplace horrors and individual suffering. The Vietnam War lingers in many of our memories as a series of still photographs which provided evidence of particular events, but at the same time symbolised needless loss of life and cruelty. Malcolm Brown's image of a Buddhist monk's protest self-immolation, Eddie Adams's still of a police chief in Saigon executing a Vietcong officer with his pistol, and, of course, Huyn Cong Ut's unforgettable photograph of a naked girl, burnt by napalm, running towards the camera: these and other images had a profound effect on how that war was understood. But their effect depended upon their being reliable as documentary evidence for what they appeared to depict. Without the causal link back to a real event, these images would have been simply manufactured propaganda and would not have had the eyewitness status that they in fact did have. Readers of the magazines and newspapers in which they appeared quite reasonably took these to be photographs of real events, presenting in a legible way images of what actually happened. The convention of interpreting news photographs was based on trust: trust that the photographer wasn't duping picture editors about what his or her photographs really showed.

Now, in the age of the electronic darkroom, the informed viewer of a photograph should be sceptical about its origins, or perhaps even acknowledge that the old conventions of photography were based on an outdated cliché which we can no longer accept, that the camera never lies. In other words, from today photojournalism is dead. Theorists such as William J. Mitchell suggest that we have already moved into a post-photographic era.[4] It's just a matter of time before the newspaper-reading public catches on. Or so the story goes.

But this pessimistic view is mistaken. It is based on myths about the nature of photojournalism and the kinds of evidence it can provide, and about the kinds of evidence it has traditionally provided. The more optimistic line I want to take is that new technology should force photographers and picture editors to be far more aware of the moral implications of their practices.[5] Far from signalling the death of photojournalism, and particularly of ethical photojournalism, the electronic revolution could be the catalyst for its rejuvenation.

Is new photography different from old?

The claim that we are moving into a post-photographic era is based on the belief that electronic photography is fundamentally different from its optico-chemical forebears. With the new technology, so the argument goes, a new relationship between object, image and viewer is set up, and so the conventions surrounding photographic image production and reception must be transformed accordingly. The relevant features of new photography that distinguish it from old photography are:

(1) *Ease of manipulation*: Whilst the manipulation of photographs by means of cropping, dodging, burning in, composite printing and a whole range of darkroom procedures, has been possible for most of photography's history, the electronic darkroom facilitates such manipulation to an unprecedented degree. For instance, in order to produce a plausible photographic image of a footballer committing a handball offence in the penalty area, using as raw material a photograph of the same footballer with the ball at his feet, you would, if you used traditional optico-chemical methods, have to be a skilled photographic technician. Another way of producing a similar effect would be to use an airbrush; but, again, you would have to have quite a high level of skill to do this in a way that would be convincing. With computer-assisted manipulation of images, this sort of transformation of a photograph is relatively straightforward even for a novice. It could probably be done in a few minutes. One consequence of this is that virtually anyone with access to the appropriate machines can perform this sort of transformation.

(2) *Undetectability*: This has two aspects. First, the ways in which an image has been manipulated electronically can be undetectable. Seamless collage is a genuine possibility with the new media, whereas it was something less frequently achieved with the old. In the above example, no evidence of the original position of the ball would remain. Second, the electronic darkroom need not leave anything that you can go back to to check the accuracy of the print. Unlike the traditional forms of photography which, Polaroids and slides apart, left a negative as a touchstone against which subsequent manipulations of an image could be measured, video stills cameras need not leave any such objects. An edited picture file need not reveal that it has been edited, and the original can simply be deleted. Thus anyone attempting to demonstrate how an electronically produced photographic image has been manipulated has a difficult task.

(3) *Change from analogue to digital*: Traditional photographs are analogues of what they represent: every variation on the negative can in principle have a representational function. New photographs are digital, which means that they are genuinely reproducible, since the state of every pixel can be encoded. Perfect reproducibility is a new phenomenon for photography (even though at its inception old photography was hailed as intrinsically reproducible); however, it is not a relevant feature of photography for the present discussion.

(4) *Transmissibility*: New technology allows digitally produced images to be transmitted electronically without loss of quality. This has important implications for how photojournalists work, but is not relevant to the present discussion.

Of the four features of new photography outlined above, only the first and second, the ease and the undetectability of manipulation, are directly relevant to the issue of photographic truth. It should be noted that neither of these constitutes a difference in kind from traditional photography, only of degree. Everything that the new technology does in terms of manipulation has had its equivalent in pre-electronic photography. Skilful technicians have managed to produce equally undetectable images using traditional techniques. Besides which, most of the most successful deceptions using photography have been carried out outside the darkroom. Think of the case of the Cottingley Fairies which duped 'experts' for almost half a century,[6] or of Capa's 'Republican soldier at the very instant of his death', the authenticity of which has frequently been questioned, but never on the grounds of illicit photographic manipulation.[7] The new technology only speeds up what photojournalists could always do anyway: there is no relevant qualitative difference from this point of view between what the new electronic technologies can offer and what the optico-chemical ones always provided.

The ethics of news photography

So, the ethics of photojournalism in general is the real issue, not just of electronically based photojournalism. In order to address the central questions about the ethics of photojournalism, it is necessary to say something about photojournalistic conventions. Photography is clearly used in a wide variety of ways. Here I concentrate on news photography, and in particular on the use of photographs as evidence that an event took place. My concern is not with issues about the subject-matter of photographs, whether news photographers are insensitive, intrusive, irresponsible in their invasion of the private lives of public figures and so on. Rather I want to concentrate on the ethical questions about how they produce the images that they do, and whether or not they dupe viewers of those images about how they have been produced.

Imagine the following scenario. You pick up your morning tabloid on the way to work. On the front page is a photograph of a member of the royal family, a married princess no less, topless and in a compromising position with her bodyguard on a public beach. The picture is not in any way ambiguous. You can see who is involved and precisely what they are doing: no innocent explanation would be in the least bit plausible. The photograph is proof of what they did.

The photograph provides us with proof, or at least that is what we take for granted, because we have, consciously or unconsciously, acknowledged the conventions about how photographs are used accompanying news stories. We assume that the photograph really is a photograph of whoever the caption claims it is; we assume that what looks to be happening really was happening; we assume that the image before us is a photograph and not a skilfully executed painting, and so on. We might exercise a little healthy scepticism about how representative the depicted scene was of what was actually going on on the beach, but, as newspaper readers who have grown up with the conventions of photojournalism, we do not expect anything but a documentary photograph to accompany a news story. The photograph gives us convincing evidence of a special kind about what happened.

Now, consider how the image was made. The photographer climbed a tree with his camera and hung around for several hours until the couple emerged. He could scarcely believe what he was seeing through his tele-photo lens. He shot a roll of film, then sneaked off to have it developed, confident that he'd just made a year's salary in a few hours. To his dismay, a fault in the film meant that only half of the shots had come out; none of the more compromising ones were printable. But all was not lost; he scanned the photographs that had come out into his computer and within half an hour he had produced a composite picture showing more or less what he had seen through the telephoto lens. He felt justified in what he had done because he knew that the photograph was not misleading in any important way. He was committed to revealing the truth, and what better way to reveal the truth than with this striking image.

He sent the image electronically to the picture editor of his newspaper, who decided to make it the lead story. However, just to cover himself, the picture editor telephoned back to check that the photograph wasn't mis-leading. He asked the photographer whether it showed what really hap-pened; the photographer answered, honestly, that it did. So the photograph appeared on the front page of the newspaper the next day. None of the newspaper readers were aware of precisely how the photograph had been made, nor was the picture editor. They assumed that it was a straightfor-ward documentary photograph. Consequently they took it as incontrover-tible photographic evidence of the princess's misdemeanours.

Setting aside any issues of invasion of privacy, is there anything wrong with what the photographer did? The answer is surely yes. There are at least three reasons for this:

1 The image he sent down the wire to the newspaper wasn't *photographic evidence* for the action it seemed to show.
2 What the photographer did involved *deception* about how the image was made.
3 His deception took a step down a very *slippery slope* that could lead to the demise of news photography altogether.

We'll consider each of these reasons in turn.

Photographic evidence

Still photographs, because of reasonably direct and traceable causal links, can be good evidence for what they are indexically of (i.e. whatever was in front of the lens and left its trace on the light-sensitive film). Moving images tend to carry much more, and more accessible, information than still photographs; some aspects of most still photographs are ambiguous or indeterminate. But provided that you have external evidence about the conditions under which the photograph was taken, you may well be able to read off all kinds of information.

For instance, think of a photofinish in an Olympic 100 metres final; we can tell who crossed the line first, but only if we are confident that the camera angle is not misleading. We also have to know who was in which lane.[8] Aerial photographs can help us to construct maps if we know the height from which they were taken and possible distortions arising from weather conditions or other factors. X-rays and ultrasound images can give us a great deal of reliable information about the condition of bones, foetuses and internal organs, but they require specialist interpretation and are only usually produced in highly controlled conditions. And so on. The information in each case is there in virtue of such photographs being direct traces of their causes. We read information from these traces almost as if we were looking at the real things. Photographs picture their causes as well as being traces of them. But in some of the above cases appearances alone can be misleading, so we rely on other factual evidence from which we hypothesise the probable causes of the photographs' appearance.

However, most photojournalistic uses of photography differ significantly from the informational ones mentioned above. Typically the viewer does not have detailed information about the conditions under which photojournalistic images were taken. Minimal information is usually carried in captions, accompanying text, or else is implied by the context of presentation. This point is well illustrated by a famous case in France. Robert Doisneau photographed a young woman in a café on the Rue de Seine drinking a glass of wine and sitting next to an older man. The photograph was used to illustrate the dangers of alcohol in a leaflet issued by the temperance league; it was then used to illustrate a story in the magazine *Le Point*, where it appeared with the caption 'Prostitution on the Champs-Elysées'.[9] In both uses, the photograph looked right: there were no incongruous details which undermined the interpretation suggested by the caption. However, in both cases the captions misled: neither of the people photographed was an alcoholic, and neither of them a prostitute. However, viewers of the photograph in these contexts would not have been able to read off these facts from the image itself.

Photojournalistic images have meaning in virtue of three interrelated aspects:

1 what they are of, in the sense of what caused them;
2 what they look to be of;
3 how they are used in a particular context.

The legibility of documentary photography depends on a relation of trust with the photographer or picture editor; in the case of news photography the viewer trusts that he or she is not being misled about the way the image was produced and what it appears to depict. The context of presentation communicates directly (through captions, accompanying stories, etc.) and indirectly (through implicit conventions) a way of interpreting the image. In most cases there is nothing within the photograph which will inform the viewer whether or not the photograph is of what the context of presentation suggests that it is. For example, as I suggested in relation to the Capa photograph of a Republican soldier, external evidence is needed to confirm our interpretation of it as of a Republican soldier at the very instant of his death and not, as has been claimed, of a Republican soldier stumbling in training. So we rely on the sincerity of the presenter and on any external evidence we might happen to have.

In the imaginary case of the photographs of the princess, the image that the photographer used wasn't direct evidence of the event. His wasn't an informational photograph about the event depicted (though if you knew enough about how he actually made the photograph you would no doubt be able to read off many factual details from the direct evidence which the image carries). Nor, however, was it a documentary photograph of the event, since the event did not play the appropriate and implied causal role in the image's construction. Its value as evidence for that event was on a par with an artist's sketch made partly from memory. It was a *pictorial* photograph of that event masquerading as a documentary one:[10] in fact it was a deliberately deceptive quasi-documentary photograph.

Deception

What is most disturbing in such cases is that the viewer is deceived – not deceived about what went on between the princess and the bodyguard, but deceived about how the photograph was made, and so about the kind of evidence being presented. The context of presentation on the news pages of a newspaper implicitly communicates to the viewer that the conventions of documentary news photography have been adhered to. But in fact they haven't. A set of conventions has grown up about photographic communication of news. Roughly, readers of daily newspapers expect that the photographs used alongside news stories are not just photographic illustrations, not simply pictorial interpretations of events, but are reasonably direct traces of what they depict. In other words, if a photograph of a princess and her bodyguard is presented as part of a news story, then the readers will quite naturally assume that they are being presented with a documentary photograph, one which was produced by taking a photograph of the couple in question while they were doing what they appear to be doing in the photograph. Clearly many photographs have the potential to be misleading about what was going on, so it is part of the picture editor's job to select images which are as unambiguous as possible, and at least not misleading on substantial issues. If you present a documentary photograph of a particular princess performing a particular act, then her performing that act must have played a direct causal role in the production of the photograph; if you got a look-alike to enact what had happened and photographed that, it could only serve as a photographic illustration of what happened.

Presenting photographic illustrations is acceptable, provided that you make clear from the context, or explicit in the caption that that is what you are doing. The effect of seeing a photograph apparently of a Second World War bomber crash-landed on the moon is, for most people, disbelief. The front page headline for the *Sunday Sport* on 24 April 1988 was 'World War 2 Bomber Found on Moon', but the headline was no more credible than the photograph accompanying it. This would have been so even if the photograph hadn't appeared on the front page of the *Sunday Sport*, but on the front page of, say, *The Independent*. The photograph reveals itself as pictorial because of the nature of the event it depicts as having actually occurred. It is largely irrelevant as to how the image was produced, whether by composite printing using conventional optico-chemical methods, or by electronic, digitally-based procedures. However, a front page photograph of the princess and the bodyguard would carry different expectations wherever it was published: the photograph depicts an event which could plausibly have taken place. This is the kind of news story deception that we should be concerned about: a form of lying by implication about the kind of visual evidence being presented.

The photojournalist in my example deliberately deceived the picture editor and thus the public about the nature of the photograph. What seems to be documentary evidence, is really just an illustration of the event it purports to reveal. It is a quasi-documentary photocollage. 'So what?', the photojournalist might say, 'I've laid bare a more important truth. What I've done is the equivalent to a white lie. A small lie to communicate a more important truth.'

His point is that the photograph may not be in a direct optico-chemical causal link back to the situation it depicts. Nevertheless it does actually convey what did in fact happen. The precise details of posture and nuance may be missing; but they would equally be missing from an eyewitness's testimony of the event, since the photographer did everything in his power to recreate the frame that he had expected to find on his reel of film when it was developed. The photograph communicated the important truth about the events, and that, surely, is what really matters in such cases.

Furthermore, parts of the photograph do have direct causal links to the situation depicted; no actors were involved, for instance, so there is fairly direct evidence about what the two were wearing, their hairstyles, and so on. In other words, parts of the photograph do carry the traditional sorts of photographic evidence. So there are some direct and some indirect causal links back to the depicted people and events, and the truth of what did happen is conveyed in a manner which remains, in all but minor incidental details, true to what took place.

Besides, it seems unreasonable to demand more than this, since in print journalism a certain amount of tidying up of quoted speech is tolerated and even encouraged. For instance, if a hesitant speaker included many 'ums' and 'ers' in his press briefing, no one would be likely to challenge a printed quotation that omitted these. What is important in print journalism is that the content of what was said is not distorted by the process of tidying it up. Newspaper readers don't usually want to read verbatim transcripts of speeches, but rather edited versions of them. Why then worry about whether a photograph presents direct evidence of what it depicts just so long as what it depicts did actually occur?

This sort of response rests on a misunderstanding of the conventions surrounding the use of news photographs and of the consequences of changing those conventions. These conventions include the toleration of minor deceptions in order to produce a legible image; it is usually acceptable to adjust contrasts, to 'burn in' important details and to crop out extraneous details. However, these conventions do not tolerate any manoeuvre which distorts the viewer's appreciation of the relationship between the photograph and its main subject. It is a matter of professional integrity for photojournalists to abide by these conventions. The role responsibilities of the photojournalist must surely include not deceiving the public about how your images were made. In my imaginary case of the princess, the bodyguard and the news photographer, it is not the fact that the photographer used electronic wizardry to produce the effect that makes it unacceptable; it is the fact that the photographer disguised the nature of the causal relationship between what happened and the photograph.

Quite apart from issues of personal and professional integrity, every case in which a deception like this is allowed into print (and subsequently exposed for what it is) serves to undermine the public's trust that the implicit conventions of photojournalism are generally being adhered to. This sort of point has frequently been made about lying in general. For example, it is the line taken by the philosopher G. J. Warnock:

> It is, one might say, not the implanting of false beliefs that is damaging, but rather the generation of the suspicion that they may be being implanted. For this undermines trust; and to the extent that trust is undermined, all co-operative undertakings in which what one person can do or has reason to do is dependent on what others have done, are doing, or are going to do, must tend to break down.[11]

In other words, what is wrong with lying is not that it tends to result in people acquiring false beliefs, but that it destroys the trust that is necessary for most co-operation and communication. Applying this sort of point to news photography we get the conclusion that what is wrong with what the photographer did in my example is that he contributed to the undermining of trust and thus of the possibility of photographic communication. If trust were substantially undermined in this area, there would no longer be any point in sending photographers out to take news photographs. Provide them instead with access to a picture library and a computer and they will be able to come up with plausible-looking illustrations of whatever story print journalists care to write up.

Slippery slope?

Toleration of minor deceptions for the sake of truth is the first step down a slippery slope towards general deception with total disregard for the truth. If you allow people to manipulate photographs without informing their viewers, then you will soon find yourself allowing photographers to invent reality. The force of this, like most slippery slope arguments, depends on whether or not you believe it is possible to arrest the descent and say 'Here and no further'. However, in most situations in which slippery slope arguments are used it is relatively easy to say how far down the slope we have already travelled. In the case of photographic deceptions, however, because they can be so difficult to detect, it is not easy to say on what kind of scale and to what degree such deceptions are currently being perpetrated. This in itself provides a reason for discouraging even minor sorties on to the slope.

Why have the conventions at all?

But why do we have a convention of presenting photographs which picture their causes in a legible way? Why not simply choose the best illustrations for news stories. In other words, what, if anything, is wrong with setting up a plausible tableau vivant and photographing it? What, if anything, is wrong with producing a composite picture by electronic means and publishing it on the front page of a newspaper? Both methods would serve to communicate a fact visually.

There are two principal reasons for preferring documentary photographs to pictorial ones in the context of news reporting. One is related to their status as evidence; the other to the psychology of looking at photographs.

Documentary photographs as evidence

Documentary photographs are themselves evidence, whereas pictorial ones are not themselves evidence; they are like implanted 'memories' which, even if their content happens to be true, are not genuine memories, no matter how realistic they seem to us. News photographs contain all sorts of information which wasn't consciously chosen by the photographer. However, one possible response to this point is that most of this information is inaccessible to the average viewer, requiring as it does a great deal of background information to interpret it. This suggests that there is more to documentary news photography than evidence alone. One additional aspect of news photography is the way that particular depicted events can take on a universal meaning, or at least the part can imply the whole in a kind of visual synecdoche. But this would still be possible if news photography were entirely pictorial. The further aspect of news photography that I believe is essential to understanding the impact of a documentary as opposed to a pictorial image is a feature of the psychology of looking at pictures that we know to be traces of what they depict.

The psychology of looking at relics

Because documentary photographs are traces as well as depictions, they have a reasonably direct causal contact with what they are of and this gives them the status of relics. This is equivalent to the effect of seeing the very shirt that Nelson wore at the battle of Trafalgar rather than a visually indistinguishable one. News photographs are relics of what has happened: events have left their trace on the world, albeit under the direction of a photojournalist. It is just a fact about human psychology that knowledge of such a direct link to events can have a profound effect on the viewer of news photographs. It's not just that the photographs seem to be declaring 'this happened', but rather that they give us the sense of being there when it did happen, and this not simply because of accuracy of detail.

Given the choice, most of us would prefer to have contact with the real world rather than a perceptually indistinguishable one produced by some evil scientist with a virtual reality machine. As Robert Nozick has put it:

> plugging into an experience machine limits us to a manmade reality, to a world no deeper or more important than that which people can construct. There is no *actual* contact with any deeper reality, though the experience of it can be simulated. Many persons desire to leave themselves open to such contact and to a plumbing of deeper significance.[12]

A benefit of contact with reality and not an imaginary version of what someone else takes reality to be is suggested by Harold Evans's remarks made in the context of discussing photographs after Auschwitz had been liberated:

> It is one of the central contributions of photojournalism that it goes beyond the limits of imagination. It makes the unbelievable believable.[13]

In exceptional cases news photography can make us realise the limits of our imagination. Some events are simply beyond our conception until we have seen photographs of them. This is not, of course, to say that the relation between a photograph and what it shows us is an unproblematic one: photographs aren't simply windows on to the past.[14] But they can carry a distinctive kind of evidence, and they can put us into a closer relationship with their subject-matter than any other kind of still picture; and this is why the conventions of documentary news photography are worth preserving even in the age of the electronic darkroom.[15]

Notes

1 René Descartes, *Discourse on Method and the Meditations*, trans. F. E. Sutcliffe (Harmondsworth: Penguin Books, 1968), p. 100.
2 For a useful bibliography on the subject of digital photography, see *History of Photography* 20 (1996), pp. 336–8.
3 For details of this case and others like it, see Fred Ritchin, *In Our Own Image* (New York: Aperture, 1990).
4 See, for instance, the subtitle of his book *The Reconfigured Eye* (Cambridge, MA: MIT Press, 1992): *Visual Truth in the Post-photographic Era*.
5 For a discussion of Susan Sontag's claim that photographs can't communicate moral knowledge, see Nigel Warburton, 'Photographic communication', *British Journal of Aesthetics* 28 (1988), pp. 173–81.
6 For a detailed and completely convincing account of how these photographs were produced and how so many people were taken in by them, see the series of articles by Geoffrey Crawley in the *British Journal of Photography*, from 24 December 1982 to 8 April 1983.
7 For a discussion of the philosophical implications of this photograph see Nigel Warburton, 'Varieties of photographic representation', *History of Photography* 15 (1991), pp. 203–10.
8 Joel Snyder and Neil Walsh Allen discuss the sort of evidence provided by the photofinish in their important article 'Photography, vision and representation', *Critical Inquiry* 2 (1975), pp. 143–69.
9 This case is described in Gisèle Freund, *Photography and Society* (London: Gordon Fraser, 1980), pp. 178–9.
10 For a discussion of the distinction between documentary and pictorial uses of photography see Warburton, 'Varieties of photographic representation'.
11 G. J. Warnock, quoted in Sissela Bok, *Lying: Moral Choice in Public and Private Life* (Brighton: Harvester, 1978), p. 287.
12 Robert Nozick, *Anarchy, State and Utopia* (Oxford: Blackwell Publishers, 1974), p. 43.
13 Harold Evans, *Eyewitness: 25 Years Through World Press Photos* (London: Quiller Press, 1981), p. 8.
14 For an attempt to show that we can quite literally see through photographs to what they are of, see Kendall Walton, 'Transparent pictures: on the nature of photographic realism', *Critical Inquiry* 11 (1984), pp. 246–77. For a critique of this view, see Nigel Warburton, 'Seeing through "Seeing through" photographs', *Ratio* NS 1/1 (1988), pp. 64–74.
15 I am very grateful for Matthew Kieran's comments on an earlier version of this essay.

11 Is the medium a (moral) message?

Noël Carroll

Introduction

The question to be addressed in this essay concerns the moral significance of the television medium. By 'medium' here I am not referring to television as a business that churns out countless stories. Rather, I am referring specifically to the historically standard image, especially in regard to fiction, and to the ways in which it is typically elaborated by structures like editing, camera movement, narrative forms, and the like. Moreover, I will be concerned with the moral status of the television image as such, irrespective of what it is an image of.

Though the distinction between form and content may be historically outmoded and ultimately unsatisfactory, perhaps I can at least provisionally demarcate my domain of interest by initially adopting the distinction and by saying that this is an essay about the putative moral significance of television from the viewpoint of some of its typical formal features – or, at least, from the viewpoint of a number of its formal features that are alleged to be typical.

Furthermore, throughout this essay, I shall be primarily interested with charges that, in some way or other, the relevant television forms are morally suspect – that they have moral implications or consequences that should be ethically worrisome. I dwell on the negative perspective of the medium, rather than on perspectives that see it as positive or beneficial, since negative prognostications represent the dominant tradition; most commentators prefer to scorn television rather than praise it.

I suppose that there can be little debate about whether television has some moral consequences, though there is certainly a legitimate disagreement about how extensive these are. On the positive side, there is evidence indicating that people can learn about alternative lifestyles from televison and that this can bring ethically significant changes in their everyday existence. People from Third World cultures can learn about ways of life in the First World and women can learn about male culture, and this exposure can encourage them to alter their lives. It is said that access through television to western ways of life contributed to the dissatisfaction and subsequent political resistance on the part of the citizens of the former Soviet empire. Likewise, a case can be made out that at least *sometimes* television befouls the moral atmosphere, perhaps by reinforcing oppressive social views. Obviously, certain programmes may traffic in outright propaganda and thereby stoke the flames of racism.

Such consequences as these, if and where they obtain, however, appear to be more a matter of the content of certain programming rather than the result of the historically typical forms of the medium. But the question before us is whether these historically typical forms of television – like the image – are morally significant. Specifically, are they inherently morally suspect?

Why would anyone think that they might be? Maybe one consideration has to do with the inordinate amount of time that the average viewer is said to spend watching the screen. These estimates seem to rise every year. One is often left with the impression that one's fellow citizens spend almost as much time watching television as they spend working and sleeping. Surely, the argument might go, it is reasonable to assume that if so much time is spent doing this, it must have some influence. Moreover, it also seems not implausible to assume – at least as a bit of armchair psychology – that part of that influence must be a result of the mode of presentation. For example, we often hear that the structure of program- ming has shrunk the audience's attention span, thus incurring a cognitive deficit. Analogously, one might conjecture that comparable moral deficits are also probable. Again, this hypothesis might be thought to be compel- ling just because television takes up such a large proportion of everyday life in the industrial world.

A second line of support for the view that the medium is morally significant might originate in the McLuhanite mantra that the medium is the message. That is, McLuhan urged a generation of researchers to look for the significance of television not at the level of its manifest content – its soaps and game shows – but at the level of its latent structure. McLuhan, himself, found a morally salutary message there: the prophecy of neo-tribalism and the global village. But since after half a century of television the world seems to many no better and perhaps worse, those who are convinced by McLuhan's mantra may begin to worry that the medium's message is far from wholesome. This is probably abetted by indulging the *post hoc, propter hoc* fallacy: since things have supposedly deteriorated morally to such a striking degree since the advent of televi- sion, it must be due, at least in part, to its emergence as a major medium of communication.

Of course, these suspicions are rather broad. The historically standard medium *might* have moral repercussions. Anything might. But before we become morally alarmed about these prospects, we want to be reassured that we are confronted by more than abstract possibilities; we want to have grounds for believing that some unsavoury moral possibilities are actually realised by existing television as we know it. This places a certain burden of proof on the critic. He or she must come up with some plausible compromising effect of the medium that is reasonably traceable to the traditional television formats (in the way that reduced attention spans at least *seem* to be a possible outcome of abbreviated televisual forms like advertisements, music videos and the rushed segmentation of game shows, headline news programmes, sit-coms and the like).

Another way to put this is that before we start being concerned that the medium carries untoward moral consequences, we will want to hear some concrete hypotheses about its likely immoral effects in conjunction with explanations of those features that are apt to bring these effects about. That is, we expect the critic to specify some mechanism that accords plausibly with an appropriate description of the medium and also seems of the kind likely to have unhappy consequences or implications for the moral life of viewers.

In this essay, I will consider three such hypotheses about such conjunctions of effects and mechanisms: what I call realism, escapism and hypnotism respectively. Though I believe that the tendency to resort to mechanisms like these is frequent in critical discourse about television, I also concede that my characterisations of them are ideal types. Television criticism is often quite fragmentary and elliptical, leaving many of its underlying premises unstated and unarticulated. What I will attempt to do is to give theoretical body to many of the intuitions that appear to be presupposed in some of the more frequently recurring diatribes against the medium. Thus, what follows is a rational reconstruction in theoretical form of what I take to be several of the leading anxieties about television's moral status.

However, since I intend to question each of these arguments against television, it might be objected that by 'rationally reconstructing' these viewpoints in order to confute them, what I am really doing is rigging the game from the start, assembling straw men for the purposes of igniting them. Against this, I would not only respond that these straw men are composed of real straws, gathered from the existing literature, but also that if there are better arguments than the ones constructed by either previous critics or me, then the burden of putting them forward now falls to the aspiring moralist.

The arguments about the degraded moral status of television that I am about to review – realism, escapism and hypnotism – are not peculiar to this medium. Some details derive from long-standing debates about popular art and media, especially visual media. Some elements in these arguments hark back to Plato and they have surfaced again and again in attacks on movies, comics, pulp literature, music and so on. In many cases, the recurring arguments against television seem to be a matter of far from new wine in very old bottles. This, of course, is to be expected, given the incremental evolution of culture, its tendency to accommodate the present by grafting it to elements of the past. But, if anything, this should lend more credence to my reconstructions of the arguments against television, since the gaps in those arguments can be so readily filled, in as much as they rely heavily on beliefs already abroad in the ongoing discussion of popular entertainment in culture.

Realism

The standard television image is pictorial – a close-up of Johnny Carson's face or a long shot of Deep Space-Nine. Pictures, moreover, are processed by the same visual capacities that we use in everyday life. Arguably we use pretty much the same perceptual processes to recognise typical pictures that we use to recognise their referents in, so to speak, 'nature'. Picture recognition may, in fact, be a hardwired perceptual capacity. This, in turn, may provide part of the explanation of how television can be so accessible to such wide numbers of people, since the basic images in its system of communication are things that nearly everyone has access to in virtue of their innate perceptual capacities.

Of course, even if we prefer to speak of codes or conventions of perception rather than of hardwired recognitional capacities, we may still agree that the so-called perceptual codes used with respect to pictures, on the one hand, and with respect to the world, on the other hand, are pretty closely related. It is in this regard that the television image (as standardly used) is realistic: the visual codes or recognitional capacities that we use to navigate its images are the same or pretty much the same as the ones that we use to navigate everyday life.

It didn't have to be this way. The early technologies that gave rise to television were developed in order to broadcast words and sentences – such as financial news – over great distances, such as oceans. Had its evolution continued under that programme, if it had become an art, then it would have been more in the tradition of the novel, it might have been a delivery system for novels rather than in the tradition of the theatre and film.

But that is not how things happened. And, as a result, the standard small-screen image is realistic in the sense that it is normally processed in much the same way that we view ordinary objects, as opposed, say, to the way that we read words. The medium trades in visual appearances and those visual appearances trigger perceptual processes akin to those triggered by their real-world referents.

The association of television as we know it with realism is also bolstered by its relation to camera technology. Television stands in the cultural lineage of photography and film; indeed much of its material is initially generated by means of cinematography. Moreover, such camera technologies are associated with recording – both historically, given some of the original purposes of photography, and formally, since whether made on film or video, television imagery is standardly a record of events in the world, even when the event is people acting out a drama or fiction. The relation of television to recording, then, supplies further grounds, though different grounds, for calling its image realistic, since it typically derives from reality, a reality that includes the acting out of scenes later to be taken as fictional.

According to Plato, picturing involves little more than holding up a mirror to nature. It deals in visual appearances (and, for Plato, for this very reason, picturing is epistemically defective when compared to the knowledge available from contemplating the Forms). Whether or not painters ever proceeded in such a mechanical manner, certain views of the television image are that it is little more than an affair of mirrors, mechanically or electronically recording, it might be said, the appearance of real things in such a way that our ordinary, low-level object-recognitional capacities are activated or triggered.

If we regard television realism in this way – as engaging ordinary, everyday perceptual capacities through processes that, in part, involve recording – the idea seems at least credible. However, critics believe that along with this variety of perceptual realism comes another effect, which we may call the naturalisation effect. Through realism of the previous sort – through verisimilitudinous appearances and recording – the image imbues whatever it presents with the aura of being natural, that is, of being a representation of the way things (really) are (and must be).

Realistic imagery in our previous sense, in other words, is said to carry a certain rhetorical force, namely it leaves the impression that what it depicts is the case. Perceptual realism tends to convince viewers, in some sense, of the veracity of what they are seeing. Thus, if television imagery presents racial stereotypes via perceptually realistic imagery, viewers, it is thought, will be disposed to accept those stereotypes as true representations, for example, of the behaviour of black people.

Images that proceed by means of perceptual realism, it is claimed, have a spillover effect that inclines viewers to greet them as, to speak loosely, representations of the way things are. Images of black men as confidence artists, lay-abouts and rascals, that is, are thought to confirm, by dint of their perceptual realism, that this is the way these kinds of people actually behave.

Furthermore, this spillover effect is supposed to be even stronger than I have thus far indicated. The thesis has a powerfully deterministic flavour, connoting not merely that what is depicted realistically is somehow the case, but also that it must be the case; that the relevant modality is not just actuality, but some kind of necessity. For example, repeated realistic representations of nuclear families in television sitcoms – from *The Dick Van Dyke Show* to *Roseanne* – not only are thought to imply that the nuclear family *is* the basic social unit, but that it *must* be – that this is a fact of human nature, that it is natural.

Hence the naturalisation effect ultimately is thought to engender in viewers convictions about the inevitability of existing social relations. This effect is particularly relevant for morality, since if it indeed obtains, then it would blinker the moral horizons of viewers. It would obstruct their recognition of alternatives to existing social arrangements. This causes especial alarm for moral reformers who, for example, oppose the notion that only heterosexual marriage is natural and so oppose any sort of representation that precludes the possibility of other sexual relationships. Thus, the putative naturalisation effect is of particular interest to reformers who worry that it is used in a way that inclines ordinary viewers toward complacency about existing immoral and unjust social relationships.

By means of perceptual realism, the television image is thought to lend credibility to various immoral and oppressive social relations. Ethnic, racial, sexist and heterosexist stereotypes are presented and naturalised as are all manner of other relations, such as: those between employer and employees; between the police, the criminal class, and law-abiding citizens; between doctors, nurses, and patients; lawyers, judges and clients; parents and children; and so on. Perceptual realism supposedly suggests to the audience that these relations are not only the way things are, but the way that things must be – that father indeed inevitably knows best (or, if not, mother does).

Moreover, if ought implies can, then the television world limits the viewer's conception of what is morally possible to whatever is endorsed by the putative rhetoric of perceptual realism. That is, if the spillover effects of perceptual realism suggest that things cannot be otherwise, then the image short-circuits moral reflection about the types of social and interpersonal relations it depicts.

Furthermore, if the hypothesis about the naturalisation effect is coupled with certain observations about recurring portrayals of social relations on television, then the medium as we know it presents a clear and present moral danger. For its 'world' is generally at great variance with the real world. There is far more violence there, more doctors, fewer poor people, a disproportionately large number of white males, and so on. Thus, the 'world' that television offers viewers in a perceptually realistic way is a distortion of society. Implicitly, it is a prescription masquerading – in the cloak of perceptual realism – as a description. Consequently, if some correlative, naturalising, spillover effect disposes audiences to view the 'television world' as the way that things must be, then the spectators' parameters for moral evaluation will be effectively undermined. Therefore, the television image as such comes to be regarded as morally problematic.

This hypothesis proposes both an effect – that the image inclines viewers to the conviction that things (especially social relations) cannot be otherwise, and a mechanism – naturalisation via perceptual realism. Both these postulations seem dubious. Let us look at the effect first.

Is it plausible to suppose that television disposes viewers to believe that things cannot be otherwise, specifically that they cannot be improved morally? This seems hardly likely as a generalisation about all television, since much of it is of a strongly reformist bent. Many movies made especially for it, for example, are 'problem films', presenting issues like racism, child abuse, wife-battering, AIDS and so on for the express purpose of convincing audiences that the relevant social ills can and should be remedied. I have little reason to disbelieve that these efforts are sometimes effective in moving some audiences morally. Therefore, it cannot be the case that by deploying perceptual realism, television cannot propose that things can be otherwise in morally significant ways.

Moreover, researchers in the area called cultural studies regard television as a site of resistance, by which they mean that viewers contest many of the implications of the programmes. For example, Native Americans may cheer when white settlers are massacred; they do not docilely accept the inevitability of white imperialism. Perhaps people in cultural studies exaggerate the amount of resistance that is abroad with respect to people's viewing. But they have established that there is some resistance and that is enough to call into question the hypothesis that the so-called naturalisation effect automatically reduces viewers to moral inertia.

Of course, one always wonders about the theoretical grounds for postulating the naturalisation effect. Supposedly perceptual realism gives rise to certain spillover effects: the impression that what is represented is how things are and, in consequence, how they must be. The first step in this deduction appears to ride on an equivocation.

Realism as a style, it might be said, implies a commitment to representing how things are; thus audiences take realistic representations that way. But *perceptual realism* is not realism in this sense. It is committed only to presenting things in such a way as to activate ordinary visual processes, specifically recognitional capacities. It carries no commitment to representing the world, especially the social world, accurately. This should be obvious, since it is, in principle, compatible with fiction. The audience realises that perceptual realism is not, in principle, committed to an accurate representation of the world. They know that Amos and Andy are not existing persons. So why suppose that viewers take perceptually realistic television images to show how things really are?

At this point, it might be said that it is not particulars that audiences take to be real, but rather certain social types and situation types. Audiences know that Andy and Amos do not exist, but perceptual realism convinces them that types, such as the ones portrayed by Amos and Andy, are accurate. But, even if we are not Platonists, the question remains as to why perceptual realism would have any special relation to shaping viewers' conceptions of types, since its domain is generally particulars: individual persons, actions, objects and events. What is the psychological mechanism that gets us from the appearance of particulars in whose existence we do not believe to types whose accuracy we accept?

If the connection between perceptual realism and the conviction that 'this is how things are' is doubtful, then the connection with the impression that 'this is how things must be' seems even more strained. Why should perceptual realism lend an aura of fatalistic determinism to what is represented? The application of our standing perceptual processes to events in the world does not come in concert with fatalism; when I see that my den is in a mess up, I do not surmise that it cannot be otherwise (or if I do, my wife doesn't). So why should the operation of our normal perceptual processes while watching television leave us convinced that things cannot be changed?

If the answer here is that it is not perceptual realism that secures this effect, but narrative structure, then we shall need to point out that television narratives often herald social change in morally beneficial directions. That is, many such narratives behave in a way opposite to that which proponents of the naturalisation effect predict.

Thus I conclude that anxieties about the moral status of the television image as such, which are based on the perceptual realism of the medium, are woefully ill-founded.

Escapism

One of the most frequent charges against television in the name of morality is that it is escapist. This charge is problematic at first blush because so many things can be meant by it, not all of which are bad. For example, if 'to escape' merely means to change one activity for another activity, which other activity may be rewarding (say, listening intently to classical music), then no necessary opprobrium should attach to the term. However, when television is called 'escapist' critics have something pejorative in mind.

One thing that might be labelled 'escapist' in the pejorative sense could be a tendency to do one thing when one should be doing something else. Shirking one's responsibilities and watching television instead would be escapist in this sense. This notion of escapism would appear to be in play when one is chided for spending too much time in front of the screen rather than improving oneself or undertaking political activity. But here the wrongness would appear to attach to one's avoidance behaviour and not to the medium itself, since it would be equally escapist in this sense to start working when one was supposed to be visiting a sick relative whom, perhaps, one dislikes. Thus when the label 'escapist' is used the critic must be referring to something else.

Perhaps it is this: escapism in this context has to do with the tendency to indulge in fantasy. Television, then, it is alleged, has something to do with inducing fantasy, where fantasy itself is regarded as morally disreputable. If this is what critics are arguing, then we need to know both what might be disreputable about fantasy and how it is that television, in particular, encourages it.

But what could be wrong with fantasising itself, especially where it is not the case that we are fantasising when we should be doing something else? One idea might be that fantasy involves decoupling our emotional responses from action. When we fantasise events – when we daydream – we undergo various emotional states, but these are divorced from action. We savour our indignation over various injustices around us, but we need not act; daydreaming disconnects affect from responsibility. This might be thought to be fraught with potential moral dangers, including: that by emoting indignation in our imagination, we deceive ourselves into thinking we have met the demands of morality; that we come to prefer emoting for the fantasised objects over real-world ones (for imagined poor people rather than real ones); that we come to prefer emoting over acting (putting watching television over community service).

But even if these specific problems are merely abuses that *might* arise from fantasy, it may still be argued that the bottom line is that it is of the nature of the structure of fantasy – its contents notwithstanding – to disconnect emotion and action. And this, it might be thought, is always a perversion of the normal function of our psychological system. Just as masturbation is alleged to pervert the sexual function, fantasy might be said to be a perversion of the emotion–action system. Detaching affect from action endangers the smooth functioning of the system; perhaps it makes us more likely not to respond to certain real-world events, just because we have accustomed ourselves to emoting without acting in our fantasy life. Thus, in so far as fantasy erodes or is likely to erode the linkage between emotion and action, and the linkage between emotion and action is essential for moral behaviour, fantasy as such – no matter what its contents are – is ethically suspect because it tampers with the conditions for moral activity. It leaves us satisfied with feeling the emotion without acting on it.

Moreover, it may be alleged that television is especially conducive to fantasy. That is, it encourages fantasy in a non-accidental way. Just as narcotics abet pure affective reveries divorced from action, so too does television. This is not simply a matter of people in certain circumstances turning to television when they should be otherwise engaged. The point about fantasy-encouragement is that it is supposed to be common to all television viewing, whatever the circumstances. It is about the medium as such and its inherent escapist proclivities. Moreover, this argument can be made without reference to any particular fantasy contents, such as the alluring (perhaps compensatory) imagery of wealth, sex and power. For the charge is that the medium itself encourages fantasy and fantasy as such is morally dubious.

But what is it about the medium that makes it complicit with fantasy? Here it may be argued that the its images are illusionistic. Their compelling perceptual realism cause us involuntarily to suspend our disbelief about the existence of a creature such as the 'primate worm' in the *X-Files* episode entitled 'The Host', and, as a result, we experience the thrill of fear without the impulse either to flee or to fight. Likewise we feel outrage at the treatment of children in a television movie such as *Miss Evers' Boys*, but we don't have to do anything about it. Moreover, this process is based on a deception: our acceptance of a false belief, i.e. that the illusion before us is a real, occurring event – thereby adding lying to the moral harm involved in this characterisation of escapism.

Illusion, then, is the mechanism that enables the television image to promote fantasy, where fantasy itself is an escapist tendency in the morally pejorative sense. Since Plato, there has been a disapproving correlation of the visual and the emotional, though in the present argument it is not the emotions themselves that are subject to moral criticism, but rather the condition of undergoing (and enjoying) emotions divorced from action and the responsibility to act. Television activates the emotions illusionistically, but in a way so as to function as a kind of electronic prosthetic fantasy – prosthetic in the sense that it does our imaging for us, but still a fantasy, since it requires no action on our part.

Television, then, is escapist because it encourages fantasy – an escape from the burden of action by its very nature – and it encourages fantasy through its deceptive or illusionistic imagery. But this argument seems flawed on two counts: both in its suspicion of fantasy and in its conception of the image as illusionistic.

The suspicion of fantasy seems to be based upon too narrow a conception of the psychology of the emotions. The emotions are typically connected to action and the linkage between the emotions and action is crucial to moral behaviour. However, this does not entail that entertaining emotions without acting is a perversion of human nature. The human capacity to undergo emotional states without the necessity to act is highly adaptive and, indeed, can make for more effective future action.

That children can be frightened by descriptions of counterfactual circumstances of danger prepares them for future predicaments. That we can envision future activities and undergo emotional responses with respect to our imaginings gives us information of what it would be like to do such and such, and, thereby, helps in making practical, and moral, decisions. Our capacity to emote without acting also enables us to simulate conspecifics and, in consequence, to modulate our responses to them, morally as well as prudentially. In all these cases, and many others, the capacity to decouple emotions and actions is an advantage to human psychology overall, not a perversion, and it is often relevant to, rather than disruptive of, moral behaviour.

Thus, where 'escapist' is opposed to 'adaptive', the bare faculty of fantasy is not necessarily escapist, nor is it necessarily alien to the moral life, since the capacity to imagine emotively without acting is at least relevant to deliberating morally about our own future actions; to learning to size up counterfactual situations, including morally significant ones, that may one day become factual; and for gathering information, including morally pertinent information, about others both in terms of what they are feeling and what they are likely to do. Thus there is nothing morally wrong with fantasy in principle, but only with specific fantasies.

Similarly, if there is any special connection between television and fantasy, there would be no problem then apart from the specific fantasies – abetted by specific programmes and their content – in question. And even if there is no special connection, but only a connection that television shares with other media, there is also no call to presuppose that everything it encourages us to imagine emotively is morally compromised. Indeed, if fantasy – imagining emotively – can be serviceable in moral living in general, then there are no grounds to think that television as prosthetic imagining can't be serviceable too. Perhaps responding emotionally to fictions depicting racism and sexism can prepare us to focus in emotionally appropriate ways on comparable real-world occurrences of racism and sexism.

Of course, there is also something wrong with the story rehearsed earlier about illusionism. Supposedly, the television image is an illusion which leads us to suspend our disbelief about whatever is represented. This makes it possible for us to respond emotionally, since it is supposed that an emotion requires belief, and the suspension of disbelief puts us in the requisite condition: it leaves us believing what we are seeing.

However, one wonders whether there aren't at least two steps too many in this scenario. For if emotions can be generated by imaginings – thoughts entertained in the mind but as unasserted with respect to truth – and if perceptual realism alone, without any supposition of illusion, can provide the grounds for imagining (for example, that Miss Evers' boys are being treated unjustly), then we can dispense with talk about both illusion and the suspension of disbelief at a stroke. And this would be all to the good anyway, since both ideas appear to suggest that viewers believe what they see before them, leaving it a mystery, then, why they don't match their emotions with actions.

Thus, the view that television is escapist because its illusionist image abets psychological perversity appears ill-advised, both because fantasy – emotive imagining decoupled from action – is not necessarily escapist in any morally pejorative sense and because the image in question is not illusionistic. The television image is typically perceptually realistic, but this does not involve one in taking on false beliefs, but only recognising what visual arrays represent. And though perceptual realism may support emotive imagining, the moral status of such imagining depends on its content, not upon the kind of mental state it is.

Here it might be argued that I have changed the terms of the argument by talking about imagining rather than fantasising. But if fantasising is just the name for naughty emotive imagining, then clearly once again it is the content of the state, not the category of the state that we are assessing.

It is true that television supports emotive imagining (though not by morally disreputable illusions), but since there is nothing wrong *per se* with emotive imagining, the medium as such is not escapist in any morally problematic way.

Hypnotism

If the problem cited in the escapism argument is that, in one sense, the medium encourages too much space for imaginative activity (abusively called fantasy), then the problem at issue in the hypnotism argument is that television allows virtually no room for the imagination at all. The hypnotism argument begins by taking note of the unexceptionable fact that the point of television is to draw our attention to it. Producers want us to watch it. In this they are no different from film makers.

However, in various respects, the movie maker has certain advantages over the television producer when it comes to compelling our attention. The film image is standardly much larger than the television one; the film screen is usually bigger than we are, whereas typically we tower over our television sets. Moreover, the resolution of the television image is typically not as bright or lustrous as the film image. Thus, along certain dimensions, the power of the former image can be said to be weak, particularly when compared to film. Whereas in a darkened screening room, our eyes are drawn to the large, illuminated film image – in truth we have little else to look at – in our living room, the duller, low resolution television screen competes for attention with other objects. It is easy for our attention to drift away from it. Thus, a primary task for the producer, given the tendency of our attention to drift, is to keep our eyes riveted on the screen.

A major resource for the television producer in this regard is the organisation of the image track. Our perceptual system is calibrated to be especially sensitive to change and movement. The obvious adaptive advantage of this is straightforward: movement in the environment in the early days of humankind was often the signal of the arrival of either predators or prey – of either danger or food. Thus our eyes are drawn to movement and change by reflex. The producer can make use of this in order to keep our attention on the screen by organising the image track structurally so that it bristles with movement and change.

Some of the relevant devices available for this purpose include: editing, camera movement, zooming, superimpositions, fades and so on. These sorts of visual devices, of course, are also available in film. However, their incidence in television – especially certain kinds (such as advertisements and music videos) – is often higher than it is in film. If we call the use of these devices 'structural articulations', then some commentators estimate that there are usually as many as eight to ten structural articulations per sixty-second interval in a commercial television programme and as many as ten to fifteen structural articulations per thirty-second interval in the average advertisement. Of course, the ration of structural articulations in commercial action programmes like *Miami Vice* can be even higher than the average for commercial programming, and cutting in music videos is frequently as high as nearly twenty shots per minute.

Needless to say, television not only deploys technical or structural changes of this sort. Fast movement inside the frame also commands our attention. This is why television loves basketball and football more than it loves baseball. Moreover, it is no accident that situation comedy is typically structured around rapid-fire repartee – trading insults in fast-paced *badinage* – because the cascade of punch lines, accompanied by rapid switching of shots from one person to another, holds our attention in the absence of compelling plot developments. Likewise, headline news programmes are always changing the story briskly, and cutting to the next visual, never giving our attention an instant to flag. Indeed, I have seen news reports where the visual cuts are repeated twice, presumably in order to maximise the number of cuts in the segment.

One pretty obvious function of the plethora of structural articulations on the visual track is to compel our interest in what is going on in the image by triggering our innate tendencies to fixate on movement and change. By means of structural articulations like cutting, the producer introduces movement and change into the visual array, often at a fairly pronounced pace. This is attention-grabbing; the structural articulations, so to speak, renew or rejuvenate our attention on almost a moment-to-moment basis, and they work against the tendency of our attention to drift away from the screen. The structural articulations, it might be said, trap our attention; they lure us into the imagery. They rivet our attention and stimulate our natural expectation that something significant is about to happen, since that is what our movement detectors are adapted to expect. Thus the structural articulations keep us watching and draw us ahead, deeper into the programme. Our attention, it is suggested, is locked involuntarily on the image track, as if we were in a hypnotic trance. Perhaps it might be added that this is part of the reason that people watch such an enormous amount of television.

But why, if structural features of the medium do function this way, is this morally problematic? Here it may be alleged that the way in which television holds our attention has us, in a manner of speaking, 'chasing after the image'. We have to keep up with the image track as one structural articulation comes fast on the heels of the previous one. We are so busy trying to deal with the onslaught of structural articulations that we have little time for thought – little time, for example, to exercise our powers of imagination. The exercise of our attention in tracking the rush of structural articulations squeezes out the opportunity for any other kind of cognitive activity.

That is, because producers exploit certain possibilities of their medium in such a way that the image captures attention to an extent that precludes or crowds out the operation of other relevant cognitive powers, television in its standard form, with its emphasis on a high incidence of structural articulations, is morally problematic. This judgement, of course, is connected to the specific cognitive powers that the critic alleges are thrust in abeyance by the intensive preoccupation of attention to the changing image track.

These cognitive powers are at least two in number: our critical powers and our imagining powers. The imagery purportedly goes by so fast that we are so busy keeping up with it attentively that we do not have time to assess it from the point of view of moral criticism. But an even more worrisome possibility is that the way in which attention is swamped with stimuli closes off the operation of our imaginative powers.

Here, the hypnotism argument shares a premiss with the realism argument. The imagination is said to be an essential feature of moral thinking because it is the power to envision alternatives. Moral judgement presupposes the recognition that things could be otherwise. The rapid succession of structural articulations, like cutting, does not allow the spectator the time to imagine moral alternatives; one is so occupied in simply attending to the visual array that there is no space for the moral imagination to take root. Thus, by precluding the operation of the moral imagination with respect to fictional and documentary material that calls for moral judgement, the typical structuring of television imagery is morally suspect.

Both the realism argument and the hypnotism argument maintain that what is morally problematic about the television imagery is that it prevents the spectator from envisioning alternatives, from thinking that things could be otherwise than the way they are portrayed on the screen. However, the two arguments reach this conclusion by different routes. The realism argument alleges that this effect occurs through naturalisation – through imparting the impression that 'this is the way things are'. The hypnotism argument maintains that the imagination is stultified by overwhelming our attention with unrelenting sequences of structural articulations.

The hypnotism argument can also be connected to certain notions of escapism. If the concept of escapism that we have in mind is that behaviour is escapist when we are doing one thing when we should be doing another, then it may be alleged that television, organised breathlessly around the succession of structural articulations, contributes to escapism by, so to speak, holding our attention to the screen captive. It is not entirely our fault that we continue to watch when we should be doing other things – improving ourselves, engaging in political activities, and so on – because producers are, for their own purposes, manipulating features of our perceptual make-up in ways that reinforce inertia. In other words, it is not entirely a result of our own character failings that we are couch potatoes. We have been hypnotised by the way television is typically articulated, irrespective of the content of the imagery.

All those people who watch so much television are virtually trapped by televisual images. But not only are they held in thrall before the screen for hour after hour. While they sit there, their powers of imagination, notably their powers of moral imagination, are effectively anaesthetised. Their attention is so engaged negotiating the imagery that moral judgement goes on holiday. And this makes the typical television format morally problematic in its own right.

There is no question that the image track is structured so as to secure maximal attention from spectators. In this, the proponent of the hypnotism argument is on solid ground. However, the question is whether or not the hypnotism argument overestimates the effectiveness of the medium in this matter. In my view, the hypnotism argument vastly exaggerates the power of the image track to hold the audience spellbound. It may characteristically be designed as a solution to the problem of wavering attention, but it is hardly 100 per cent successful in this regard.

Much viewing occurs in a highly distracted way. As a successor to radio listening, television viewing is often pursued in concert with other activities, including household chores. As the family sits around the set, what is on the screen often takes a back seat to conversations. Some commentators characterise our typical way of looking at television as 'the glance' as opposed to 'the gaze'. The notion of the gaze refers to the intent looking that marks our attention to movie images in cinemas. The glance is a more casual mode of attention, such as that shown by students who look up from their homework and catch a glimpse of the programme before returning to their algebra. I would not wish to argue categorically that television viewing is always a matter of 'the glance' in contrast to movie viewing which is always a matter of the so-called gaze. Nevertheless, it does seem to me that the television image is not as hypnotic as critics argue. However much structural articulations incline us to continue watching, it is very easy to escape their grip, as should be clear from the fact that people often half-watch television while they are doing something else.

The fact that one can do this also raises doubt about the extent to which television really crowds out the possibility of other occurrent cognitive activities. Certainly it does not preclude imagining: one can easily indulge in a bit of daydreaming while following an episode of *Star Trek*. Indeed, it seems wildly wrong to suspect that television precludes imagining, since certain forms of imaginative activity are probably required or presupposed in order to understand what is going on in any given programme.

Television programmes are edited, often intensively edited, as we have already noted. But in order to assimilate the meaning of those edited arrays, the mind must be engaged in some form of constructive activity and this, presumably, involves the operation of the imagination. The structural articulations we have discussed cannot preclude the operation of the imagination entirely; we cannot merely be attending to the parade of structural articulations in a frenzy of cognitively impenetrable reflexes.

Otherwise the array would appear meaningless. But since these arrays characteristically appear meaningful, we must suppose that some form of constructive, imaginative mental activity is in play.

Moreover, not only is it the case that the operation of our constructive powers of imagination are engaged by watching television. Our powers of moral imagination must be in gear as well. Typical programmes – both fictions and news programmes – constantly call upon their audiences to make moral judgements. This presupposes the activity of the moral imagination. If we are to recognise that a certain character is evil, we must be able to recognise that his behaviour can be otherwise. How could typical TV programmes elicit the moral uptake they require in order to be intelligible if they, at the same time, shunt the moral imagination to the sidelines? Clearly, the moral imagination could not be so neutralised, if the programme is intended to communicate to viewers in a way that requires moral judgement. And just as clearly, the imagery does not neutralise our powers of moral imagination, since it does so frequently elicit the requisite moral judgements from viewers. In order to follow the programme, viewers must be making certain moral judgements. That they do follow such programmes indicates that their powers of moral imagination are suitably engaged. Following the image track in terms of attention, then, does not preclude following it with an alert moral imagination.

Nevertheless, here it might be argued that the moral imagination is shackled or constrained by television. We make moral judgements all right, but only the moral judgements that the producers want us to make about the content of their programmes. Yet this is palpably false. How could it be true at the same time that critics, including ordinary citizens, rage about violence and sex on television? Producers certainly are not happy about those moral responses, and did not intend them. Nor were the exercises of the moral imagination that were called on to make those responses in any way stultified by the organisation of the image track. In this regard, there is no reason to suspect that television as such, in its style of representation, necessarily poses a threat to the operation of the moral imagination. The hypnotism argument is no more compelling than either the realism or the escapism argument.

Nor does it seem very likely that the hypnotism argument explains why people watch so much television. The way the sequence of images is organised may draw attention to the screen, but its holding power is extremely limited; it takes a minuscule amount of effort to elude its grasp. That this is obvious perhaps explains why we often feel a guilty conscience for having overindulged our television habit.

If we watch too much television that is probably a function of the fact that in our culture we do not spend much time training people how to use the medium: how to integrate it in a fulfilling life-plan. This, of course, may itself reflect an unwillingness in certain societies to include as part of basic education thinking about how one might lead one's life and the habits one needs to develop to pursue such lives. The problem of excessive television viewing, then, is a moral problem, if it is a moral problem, because of a larger cultural failing. It is not an ailment to be attributed to the medium as such, nor to its characteristic stylistic elaboration of the image. Neither the medium nor the image is inherently immoral, though our systematic failure to educate people about how to use it may be socially irresponsible.

Bibliography

Carroll, Noël, 'Conspiracy theories of representation', *Philosophy of the Social Sciences* 17 (1987).

Carroll, Noël, *A Philosophy of Mass Art*, Oxford: Oxford University Press, 1998.

Dyson, Kenneth and Homolka, Walter (eds), *Culture First/Promoting Standards in the New Media Age*, London: Cassell, 1996.

Ellis, John, *Visible Fictions*, London: Routledge and Kegan Paul, 1982.

Fiske, John, *Television Culture*, London: Methuen, 1987.

McLuhan, Marshall, *Understanding Media*, London: Routledge and Kegan Paul, 1964.

Mander, Jerry, *Four Arguments for the Elimination of Television*, New York: Quill, 1978.

Meyerwitz, Joshua, *No Sense of Place*, Oxford: Oxford University Press, 1985.

Plato, *Republic*, Harmondsworth: Penguin, 1974.

Tester, Keith, *Media, Culture and Morality*, London: Routledge, 1994.

12 Sex and violence in fact and fiction

Gordon Graham

Controlling pornographic production

The claim that pornography, whether of a sexual or violent nature, leads to the real thing, forms the basis of the most common case made for its social regulation, a line of argument made famous by the representations of Catherine MacKinnon and Andrea Dworkin to the City of Minneaplois in 1983. This is an old and well-trodden line of thought, but it is one that has been put with increasing frequency of late, not merely because the volume of pornographic material is widely believed to have grown, but because there are new media deployed in its distribution: the VCR, satellite television and the Internet. These new media have extended the reach of pornography considerably, at the same time as weakening social systems for its control. Whereas formerly pornographic magazines, for example, could be seized and destroyed, it is not possible to make seizures on the Internet.

Forms of control adapted to the new media are actively being investigated, it is true. The government of Singapore, for example, has attempted to create restrictions on individual access to the Web, and there are systems of self-censorship under discussion by the chief suppliers of access in the USA and Europe. Experience suggests, however, that even the most determined states can exercise only limited control. Iran for instance has found it hard to block or restrict satellite television despite the perpetual vigilance of the religious authorities. Similarly, while children and young adults can be physically stopped from entering cinemas, it is much more difficult to prevent their watching television or videos in their own homes, bedrooms even, or discovering pornographic materials when surfing the Internet.

Combined with the scale and availability of the new media, there is, too, a widespread belief that because all these new media are largely visual, they are more dangerous, since the visual depiction of sex and violence is more powerful than the mere written word. With such a rising tide of pornography, is it surprising that sexual violence should also rise? Could there be any serious question but that we are confronting new dangers?

Spelt out in full, the argument against pornography runs like this:

1 The depiction of certain sorts of action causes occurrences of those actions.
2 These are actions of a socially harmful kind.
3 Society has the right to constrain the activities of individuals in order to prevent harm.
Thus:
4 Society has the right to constrain the activities of those who would produce and distribute pornography.
Consequently:
5 Society has a right to confine the activities of those who want to view it.

This argument has been given a new twist recently by its extension from fiction to fact. The multiple murders by Martin Bryant in Tasmania, Australia in 1996 followed so hard on the heels of the slaughter of children by Thomas Hamilton at Dunblane in Scotland a few months earlier, it was inevitable that someone should ask whether there might not be a connection between the two. At least one psychologist was reported as expressing the opinion that more discreet handling of Dunblane by television and newspapers would have reduced the chances of a repeat event in Tasmania. This, if true, seems to place a special burden of responsibility on reporters and editors. It implies, in effect, that their activities were a contributory cause to the deaths and injury of many people. This is a much more serious implication than those who draw it often seem to realise, one that needs to be weighed with the greatest of care.

The same charge is not less serious when it is made against pornographers. Though they are socially less respectable than (most) newspaper and television reporters, it is still a grave matter to accuse pornographers, previously thought of as seedy rather than vicious, of being responsible for the deaths of innocent people. In fact, the grounds upon which such an accusation might be made do not differ significantly between the factual and the fictional cases. The idea is just that the depiction of sex and violence in either fiction and fact can be a serious contributory factor in the production of social harms, and for this reason I shall use the label 'pornography' to cover both factual reporting and fictional imagery.

The argument as I have set it out rests upon a number of assumptions. In the first part of this essay I identify and examine some of these assumptions. I shall argue that once this is done, the argument is revealed as inherently weak. It follows that if reservations about the depiction of sex and violence are to be given a proper grounding, it is necessary to take another approach, one not based on the idea of causing harm, and in the second part of the essay I shall sketch what that approach might be.

Harm and pornography

The most obvious assumption at work in the argument is the truth of the first premiss: the depiction of certain sorts of action causes occurrences of those actions. How is this claim to be established or assessed? It is worth noting that abstract reason is no use to us here. People often say 'it stands to reason' that the more violence there is displayed on our screens, whether fictional or actual, the more there will be in our streets. When pressed for evidence, some have even argued that no evidence is needed. In this spirit Janet Daley writes,

> It is not necessary, nor is it possible, to establish a direct mechanistic link between the watching of a particular film and the carrying out of particular acts.
> There is nothing special, in this respect, about the relationship between video violence and actual violence. This is simply a universal truth about human psychology. No definitive causal link can ever be proved between any experience and any subsequent behaviour . . . [but] . . . If a link cannot ever be proved, then it does no damage to an argument not to have proved it. What is beyond dispute is that the saturation of popular culture with images of cruelty normalizes violence.
> This is not a statement that requires proof. It is self-evident.[1]

Philosophers generally hold that no factual proposition can be self-evident in the strict sense; such claims can only be made on the basis of empirical evidence. Daley, presumably, would deny this, but whatever the truth on the general point, her argument rests upon two important mistakes. First, even if it is true that we cannot establish a direct mechanistic link between the watching of a particular film and the carrying out of a particular act, it may yet be possible to make general statistical connections between images and actions of those types. Second, the fact that a statement by its nature is not *provable* does not release us from the obligation to believe it only if it has been shown to be *probable*. David Hume's dictum that we should proportion our belief to the evidence[2] applies just as well when there is an acknowledged absence of conclusive proof, and where all we have to go on is probability. Indeed, since most of our beliefs fall into this category, rationality requires us to make reasonable judgements of probability almost all the time.

A parallel which illustrates both these points will be found in the case of passive smoking. It is tempting to assume that if smoking damages health, 'it stands to reason' that other people's smoke will damage health as well. Many people do hold this to be self-evident, and faced with a demand for evidence, an adherent of this inference could rightly claim that given the multiplicity of factors, it is never possible to link some one bit of passive smoking with a particular death. Nevertheless, claims about passive smoking can be put to both clinical and statistical tests and so far the results seem to show that what is held to 'stand to reason' is not in fact very likely to be true.

Now it seems to be the case that convincing evidence of the harmful effects of pornography is also lacking.[3] No study has revealed any clear statistical connection, and even the seemingly plainest and most telling instances do not clinch the matter. This is partly because the theories of psychological motivation with which they must ultimately be supported allow interpretation in different directions. The most compelling examples usually cited are those of killings or rapes which appear to act out some video nasty. The difficulty is that even if we know of a connection in the mind of the person who acts out the fantasy, this in itself gives us no reason to regard it as that of cause and effect. It may as easily, and perhaps more plausibly be that the psychology of someone who is fascinated by such images is also the psychology of a killer or a rapist.

Something of the same is to be said about the extension of the argument from fiction to fact. From time to time it is alleged that the reporting of violence stimulates crimes by providing ideas and models for criminals, and provokes so-called 'copycat crimes'. For example, it is a familiar complaint that the BBC's *Crimewatch*, designed to alert us to and help catch thieves and criminals, actually suggests new ways of criminal behaviour to feckless viewers. On this theory, newspaper and television reports suggest ideas to would-be criminals, which they then set about realising in their own locality. It seems quite likely that this does indeed happen, but where crimes appear to be copycat, this shows only that their *form* has been determined by reports from elsewhere; it does not show that the impulse to crime itself has been prompted by the reporting. It seems not implausible that those waiting to commit crimes sometimes change their plans to imitate exploits of which they have read in the papers; it is much less plausible that until they picked up the newspaper no thought of crime had entered their heads. Once again, in order to establish a significant causal connection between the occurrence of crime and its depiction, whether in fact or fiction, we need hard empirical evidence, both about patterns of crime, and about the motivations of actual criminals. Claims of 'self-evidence' are not enough.

The example of Dunblane and Tasmania illustrates this. Martin Bryant, the Tasmanian murderer, may or may not have been mad, but at a minimum the evidence of his mentality shows it to be bizarre. In this it is like the mentality of most multiple murderers. Careful studies of the Boston Strangler, Jeffrey Dahmer, Dennis Nilson and so on, reveal that even where there is no clinically identifiable form of madness at work, the relation of belief, desire and action in such people is extremely hard to understand, if indeed it is intelligible at all.[4] A large part of the difficulty is the non-standard ways in which belief and action are related. The degree of importance that such people seem to attach to the wholly inconsequential, for instance, and strangeness of the desires and interests they have, puts their mental and emotional life at some considerable remove from the normal ways in which actions are motivated and controlled. Precisely because of this, however, it is naïve to imagine that we can estimate the contribution that watching television reports (or even pornographic videos) might make to the balance of forces within such a mind. The distinguished American psychiatrist Willard Gaylin has freely admitted that confronted with the strange mentality of the multiple murderer most experts 'are aware how trivial, ephemeral, descriptive and mean-ingless are psychiatric diagnoses' in these cases.[5] Accordingly, even if we knew that Bryant dwelt on the events of Dunblane with intensity, we could not attribute any clear causal weight to this. There is no more reason to think that this was the cause of his deranged state than that it was simply more evidence of it.

This line of argument may be applied more generally. It is a familiar thought that people whose newspapers and television screens are regularly filled with reports of violence will, so to speak, become inoculated against its horror, or worse, positively develop a taste for it. This is perhaps what Daley means when she says that images of cruelty normalise violence. That is certainly one possible outcome. It is equally possible, however, that the reporting of violence increases people's revulsion in the face of its con-sequences, and strengthens their repudiation of it. Neither one of these reactions is any more or less possible than the other, and that is as far as reasoning in the abstract can take us. To discover most people's actual, as opposed to possible, reaction we need solid, and extensive, social enquiry. This would provide some hard evidence, but it is evidence of a sort that we do not have as yet. Studies that have been attempted along these lines have resulted in very uncertain or conflicting conclusions.

There is reason to hold, I think, that violence begets violence. We ought not to confuse this with a quite different thesis, that the *depiction* of violence (factual or fictional) begets violence. This is a much more ambi-tious thesis, and one waiting to be established. Certainly pornography is to be found associated with violence, but the fact is that human history before radio, television and full colour magazines is littered with specta-cular acts of cruelty, and most present-day violence can be causally con-nected with videos, television and so on in only the most tenuous way. Even today, in countries far too poor for any of these, truly staggering violence, rape and bloodshed can take place, as it did in Rwanda in 1995.

However, in order to expose the full weakness of the argument with which we began, let us suppose, contrary to these reflections, that there are some grounds for thinking that a proliferation of pornographic images leads to an increase in the real incidence of such actions. A second assumption at work in the argument we are considering is that these effects are necessarily harmful. This seems an odd assumption to question, but the fact is that the radically altered attitudes to sexual conduct which pornographic materials may induce are regarded by some as liberating rather than corrupting.[6] The once infamous Marlon Brando, Maria Schneider film *Last Tango in Paris* was hailed by the New Yorker's great film critic Pauline Kael as 'the most liberating movie ever'. It might be replied, of course, that while sexual pornography could be regarded as liberating, the same thing could hardly be said about the depiction of violence. The issue is not so clear, however. Long ago Aristotle argued that dramatic depiction can have a cathartic effect, dispelling emotions that would be harmful if given vent to in reality.[7] Now if it is true that the depiction of violence can have a cathartic as well as a provocative influence this means that as well as prompting violence, it forestalls it, by providing a fictional release for otherwise destructive emotions. In this sense, it too might be liberating, and if it is there will be a question whether the benefits do not outweigh the costs.

This line of thought can be expanded. Many people die as a result of motor vehicles on modern roads. The causal connection here is far better established than any connection between violence and pornography. But the public mind accepts these negative outcomes as a price worth paying for the benefits modern transportation brings. In principle the same point applies to VCRs, satellite television and the Internet. Of course, it is true that if one could have the benefits without the harms, this would be better still, but if we cannot, it may still be rational to accept the harms. It needs to be shown, therefore, that as things stand, the social and cultural condition to which we have been reduced is so bad as to warrant the elimination of much that is good.

The proponent of social controls will argue, of course, that this is not what is proposed. It is proposed only that society should, in the interests of self-protection, constrain the freedom of individuals with respect to the production and consumption of pornography. This reply reveals a further two assumptions. The first is that such controls can be effective. This I am inclined to doubt. The efforts of the western world to control illicit drugs is salutary in this respect. Many years of highly expensive law enforcement has resulted in a world in which trade in drugs is even more vigorous, as the enforcing agencies themselves declare. If there is a demand for pornography, which there obviously is, the black market will find ways of supplying it, and, if our experience with drugs is any guide, under legal proscription it will do so in even less well controlled ways, while at the same time generating the huge cost of an unsuccessful effort to contain it. This certainly was the experience under Prohibition in the United States. The attempt to make alcohol illegal simply pushed it underground.

The harm principle

But suppose effective control *is* possible, and that, further, we leave aside the question of who is to exercise it. A second assumption comes to the fore: that the prevention of harm is a sufficient justification for the exercise of social coercion. Here, we encounter the 'one simple principle' which John Stuart Mill elaborates in his classic essay *On Liberty*, a principle that has had considerable influence on public policy, notably in the reform of the law on homosexuality in England and Wales. Mill's principle still commands widespread assent, and yet philosophical discussion long ago revealed its weakness. The causing of harm to others is neither a necessary nor a sufficient condition of making something against the law. That is to say, to show that a class of action is harmful is not enough to satisfy the basic requirements of justified prohibition. Nor does harm in itself provide an adequate ground. Causing harm is not a necessary condition of unlawfulness because there can be violations of right that are not in any straightforward sense harmful – invasion of privacy is a good example – and it is not a sufficient condition because there are actions that seriously harm the interests of others which society must nevertheless permit; free competition in the market-place is one clear instance. I can invade your privacy without harming you, and I can seriously harm your means of livelihood simply by trading more efficiently and effectively.

The upshot of all this is that scarcely a proposition in the argument with which we began can be sustained. We cannot confidently assert that pornographic depiction is causally connected with the sort of action depicted; even if it were, we could not unequivocally declare those actions harmful; even if we could, the costs of attempting to control them might well outweigh the benefits; and in any case, the fact that something is harmful does not automatically justify its social proscription.

Once all these points are put together, the upshot is plain; the case against pornography on the grounds of the social harm it does is at best very weak. Possibly it is no case at all, and this is a rather striking conclusion since, as I remarked at the start, the appeal to the harm pornography does is the commonest case against it.

To draw or advance such a conclusion is often taken to mean that there is no reasoned case to be made against pornography, and that the root of objections to it must lie in personal revulsion. In turn this seems to imply that while people are entitled to express disgust, this is in all probability a matter of the residual feelings of older generations and should not be allowed to confine the activities of those who do not share these feelings. Such is the position, generally, of those who take a more relaxed attitude to pornography.

This retreat to subjectivism is not the only alternative, however. There are many social questions which bear thinking about in other terms. For example, we can reasonably object to the construction of drab and dreary towns and city centres, without supposing that there is only one question that matters to rational town planning: whether drabness leads to more domestic accidents or car crashes. Similarly, arguments about what sort of society it is rational to want to belong to need not confine themselves to physical or psychological harm. The argument about the harmfulness or harmlessness of pornography is essentially a legal-cum-political and social one. It takes the existence of graphic reporting and of a demand for pornography for granted, and then asks how far this is to be permitted and how far it is to be contained. One way of putting this is to say that it is concerned with the *external* control of pornographic material. A quite different approach lies in considering pornography from the point of view of the *internal* aims of the sort of human activity to which it belongs. This is the approach I now want to explore.

Pornography and creativity

The public view of pornography has moved a long way from the world in which the novel *Lady Chatterley's Lover* could be prosecuted as an obscene publication. In that trial, however, an issue was raised which continues to be relevant. Representations were made that *Lady Chatterley's Lover* could not be pornography because it was *art*, a line of thought frequently invoked in many other cases since then. What such a defence implies is that depictions are pornographic not so much because of their content or subject-matter, but because of the way this content is treated. In other words, pornographic productions fail to reach certain aesthetic standards. Early examples of pornographic literature bear out this contention. Almost without exception they have nothing of interest in the way of plot, character or dialogue, and for most readers their focus on the minutiae of sexual congress rapidly loses whatever appeal it might have had through the tedium of endless repetition. The same thing is true of the soft pornography novels which nowadays can be found on the paperback bookshelves of even mainstream booksellers. Though they may titillate, they are wholly without literary merit or distinction. So too with pornographic films in which repeated acts of sex without any narrative purpose quickly become boring. And the same can be said of stories and films that consist in repeated acts of violence.

By contrast, a book or a film which observes minimal literary standards, though it may contain sex and violence, will in fact *eschew* the purely pornographic. This is true of artistic creation that falls far short of anything aspiring to the grand title of 'Literature' or 'Art'. The reason is that literary creation of even a modest sort aims actively to stimulate new interest and value in its readers, and not merely to accept and exploit their pre-existent interests and values. Its hope is not simply to *serve* but to *create* its audience. In illustration of this point consider writing for entertainment. Among the great writers of this century who were without aesthetic pretension, P. G. Wodehouse and Eric Ambler must figure prominently. What these writers did, Wodehouse especially, was not to move from mere entertainment to high 'Art', but use their very considerable literary skills to generate a higher standard of entertainment. It is in this way that all truly creative writing, even writing whose sole purpose is entertainment, is educational (in a broad sense). It does not merely *pander* to taste but tries to *educate* it.

The language of pandering is unfashionable, and the idea of educating taste no less so. It is commonly assumed that about taste there can be no disputing, and by implication that all references to better or baser tastes is merely a cover for élitist prejudices. These assumptions are part of the subjectivism to which, as we have seen, the normal argument about pornography tends to lead. A convincing alternative, therefore, needs to challenge such assumptions, and in my view we have only to reflect briefly on one familiar area of human endeavour in order to make such a challenge convincing.

The pupil who first comes to the piano has practical abilities to learn. However boring they may be, scales and finger exercises, and those rather mechanical 'studies' which many first-rate composers have devised, are an essential part of mastering the techniques without which great works of music cannot be played. But this technical mastery is only a foundation. The main business of the music teacher lies elsewhere, partly in the development of musicality and partly in a knowledge of which pieces of music are most worth playing. It is essential to the relationship between pupil and teacher, that the teacher knows what the pupil does not. Accordingly, though (human beings being what they are) success will come more easily if pupils are quickly enabled to play the music they like, the purpose is to bring them to the point of playing music that is *worth* playing and being able to tell which music this is. It is at this point that they pass beyond the mere mastery of technique and are given a musical education. One way of putting this is to say that it is not merely the musical abilities but musical *taste* of pupils which must be educated.

Unfashionable though the idea of educated taste may be, its necessity in the real world of music, and the arts more generally, is undeniable. No good music teacher would take the preferences of the elementary pupil as sovereign; they await formation, and this is a major part of their musical education. Conversely, no sensible pupil would devote time and money to lessons if there were not valuable things to be learned. Consequently, the test of a good teacher, and of a good course of instruction, is not that pupils are pleased, or have their pre-existent preferences satisfied, but that they become good musicians. To be inducted into the world of music is certainly to be inducted into a world of pleasure and enjoyment (though in my view it is not only this). But it is also a matter of being taught which pieces of music are most worth enjoying, and which it is best to take pleasure in, a truth, I might add, which applies as readily to twentieth-century jazz as to eighteenth-century baroque. The crucial point to be observed is that the pupil–teacher relationship is one in which it is the informed taste of the teacher, not the natural taste of the pupil, which is sovereign.

It is not only, or even chiefly, those actually described as teachers who have this role and importance. Composers and other creative artists are also educators of taste in this sense, and can thus claim an authority that the mere player cannot. This is not a defence of artistic conservatism; the greatest artists are highly innovative. But it *is* a defence of discrimination, and hence an attack on the indefensible (and usually undefended) claim that the pre-formed or 'natural' taste of anyone and everyone is author-itative. There is plenty of prurience among potential audiences – of this there can be no doubt – but truly creative writing does not rest content with reflecting existing interests and desires, or worse, taking them as the principal basis of its appeal.

The same sort of point can be made about other media. Sex and violence will continue to make an appearance in films, theatre, and on television. This is not specially deplorable. There is sex and violence in Shakespeare, in the Norse Sagas, in *The Decameron*. What is to be feared is that the sex and violence come to dominate. They can do so, however, only to the extent that the internal aims of artistic endeavour itself are abandoned by those who work in these media. Such things as ratings wars, or box office competitions, can bring this about. It is easy for writers, directors and producers to succumb to popularity for its own sake, and economics often increases the pressure to do so. Nevertheless, in so far as the standards internal to good writing, television, theatre and so on are upheld, they bring a contrary pressure, one which militates *against* the depiction of largely gratuitous sex and violence. It is wrong to think of this pressure as a quite extraneous concern with something called 'morality', however. Rather, it is the special business of the creative artist to show us that there are matters *more* interesting, more entertaining, more arresting, than sex or violence, and that images of sex and violence are only fleetingly attractive unless they are set in one of these larger contexts.

If it is true that there is a rising demand for pornography, this is evidence that artists have to this extent failed the public. In this they have been assisted, I think, by declining standards of literacy, the need to fill countless hours of television time, and a widening gap between high art and folk art. Alarmists sometimes speak of a tide of pornography sweeping late twentieth-century culture. If so, it is not social policy which needs critical scrutiny so much as artistic endeavour. And there is some evidence that the failure of the artists is beginning to be more widely realised. The box office flop of the films *Jade*, *Showgirls* and *Striptease*, it has been argued, has had the effect of casting their hitherto celebrated scriptwriter Joe Esterhas in a rather less *marketable* light.

Media ethics

This same approach, in contrast to the harm argument, may also be applied to some effect in the case of reported as well as to imagined sex and violence. News reporting too has its own internal goods. To see what these are we need to ask what the point or aim of reporting is. A natural answer is 'to inform', but this as it stands is inadequate. 'The news' is not simply accurate information about what has happened recently. Otherwise the utterly trivial – the amount of petrol used by a bus between one stop and the next, say – would qualify as news; it happened, after all. A 'news story' is information in a context, and the context determines both the significance of the story and the relevance of the information it contains.

Now here, as in fiction, the writer seeks not merely to serve but to create a readership. It is editors and reporters who decide what is newsworthy. In doing so, like the artists they can adopt the role of panderer or of educator. In practice, of course, even the best journalism comprises some mix of the two. The question therefore is where the greater emphasis will fall. This is not a matter entirely for decision but something determined in large part by the history and traditions of the particular form of publication. A newspaper, journal or television programme must find and keep an audience. Consequently, what is known variously as the popular, tabloid or gutter press cannot be expected to give pride of place to investigative reporting. Nor can it reasonably be thought a failure because it does not. Nevertheless, there is still a crucial distinction to be drawn between populist newspapers and outright fiction and one which the editors and correspondents on such papers must continue to draw if they are to remain reporters in any sense at all.

Journalism, then, should be thought of as a spectrum and the question to ask is whether, at least at the higher end of the spectrum, the goods and norms internal to journalism place limits on how sex and violence are reported. At the other end of the spectrum is what is known as sensationalism. This is the publication of news items that shock, horrify and titillate. The standard of significance in such reporting is almost entirely extraneous: whatever will shock, horrify and titillate is newsworthy, and this can be true of isolated events that have no relevance to anything outside themselves. By contrast, the standard of newsworthiness in higher journalism is to a large extent internally generated. The purpose of serious news reports in the newspapers and on radio and television is not merely to recount what has happened, but to report events in a way that uncovers and explains their political, social and cultural significance. In turn, of course, this requires that some *conception* of significance be brought to the reporting, and hence to the reader.

Now the fact is that specific acts of sex and violence have relatively little significance of this sort. In fact, some of the most famous 'massacres' in history, which had enormous social and political repercussions, were modest affairs in terms of the number of deaths and injuries compared to spectacular murders such as those at Dunblane and Hobart. In the Boston Massacre, for example, which led to the American War of Independence and thus to the creation of the United States, only three people died. The same point may be made about the sex lives of political leaders. However lurid, they are generally not of any more consequence than other people's sex lives. More particularly, the express detail concerning both multiple murders and high society scandals has in general no social or cultural significance at all. Odd though it may sound, striking and shocking events can be of no moment. Thus to dwell on the details of reported sex and violence is a kind of prurience, and to devote a lot of space to it makes journalism passive rather than active in the public culture.

There is always, of course, the matter of readership to be considered. Journalism cannot succeed in a vacuum, or be forever talking down to those it hopes to make its audience. Even in what is generally called the 'quality' press, there is a need to appeal to existing interests and prejudices, and the task is to strike a balance between this necessity and the demands of good journalism itself. Nevertheless, there are, as it seems to me, some clear instances where this balance has not been correctly struck. For instance, it has always been common for court cases to be reported at length. In the past such reporting had a lot to do with matters of legal import, though some celebrated cases never had any significance other than their sensational character – nineteenth-century coverage of Dr Crippen is a good example. In recent years, however, the proportion of these has risen steadily, to the point where most cases reported in the quality press appear to be chosen for their lurid nature, not for their legal or social significance. When this is true journalism has failed by its own standards.

The truth of this claim is not specially important. I cite it chiefly as an example of the balance between the internal standards of and the external demands on news reporting, which is at the heart of anything properly called media ethics. If the public appears to have an insatiable appetite for true stories of sex and violence, this is something which journalists will accept and cater to only in so far as they have fallen into passivity and abandoned the creatively active role which is intrinsic to their profession. Just as there is something called artistic integrity, there is journalistic integrity, and it cannot be spelled out simply in terms of factual accuracy or the protection of sources. In short, if there is reason to be concerned about the level of depicted sex and violence in our culture, it is not protection from harm by government or law we should look for, but more active, less passive conceptions of journalism and the arts.

Notes

1 Janet Daley, *Daily Telegraph*, 26 June 1996.
2 David Hume, *Enquiries*, Section X, 'Of miracles', Part I.

3 A review of the evidence will be found in D. Howitt and G. Cumberbatch, *Pornography: Impacts and Influences* (London: HMSO, 1990).

4 See for instance Brian Masters, *Killing for Company: The Case of Dennis Nilson* (London: Jonathan Cape, 1985).

5 Quoted in Elliot Leyton, *Hunting Humans: The Rise of the Modern Multiple Murderer,* (Harmondsworth: Penguin Books, 1989).

6 A line of argument pursued by Nadine Strossen, *Defending Pornography: Free Speech, Sex and the Fight for Women's Rights* (London: Abacus, 1996).

7 Aristotle, *Poetics* 1449b28.

13 Censorship and the media

Anthony Ellis

Those who are in authority generally wish to regulate the views and sentiments that others express, for the power to do so makes their lives considerably easier; and this is nowhere more true than in the case of the government. It is a wish that has, in the western world, been increasingly frustrated in the last half century or so as the authority of government to regulate speech has been steadily diminished.

When we refer to freedom of speech we are, of course, not referring only to speech in the literal sense, nor just to speech and the press. There has been a growing awareness that most of the arguments in favour of freedom of speech will generalise to other forms of communication; in a recent US Supreme Court case, for instance, the Court held that nude, barroom dancing was entitled to some protection under the First Amendment – 'though barely', as Chief Justice Rehnquist put it. Article 10 of the European Convention on Human Rights speaks not of the freedom of speech but of the 'freedom of expression'.

Almost everyone agrees that speech must be protected, to at least some extent, from governmental regulation. But what are the arguments in favour of freedom of speech? And what are they supposed to show?

At this more specific level, there is, as one might expect, less agreement. As to what the arguments are supposed to show, we should note at least three differences of opinion. One concerns *scope*. There are those who think that the effective arguments show only that speech that has a political dimension should be protected; others think that they show that the protection must be more general. A second difference concerns the *weight* of the protection. The American tradition has, since the 1940s, tended to give greater protection to speech than have European jurisdictions. British common law seems now to have accepted as a principle that the value of freedom of speech should be given some weight, but the British Race Relations Act, for instance, would not pass constitutional muster in the United States. The third concerns the *nature* of the protection more generally. We could think of the protection as giving merely a negative right, the right, roughly, not to have one's speech interfered with in certain ways; or we could think of it as a positive right, a right imposing a duty on the government positively to promote freedom of speech. Taken in the latter way, as European traditions have tended to take it, the right might generate, for instance, a duty on the part of the press to make space available to some of those aggrieved by what they read therein; taken the former way, as the American tradition has tended to take it, it would not generate this right (and the US Supreme Court has refused to recognise a 'right to reply' against the press).[1] Let us briefly survey some of the more familiar arguments.

The argument that gives the least scope to the protection of speech holds that freedom of speech is necessary for the proper working of democracy.[2] This might be so for a number of reasons. One is that the government should be responsive to all preferences, and it can hardly be so if it denies some people the right to make their preferences known. Another is that, in a democracy, the government should be accountable to the people, and that it is more likely to be so, in fact and not just in theory, if it cannot stifle criticism. Another depends upon some version of the second justification, to which we shall turn in a moment: in general, it holds, we should expect political decisions to be more soundly based the more they depend upon true judgements rather than false ones, and freedom of speech is likely to conduce to the discovery of truth. There is surely something in all of these points, but few now would hold that protection for speech should be so narrowly circumscribed, offering, for instance, no protection for science and the arts except in so far as they may have political implications.

A second argument gives much greater scope. It is perhaps the most famous of the arguments and is often summed up in the slogan that the discovery of truth requires a free 'market-place of ideas'.[3] The argument has been stated in many ways, and often misunderstood; it is often ridiculed as depending on the obviously false claim that, if people are always allowed to speak their minds, then true ideas will necessarily triumph over false ones. But this misses the real point of the argument twice over. First, the argument does not depend upon the idea that the truth always drives out the false, nor indeed on the weaker claim that it generally does so. Nor does it depend upon the relativistic view that there is no such thing as truth other than what is socially accepted as 'true'. This is not to deny that some of the proponents of the argument have accepted these claims, but merely to point out that they are not essential to it. Indeed, in order to have considerable force the argument need not make a very general claim at all. The proponent of freedom of speech need not claim that speech is to be protected always and everywhere, and Mill, of course, did not claim that. All that needs to be claimed is that in our circumstances, in the modern, western democracies, allowing the government to hold a monopoly on speech is likely to hinder progress towards the truth. And that is surely true. Secondly, the argument should not in any case be stated in terms of truth, which would restrict its force unnecessarily, since we need not judge the worth of all communications – music and dance for instance – in terms of truth.

The previous two arguments have been, in the broadest sense, consequentialist: they hold that protecting speech will promote greater good. This does not mean, of course, that any particular item of speech is likely to do more good than harm, but only that allowing the government a general licence to regulate speech, or certain sorts of speech, is likely to do more harm than would the largely unfettered exercise of freedom of speech. Other justifications are quite different.[4] They depend upon the idea that in order for a government to respect the moral dignity of its citizens it must grant them fairly broad and deep free-speech rights – even if this involves considerable costs.

One argument of this type is found in Mill (though allegedly embedded in a utilitarian framework): it holds that the freedom to speak is intimately tied to the freedom of thought, and that a prohibition on what one can think is an attack on one's identity.[5]

Another non-consequentialist argument holds that to deny the freedom to speak is also to deny the freedom to *hear*, and that a democratic government must treat its citizens as responsible adults who must be trusted to hear dangerous opinions and who therefore have the right, within very large limits, to decide for themselves what they will hear.[6]

Another non-consequentialist argument would hold that we each have a moral responsibility – to others, or perhaps just to the truth – to express our views to others; in so far as the government denies us the freedom of speech it prevents us from carrying out that duty.[7]

It is perhaps a philosopher's tendency to seek the master-argument, the one argument that will do all that is necessary to justify a position. But this is unnecessary in the present case, for all of the arguments just canvassed can be thought to express a relevant truth. And the fact that some right to freedom of speech is so widely accepted may, perhaps, suggest that it has appeal from more than one point of view.

These arguments give freedom of speech different scope. The argument that rests its weight on the citizen's right to hear would clearly justify the US Supreme Court's view that nude barroom dancing is entitled to First Amendment protection, for it is as paternalistic of the government to try to protect willing consumers from this sort of expression as to protect them from political speeches.[8] It seems unlikely that the argument that emphasises the importance of speech for the democratic process would have that result. But clearly, taken together, the arguments give freedom of speech great scope.

What *weight* they give to freedom of speech is more complicated, and cannot be dealt with fully without taking account of more general issues in political and legal philosophy. No one thinks that any of them justifies absolute freedom. In the USA, for instance, any speech can be prohibited if the government has a 'compelling interest' in preventing the harm that it may cause. (Speech which, like barroom dancing, or burning one's draft card, has a substantial 'non-speech element' must pass a less stringent test: there must be a 'substantial' governmental interest.) But morality and history would suggest that, if the arguments are taken seriously, then they support considerable weight for the freedom of speech. History surely bears out the claim that government interference with the citizens' right to free expression generally produces baneful effects, and should labour under severe burdens. And in a political democracy we should surely place great weight on the claim that the government must respect the autonomy of its citizens, even at some cost to both.

The *nature* of the right to freedom of speech is also a complicated matter, not to be settled independently of general considerations about the nature of rights. I shall do little more than state a view: it is arbitrary to restrict rights to negative rights. Rights protect interests, and interests can be threatened by more than the interference of other agents. One's interest in expressing an opinion can be threatened by the lack of resources with which to do so just as much as by the positive interference of others; there seems little other than an overridable, broadly utilitarian, reason why the government should not be required to maintain, to some degree, a 'level playing field' in this area as in others. That requirement might well generate, for instance, a strong reason for allowing some right of reply against the press.

When may speech be restricted?

However weighty the right to freedom of speech may be, everyone agrees that it may legitimately be overridden. As we have seen, the USA requires that there be a 'compelling governmental interest' for ordinary speech, and a 'substantial' governmental interest for symbolic speech. The European Convention on Human Rights, Article 10 states,

> The exercise of [the freedom of expression], since it carries with it duties and responsibilities, may be subject to such formalities, conditions, restrictions or penalties as are prescribed by law and are necessary in a democratic society, in the interests of national security, territorial integrity or public safety, for the prevention of disorder or crime, for the protection of health or morals, for the protection of the reputation or rights of others, for preventing the disclosure of information received in confidence, or for maintaining the authority and impartiality of the judiciary.

Our question, then, is, 'When may the government legitimately override the right to freedom of speech?'

Harm

The most obvious justification for prohibiting speech arises when the speech causes significant harm. But what is to count as harm? And what is significant? If we take seriously the arguments of the first section, then one thing is relatively clear: we should expect the harm at issue to be restricted to speech that harms others; if there is speech that harms only the speaker, then it would be unacceptably paternalistic of the government to regulate it. Speech that harms others is, of course, a more complex matter.

Here is one slight complication. Speech may directly harm particular, specifiable people; that is the case with speech that libels individuals. It may, on the other hand, harm general social interests without harming any specifiable individuals; that will often be the case with speech that harms national security. Both are harms that the government has a legitimate interest in preventing, and so both can, in principle, generate legitimate restrictions on speech. The latter, for obvious reasons, are likely to be more problematic than the former, and we shall return to them in a moment.

The harm referred to plainly does not encompass all harms that speech may cause, but is limited to 'the substantive evils that [government] has a right to prevent'.[9] But this still leaves room for difference of opinion, since people differ about what harms it is permissible for the government to prevent. These differences, which touch on fundamental issues in political philosophy, obviously cannot be resolved here. We can, however, make some progress without resolving them, for there is considerable agreement about what concrete things count as harms even amongst people who differ about what abstract account of harm should be given. Thus few would disagree that, in principle, it is permissible for the government to restrict speech in order to protect any of the following: national security, territorial integrity, public safety, public order, public health, the reputation or rights of others, private information received in confidence, the impartiality of legal proceedings and the protection of the public from crime. (This is the list, minus one or two items to which we shall return, given in Article 10 of the European Convention on Human Rights.)

We should expect, then, broad agreement on the sorts of harms that the government may seek to prevent by restricting speech. That, of course, does not guarantee agreement about more particular issues, for the harm that is to be prevented must somehow be weighed against the harm involved in restricting speech, and people may disagree about the results of that weighing. Even here, however, we find considerable agreement. The UK has, for instance, libel laws which make it relatively easy for those who think that they have been libelled to win their cases. In the USA, by contrast, a 1964 ruling required that a public figure can win a libel case only if he can show that the libel was published with 'malice', i.e. knowing that it was false, or recklessly ignoring evidence that it was true.[10] The effect of this difference is clear. English libel law, though benefiting those who are libelled, has a discernibly chilling effect on what the media will print or broadcast about public figures, since a few unsuccessful libel suits could bankrupt even a large newspaper; it seems highly doubtful whether the resulting gains to public figures outweigh the loss to public life, and in fact few people do think this.[11]

It is also surely clear, and generally agreed, that the need to protect national security is frequently used to justify unacceptable restrictions on speech. In recent years, press coverage of war has provided ample illustration. It is widely thought that the United States lost the Vietnam War partly because television coverage critically sapped the support of the American public. Now, to the extent that the media coverage was fair and accurate, the enormous resentment that this belief fuelled was plainly out of place. Everyone would agree that press coverage may be restricted to protect military operations; protecting civilian morale is quite another matter, and a democratic people have a right to know what is happening in a war carried out in their name even if it does critically sap their support for it. That is surely clear. However, governments learned their lesson. When Britain entered the Falklands War in 1982 press coverage was severely restricted, and in ways which could not possibly have been justified by the need to protect particular military operations. The press was also used to disseminate militarily useful misinformation.[12] The American government followed the lead of Mrs Thatcher in the Gulf War in 1991.[13] In both of these cases citizens were prevented from learning information which, in a democratic society, they have a right to know.

Other cases are more difficult and there is therefore less agreement about them. There is, for instance, substantial difference between the USA and the UK in how the press is allowed to report legal proceedings. Crudely, the UK is more concerned with ensuring the integrity of legal proceedings whereas the USA is more concerned with protecting the freedom of speech. The EU countenances restriction of speech to safeguard 'the authority and impartiality of the judiciary';[14] we need not, perhaps, be overly concerned for the authority of the judiciary but the impartiality of legal proceedings is more troublesome. In the year-long 1996 murder trial of O. J. Simpson, a famous US footballer, the jury was effectively imprisoned for the duration of the trial to ensure that they could not hear the discussions which saturated the news and entertainment media. Sequestration of juries is one of the trade-offs for allowing more-or-less unfettered reporting of legal cases. Understandably, sequestration is not often practised in the USA, and it is tempting to believe that juries are often prejudiced by what they learn in the morning papers although they are typically instructed not to read them. On the other hand, there is little hard evidence to support this belief, and in the absence of good evidence it may well be that the value of free speech should prevail.

In cases such as these, hard or easy, a balancing of harms is called for. And in hard cases people will naturally differ about what the result of that balancing will be; and it may be that there will be many differences that are hard to resolve.

Some of these differences are empirical. That is so with, for instance, the continuing debate about sex and violence in the media, and particularly on television. One argument is that a continuous diet of entertainment in which violence and casual sex are a staple may contribute to the formation of attitudes in children which will later result in violent antisocial behaviour. The evidence, in fact, seems extremely thin, often relying upon fanciful definitions of violence, ways of measuring attitudes that leave much to be desired, and hasty inferences from short-term alterations in attitudes to long-term alterations. But there is nothing especially improbable about the hypothesis itself, and it should be taken seriously. And if credible evidence should be found to support it then everyone would agree that this would be relevant to the question of whether the government should impose some sort of restrictive legislation. How could it be denied? It would clearly be crazy to think that, *in and of itself*, our interest in publishing and receiving a particular sort of entertainment should trump our interest in bodily security. All that remains is the question of whether violent television entertainment actually does in fact make a significant contribution to the amount of real violence in society.

That question is largely empirical, but not wholly so. It asks whether violent, televised entertainment makes a *significant* contribution to the amount of real violence in society, and that is partly an evaluative question, requiring that we balance the value of freedom of speech against other values – bodily security, in the particular case. Here, people may differ. Those concerned with freedom of speech will, however, insist that speech must be accorded great value, much more than most of the things (alcohol, for instance) that may contribute to violence in society. Not to mince the matter, this means that we should require a higher rate of increase in crimes of violence or a higher probability of such an increase in order to justify regulating speech than to justify regulating alcohol. Speech, unlike alcohol, plays a crucial part in our political, social and personal lives, a role that requires that government leave it largely unrestricted, even at some cost to other values; or so the arguments for freedom of speech undertake to demonstrate.

Freedom of speech, then, has a cost. When the US Supreme Court decided that political life in a democracy demands sufficiently 'uninhibited, robust and wide-open' debate that public officials could not sue for libel unless they could show actual malice,[15] the justices presumably did not think that this would mean that, in each particular case, the harm to the democratic process would outweigh the harm to a libelled official, for this would clearly be false in any normal sense of harm. A cost has to be paid.[16] That emerges no less when we consider the different views about whether violent entertainment contributes to antisocial attitudes. There are those who argue that, if the evidence is unclear, caution should be our counsel and that some degree of censorship is legitimate. Those who value freedom of speech will take a different view: they will think that, if it is freedom of speech that is at issue, then this brings with it a more stringent demand that there be evidence for the harm to be prevented. They will also hold that not just any proven degree of harm legitimates regulating speech.

Blasphemy, profanity, vulgarity, indecency, obscenity

There are still many, in both the USA and the UK, who would like to restrict blasphemy (reviling God or religion), profanity ('swear words'), indecency and vulgarity in public life. Indeed, most of the complaints levelled against television programmes in the UK have concerned 'bad language'.

Here it is worth making a distinction. One may object to blasphemy, for instance, in different ways. One may think that cursing God (the traditional Jewish understanding) is simply wrong, independently of its effect on others, and that this is why it should be prohibited. By contrast, one might think that a major element in its wrongness is its tendency to offend and outrage others. A parallel distinction holds for profanity, vulgarity and indecency.

There is nowadays little support for restrictions on speech that does not adversely affect others; and in, for instance, English law, blasphemy has long been generally understood as involving the intent to outrage the feelings of others.[17] We may, then, think of blasphemy and so on merely as types of speech that give offence. Does such speech justify censorship?

Offence

Let us start with indecency and obscenity. Genuine obscenity is, and always has been, rare in the media, but indecency has not, for I take it that the public display of a woman's naked breasts for sexual titillation is indecent, as is the representation of intimate sexual behaviour common in films that are shown on television. Does the fact that people are offended by indecency give a legitimate reason for censoring it?

One response would be to say this: people certainly have a right to be protected from *bodily* assault; why should they not have a parallel right to be protected from assault on their *minds*?

This response, so far as it goes, is surely correct. I would certainly be doing you a wrong if, say, I caused you to fall into fits of pointless rage by putting drugs in your food, and this needs no argument. That the harm caused is to the mind rather than to the body is clearly irrelevant. But now we need some distinctions.

The first thing we need to do is to distinguish different ways in which things can be offensive.[18] A smell can be offensive and so too can the display of an attractive naked body. But these are not offensive in the same way. So-called 'offensive nuisances', such as smells and loud noises, are simply assaults – offences – on the senses; they are, in an important way, similar to the case mentioned above where someone's mental states are affected by drugs. To find the display of an attractive nude offensive is, however, quite different. This is no more than *to have a view* about the display; it is to think it morally inappropriate in some way, whether because it is boorish to cast off one's clothes with no thought of the embarrassment it might cause the guests at the vicar's tea party, or just because it is wrong in itself – shameful – to be naked in public. To censor such displays because they are found offensive is, then, simply to censor them because some people think them immoral. Is that a reasonable ground for censorship?

Here, we may perhaps need to remind ourselves of another distinction. There are different ways in which things can be immoral. Perhaps the most obvious is by causing harm. And when some people object to the presence of semi-naked pin-ups in newspapers they do so on the ground that it causes harm in some way, perhaps by fostering a climate in which sexual offences against women are more easily tolerated; again, people sometimes object to the display of sexual behaviour on television because it will encourage the young to experiment sexually to their, and others', detriment. We need not discuss the plausibility of such claims for they are all irrelevant at the moment; if such indecencies cause harm then *that* is the objection to them, and it was dealt with briefly in an earlier section. If the argument about offence is to bring in anything new it must be referring to a sort of immorality that has nothing to do with the allegedly harmful consequences of the displays in question. The thought that it is immoral to appear nude in public must be the thought that this is *intrinsically* immoral, simply morally inappropriate in itself, whether or not it leads to bad consequences.

Our question, then, is this: Is it reasonable to censor expression merely because some people think that it is intrinsically immoral?

I said above that there is little support for restrictions on speech that does not adversely affect others. If that is to mean anything then it must be implicit in it that speech does not 'adversely affect others' merely because they form a disapproving view of it. If it were not implicit, then we should have to accept the view for which, I said, there is little support: we must accept that speech can be censored simply on the ground that some people, perhaps a majority, disapprove of it, even though it has no (further) adverse effect on anyone. I think that most of those who campaign for more stringent standards of decency in our public life do indeed accept something like this, though often without fully realising it (for the dominance of consequentialist ways of thinking in public life have made it difficult for many to articulate their thoughts in a non-consequentialist way). But it is surely an unacceptable view.

First, we need to be clear that the argument cannot, without arbitrariness, be restricted to indecency; and this must carry with it an implication unwelcome even to those who profess to accept it. Their thought is that public nudity is just immoral, and ought not to be tolerated. That thought, however, can have no grip in our society until it has been through a democratic filter from which it will emerge as the thought that public nudity is *generally thought* to be immoral and so ought not to be tolerated; it must go through this filter, for it has to be decided whether public nudity is indeed immoral, and this must be decided in some democratic manner (by a democratically elected legislature, for instance). Now, of course, a corollary beckons: any expression, including for instance the expression of these intolerant views, could legitimately be censored if a majority disapproved of them. Such a view would effectively allow one to say only what the majority might decide that one may say. It therefore accords no value to freedom of speech whatever, for to think that freedom of speech is a value is at least to think that one's right to speak should not be dependent on majority approval. That is why the right to freedom of speech is, in the USA and the EU, enshrined in a constitution restricting the legislative powers of the government.

Even if the position under discussion could be restricted to indecency, it would still be unacceptable. Think again of some of the original arguments for valuing freedom of speech.

One of them – the idea of the 'market-place of ideas' – can be cast in terms of artistic freedom. It is unclear whether art progresses, but it certainly changes, constantly seeking the best that it can for its own time and place. This means that it must explore boundaries, and in the process it will often linger in dead ends which are variously silly and offensive; equally, it will often arrive at valuable destinations that required traversing ways which seemed, and perhaps were, silly and offensive. But the silly and the offensive are the price we pay for the sublime, for the best art does not emerge from the dictates of the majority (or from the dictates of a minority, for that matter). It is, of course, a value judgement to say that the price is worth paying. But if we deny that value judgement we should be clear about what it is that we are denying.

The argument about paternalism is also relevant here. I have often encountered things in the media of which I disapprove. But I would not, on the whole, wish for a society in which I was protected from them, even though my life might have been better in some ways if I had not encountered them. A society in which I was protected from them would inevitably be a society in which *others* decided what I should be protected from. That is not because I should need to encounter what I wish to be protected from before I could know that I wish to be protected from it, for often one wants to be protected from general types of things which can be specified adequately in advance. It is because I live in a society in which I do not myself make the relevant decisions about what I may and may not see; those decisions are made by a government more or less responsive to majority opinion,[19] and even if I had some desire to be protected from things that I myself disapprove of I should have no desire whatever to be protected from things that others disapprove of and think that I should disapprove of too. That some people, even a majority, disapprove of some expression is not, then, by itself a reasonable ground for censorship.

It may now be thought that I have misinterpreted the argument from offence. I have said that to be offended by something is to disapprove of it. But perhaps being offended is more than this, necessarily involving some unpleasant affect beyond that which is generally involved in having a disapproving view of something. The argument, it may be said, is not that the fact that people think something offensive is a ground for censorship, but the fact that they are actually *offended* by it, that they are caused feelings of indignation and outrage. Let us confine our attention, then, to things which cause offence in the sense that they cause *outrage*. Does this affect the argument in any way? Is it a reasonable ground to censor speech that it causes in some people outrage?

Here again a distinction needs to be observed. One reason for censoring speech that causes outrage is to protect the public order. This is, of course, a highly dangerous principle, and one that no government should normally countenance, for it creates the right to a 'heckler's veto': those who wish to silence speech may do so simply by threatening violence in response to it.[20] In any case, this reason is not relevant at the moment; its appeal is to *harm* that the speech may cause, and we have already dealt with that. The reason that would have to be at issue now would be that people simply have a right not to be caused outrage. But this principle is far from compelling. Our public life is disfigured by outrage on the part of too many who think they have a grievance or even just a worthy cause, and there seems little reason to honour it with legal protection. On the contrary, a healthy respect for the civic virtues requires, not only that one generally refrain from giving gratuitous offence, but that one should learn to control one's temper when it is given.

A further distinction may be worth commenting upon, though a fairly obvious one. Being offended is not the same thing as being embarrassed, though they are often confused in this context because one of the things that makes certain actions offensive is that they obviously cause embarrassment. Now, most people find it embarrassing to watch, say, representations of sexual behaviour on the television in the presence of their 11-year-old children. Such embarrassment is not at all unreasonable, and nor is the desire to be protected from it. But it does not generate any argument for censorship. The most that it justifies is a requirement of clear labelling. That can be accomplished in many ways. The BBC for many years operated with a '9 o'clock watershed'; nothing sexually explicit could be shown before 9 o'clock, when good children were supposed to be in bed. Many professed to find this inadequate on the ground that many children did not go to bed until much later. But, after all, viewers had been warned; they could send their children to bed if they did not want to be embarrassed (or, alternatively, go to bed themselves). But other methods would work better; some cable television stations in the USA, for instance, label the films that they show, indicating whether they contain nudity ('N'), brief nudity ('BN'), 'strong sexual content' ('SSC') and so on. Of course, one may switch on the film after it has started and miss the label. But if one is subsequently embarrassed, that is one's own responsibility, just as it is if one drinks a bottle of paraquat not having had time to read the label.

We have been dealing so far with indecency, but we should now be able to see our way through the other issues that I mentioned. Let us turn to blasphemy.

Laws prohibiting blasphemy have never been ruled unconstitutional in the USA, but it would now be generally recognised that to prohibit blasphemy would violate two provisions of the First Amendment: the clause prohibiting the state from establishing a religion, and the clause prohibiting the state from abridging the freedom of speech. There has been no prosecution for blasphemy in the USA since 1971.

There is no such protection for blasphemy in the UK, and it remains a criminal offence in England and Wales.[21] However, the last prosecution for blasphemy in the UK was in 1976. Mary Whitehouse, a noted agitator for stringent standards of decency on radio and television, prosecuted a journal, *Gay News*, and its publisher for a poem celebrating a union of Christ and homosexuality. Though the conviction was upheld on appeal, many thought that the absurd affair was the dying cough of the law of blasphemy. It was resuscitated however, by two events in 1988. One was Martin Scorsese's film *The Last Temptation of Christ*, which suggested that Jesus had fathered children by Mary Magdalene. Reportedly described as 'the most blasphemous evil attack on the Church and the cause of Christ in the history of entertainment'[22] it caused immense outrage in many countries. (Even Franco Zeffirelli, whose *Jesus of Nazareth* had earlier been denounced as blasphemous, boycotted the film at the Venice Film Festival.) The other event was the publication of Salman Rushdie's *The Satanic Verses*, a long novel which many Muslims held to be blasphemous. It was widely banned and burned and eventually the Ayatollah Khomeini sentenced Rushdie (and the publishers) to death, promising an enormous sum of money to anyone who would murder them. Subsequent sales of the book have made Rushdie an enormously wealthy man, but he has ever since been forced to live in hiding, guarded by policemen.[23]

Both film and book undoubtedly caused much genuine offence, though, as is common with persecution for blasphemy, the hysteria over Rushdie's book was partly political, deliberately whipped up as part of an anti-western propaganda movement on the part of extremist Muslims. And the book, which in the normal course of events, would have been read by relatively few people, became an international best-seller. The most interesting aspect of all of this, however, was the impetus it gave to the movement to *extend* the blasphemy law in the United Kingdom, a movement supported by many politicians, church leaders and others. The idea, at its simplest, was to toughen up the blasphemy law and extend it to cover all religions and not just Christianity. The argument seemed to be twofold. First, in an increasingly multi-cultural society there is a public interest in preventing the sort of offence which might lead to civil discord; and second, people have a right to have their feelings protected from outrageous attacks on their religious beliefs or on the gods in whom they believe.

But we have already seen problems with these arguments. The first seems to legitimate the 'heckler's veto'. In the present context, however, it picks up other problems too. First, it has little to do with religion, and therefore gives little support to blasphemy laws specifically. Anyone minded to offend someone from a different culture will find little obstacle in a law prohibiting insulting references to his religion. Second, and a corollary, the argument would cast the net of prohibited speech very wide indeed, and such a law, if enforced, would almost certainly exact considerably greater costs to freedom of expression than any benefits to be reaped. Third, one might expect such a law to produce its own civil discord, as those who never liked a multicultural society in the first place vented their rage on those whose cultural differences were perceived as the root cause of this restrictive prohibition.

The second argument too we can now deal with fairly quickly. It should not be confused with the argument that says that it is intrinsically immoral to insult God or religion; that could be true, but we have already seen that the mere intrinsic immorality of speech will not generate a legitimate reason for censorship. Nor is that how it is nowadays usually intended. The idea is rather that what people have a right to be protected from is the hurt to their feelings caused by *outrageous insult*. But this cannot be right. First, if we were to acknowledge such a right, then it would be totally arbitrary to restrict it to the area of religion; we should thus not really be talking about blasphemy at all. Second, certain beliefs, some religious ones included, *call for* the sort of robust attack which their adherents will perceive as outrageous and insulting; it would be wholly inappropriate to censor such speech merely to protect the feelings of those adherents. Nor should we want to allow the government to decide which beliefs could be spoken of in that way and which could not.[24] Third, as I have already said, there seems in any case little reason to give protection against outrage caused by sentiments that one does not approve of.

Notes

1 *Miami Herald Co. v. Tornillo* 418 US 241 (1974).
2 See, for instance, Alexander Meiklejohn, *Free Speech and its Relation to Self-Government* (New York: Harper and Row, 1948). Meiklejohn gave absolute weight, however, to the narrowly defined speech that he thought was protected by the First Amendment.
3 See J. S. Mill, *On Liberty*, ch. 2 (*On Liberty and Other Writings*, ed. Stefan Collini, (Cambridge, Cambridge University Press, 1989); and Oliver Wendell Holmes's dissenting opinion in *Abrams v. US*, 250 US 616 (1919).
4 There is, of course, a technical method for expressing these other theories as consequentialist theories, but it does not hide the significant difference between them and the theories that it is more natural to refer to as consequentialist.

5 See Mill, *On Liberty*, p. 15; and Rodney Smolla, *Free Speech in an Open Society* (New York: Vintage Books, 1993), pp. 10f.
6 See Ronald Dworkin, *Freedom's Law: The Moral Reading of the American Constitution* (Cambridge, MA: Harvard University Press, 1996), p. 200.
7 Dworkin, *Freedom's Law*, pp. 200f.
8 However, obscene speech, as defined by *Miller v. California*, 413 US 15 (1973), has no constitutional protection in the USA.
9 *Schenck v. US*, 249 US 47 (1919).
10 *New York Times Co. v. Sullivan*, 376 US 254 (1964).
11 'The English law of civil defamation is widely regarded as unsatisfactory' (Eric Barendt, *Freedom of Speech* (Oxford: Clarendon Press, 1985), p. 178.
12 For a balanced account of press coverage in the Falklands War, see 'Information policy and the Falklands conflict' in Shimon Shetreet (ed.), *Free Speech and National Security* (Dordrecht: Nijhoff, 1991), pp. 143–54.
13 For a detailed account, see Smolla, *Free Speech in an Open Society*, ch. 10.
14 Article 10 of the European Convention on Human Rights. On this, issue see Barendt, *Freedom of Speech*, pp. 218–23.
15 *New York Times Co. v. Sullivan*, 376 US 254, 270 (1964). For an account of this case, see Anthony Lewis, *Make No Law: The Sullivan Case and the First Amendment* (New York: Vintage Books, 1991).
16 See Frederick Schauer, 'Uncoupling free speech', *Columbia Law Review*, 92 (1992), pp. 1321–57. Schauer points out that under current US First Amendment law, those who are injured by protected speech bear the full costs, costs which ought, in principle at least, to be borne by those who benefit from protecting speech, i.e. society at large.
17 However, the conviction in the *Gay News* case was upheld by the House of Lords in 1979, the majority of the justices holding that intent to offend was *not* a necessary part of the common-law crime of blasphemy. For an account of this case, see Leonard Levy, *Blasphemy: Verbal Offense against the Sacred from Moses to Salman Rushdie* (New York: Alfred A. Knopf, 1993), pp. 534–50.
18 I have discussed this in more detail in 'Offense and the liberal conception of the law', *Philosophy and Public Affairs* 13 (1984), pp. 1–23.
19 More or less because it takes only a small minority of people – such as the members of the National Viewers' and Listeners' Association – to have a significant effect on government bodies.
20 See Harry Kalven, Jr, *A Worthy Tradition: Freedom of Speech in America* (New York: Harper and Row, 1988), pp. 89ff.
21 Parliament repealed the 1698 Blasphemy Act in 1967, but it remains a common law offence in England and Wales. There is no law of blasphemy in Scotland or Northern Ireland.
22 *The Economist*, 13 August 1988, p. 77.
23 Blasphemy has caused enormous offence in a different context; as I write, the city of Richmond, Virginia, is, probably unconstitutionally, desperately trying to cancel a contract for a concert with a Satanistic rock group known as Marilyn Manson; they had not realized, when the contract was made, the nature of the group's performance. The city councillors' outrage had been matched in many cities, and the University of South Carolina had shortly before, paid the group $40,000 not to perform a scheduled concert.
24 'If there is any fixed star in our constitutional constellation, it is that no official, high or petty, can prescribe what shall be orthodox in politics, nationalism, religion, or other matters of opinion', Justice Robert Jackson (*West Virginia State Board of Education v. Barnette* (319 US 624 (1943)).

Select bibliography

Altman, I., 'Privacy: a conceptual analysis', *Environment and Behavior* 8 (1976): 7–8.

Aristotle, *Nichomachean Ethics*, Harmondsworth: Penguin Books, 1953.

Aristotle, *Poetics*, Ann Arbor, MI: University of Michigan Press, 1970.

Attorney General's Commission on Pornography, *Final Report*, 2 vols, Washington DC: US Government Printing Office, 1986.

Barendt, Eric, *Freedom of Speech*, Oxford: Oxford University Press, 1985.

Barker, Martin and Petley, Julian (eds), *Ill Effects: The Media/Violence Debate*, London: Routledge, 1997.

Baudrillard, Jean, *In the Shadow of the Silent Majorities . . . or the End of the Social*, New York: Semiotext, 1983.

Baudrillard, Jean, *Selected Writings*, ed. Mark Poster, Cambridge: Polity, 1988.

Beauchamp, Tom L. and Pinkard, Terry P. (eds), *Ethics and Public Policy*, Englewood Cliffs, NJ: Prentice-Hall, 1983.

Bell, Martin, *In Harm's Way: Reflections of a War Zone Thug*, London: Hamish Hamilton, 1995.

Belsey, Andrew and Chadwick, Ruth (eds), *Ethical Issues in Journalism and the Media*, London: Routledge, 1992.

Belsey, Andrew and Chadwick, Ruth, 'Ethics as a vehicle for media quality', *European Journal of Communication* 10 (1995): 461–73.

Benn, Piers 'Pornography, degradation and rhetoric', *Cogito* 7 (1993): 127–34.

Bennett, T., Boyd-Bowman, S., Mercer, C. and Woollacott, J. (eds), *Popular Television and Film*, London: British Film Institute.

Berlin, Isaiah, *Four Essays on Liberty*, Oxford: Oxford University Press, 1969.

Bernays, E., *Crystallising Public Opinion*, New York: Boni and Liveright, 1923.

Bernstein, Carl and Woodward, Bob, *All the President's Men*, New York: Secker and Warburg.

Bezanson, Randall P., Cranberg, Gilbert and Soloski, John, *Libel Law and the Press*, New York: Free Press, 1987.

Birkenshaw, Patrick, *Freedom of Information: The Law, the Practice and the Ideal*, London: Weidenfeld and Nicolson, 1988.

Bok, Sissela, *Lying: Moral Choice in Public and Private Life*, London: Quartet, 1980.

Bok, Sissela, *Secrets: On the Ethics of Concealment and Revelation*, Oxford: Oxford University Press, 1982.

Bryant, Jennings and Zillman, Dolf (eds), *Perspectives on Media Effects*, Hillsdale, NJ: Erlbaum, 1986.

Calcutt, David, *Report of the Committee on Privacy and Other Matters*, Cmnd. 1102, London: HMSO, 1990.

Calcutt, David, *Review of Press Self-regulation*, Cmnd. 2135, London: HMSO, 1993.

Capa, Robert, *Slightly out of Focus*, New York: H. Holt, 1947.

Caputi, Mary, *Voluptuous Yearnings: A Feminist Theory of the Obscene*, Lanham, MD: Rowman and Littlefield, 1994.

Carroll, Noël, 'Conspiracy theories of representation', *Philosophy of the Social Sciences* 17 (1987).

Carroll, Noël, *The Philosophy of Horror*, New York: Routledge, 1990.

Carroll, Noël, *A Philosophy of Mass Art*, Oxford University Press, 1998.

Chomsky, Noam, *Necessary Illusions*, Toronto: CBC Enterprises, 1989.

Chomsky, Noam and Hermann, Edward, *Manufacturing Consent*, London: Vintage, 1994.

Christians, Clifford G., Ferré, John and Fackler, Mark, *Good News: A Social Ethics of the Press*, New York: Oxford University Press, 1993.

Christians, Clifford G., Fackler, Mark and Rotzoll, Kim B., *Media Ethics: Cases and Moral Reasoning*, 4th edn, New York: Longman, 1995.

Cohen, Elliot D. (ed.) *Philosophical Issues in Journalism*, New York: Oxford University Press, 1992.

Commission on Freedom of the Press, *A Free and Responsible Press*, Chicago: University of Chicago Press, 1947.

Cooper, Thomas W., *Communication Ethics and Global Change*, New York: Longman, 1989.

Crewe, I. and Gosschalk, B. (eds), *Political Communications: The General Election Campaign of 1992*, Cambridge: Cambridge University Press, 1995.

Curran, James (ed.), *The British Press: A Manifesto*, London: Routledge, 1978.

Curran, James and Seaton, Jean (eds), *Power without Responsibility: The Press and Broadcasting in Britain*, 4th edn, London: Routledge, 1991.

Dahlgren, Peter and Sparks, Colin (eds), *Communication and Citizenship*, London: Routledge, 1991.

Dahlgren, Peter and Sparks, Colin (eds), *Journalism and Popular Culture*, London: Sage, 1992.

Day, Louis A., *Ethics in Media Communication: Cases and Controversies*, Belmont, CA: Wadsworth, 1991.

Denton, Robert E. Jr. (ed.), *Ethical Dimensions of Political Communication*, New York: Praeger, 1991.

Deppa, Joan, *The Media and Disasters: Pan Am 103*, London: David Fulton, 1993.

Devlin, Patrick, *The Enforcement of Morals*, Oxford: Oxford University Press, 1965.

Dworkin, Andrea, *Letters from a War Zone*, London: Secker and Warburg, 1988.

Dworkin, Ronald, *A Matter of Principle*, Oxford: Clarendon Press, 1985.

Dworkin, Ronald, *Freedom's Law: The Moral Reading of the American Constitution*, Cambridge, MA: Harvard University Press, 1996.

Dyson, Kenneth and Homolka, Walter (eds), *Culture First/Promoting Standards in the New Media Age*, London: Cassell, 1996.

Eason, David L., 'On journalistic authority: the Janet Cooke scandal', *Critical Studies in Mass Communication* 3/4 (1988): 313–34.

Elliot, Deni (ed.), *Responsible Journalism*, Beverly Hills, CA: Sage, 1986.

Ellis, Anthony, 'Offense and the liberal conception of the law', *Philosophy and Public Affairs* 13 (1984): 1–23.

Ellis, John, *Visible Fictions*, London: Routledge and Kegan Paul, 1982.

Engel, Matthew, *Tickle the Public: One Hundred Years of the Popular Press*, London: Gollancz, 1996.

Ettema, James S. and Glasser, Theodore L., 'On the epistemology of investigative journalism', *Journal of Communication* 8/2 (1985): 183–206.

Evans, Harold, *Eyewitness: 25 Years Through World Press Photos*, London: Quiller Press, 1981.

Fairclough, Norman, *Media Discourse*, London and New York: Edward Arnold, 1995.

Fallows, James, *Breaking the News*, New York: Pantheon, 1996.

Feinberg, Joel, *Social Philosophy*, Englewood Cliffs, NJ: Prentice-Hall, 1973.

Feinberg, Joel, *Rights, Justice and the Bounds of Liberty: Essays in Social Philosophy*, Princeton, NJ: Princeton University Press, 1980.

Feinberg, Joel, *The Moral Limits of the Criminal Law*, vol. 2: *Offense to Others*, New York: Oxford University Press, 1985.

Feldman, D., *Civil Liberties and Human Rights*, Oxford: Clarendon Press, 1993.

Fink, Conrad, *Media Ethics*, New York: McGraw-Hill, 1988.

Fiske, John, *Television Culture*, New York: Routledge, 1987.

Fiske, John, 'Popularity and the politics of information', in P. Dahlgren and C. Sparks (eds) *Journalism and Popular Culture*, London: Sage, 1992, pp. 45–63.

Fiske, John, *Media Matters: Everyday Culture and Political Change*, Minneapolis, MN: University of Minnesota Press, 1994.

Franklin, Bob, *Newszak and News Media*, London: Arnold, 1997.

Freund, Gisèle, *Photography and Society*, London: Gordon Fraiser, 1980.

Gauntlett, David, *Moving Experiences: Understanding Television's Influences and Effects*, London: John Libbey, 1995.

Gitlin, Todd, *The Whole World is Watching*, Berkeley, CA: University of California Press, 1980.

Gluckman, Max, 'Gossip and scandal', *Current Anthropolgy* 4/3 (June 1963): 307–16.

Goldman, Alan, *The Moral Foundations of Professional Ethics*, Totowa, NJ: Rowman and Littlefield, 1980.

Goldstein, Tom, *The News at Any Cost*, New York: Simon and Schuster, 1985.

Goodman, Robert F. and Ben-Ze'ev, Aaron (eds), *Good Gossip*, Lawrence, KS: University of Kansas Press, 1994.

Goodwin, H. Eugene and Smith, Ron F., *Groping for Ethics in Journalism*, 3rd edn, Ames, IA: Iowa State University Press, 1994.

Gosschalk, B. (ed.) *Political Communications*, Cambridge: Cambridge University Press, 1995.

Graham, Gordon, *Contemporary Social Philosophy*, Oxford: Blackwell Publishers, 1988.

Gripsund, J., 'The aesthetics and the politics of melodrama', in P. Dahlgren and C. Sparks (eds) *Journalism and Popular Culture*, London: Sage, 1992, pp. 84–95.

Gross, Larry, Katz, John Stuart and Ruby, Jay (eds), *Image Ethics*, New York: Oxford University Press, 1988.

Habermas, J., *The Structural Transformation of the Public Sphere*, Cambridge: Polity, 1988.

Hargrave, Andrea Millwood, *Sex and Sexuality in Broadcasting*, London: John Libbey, 1992.

Hart, H. L. A., *Law, Liberty and Morality*, Oxford: Oxford University Press, 1963.

Hartley, John, *Understanding News*, London: Methuen, 1982.

Hausman, Carl, *Crisis of Conscience: Perspectives on Journalism Ethics*, New York: HarperCollins, 1992.

Hewitt, Patricia, *Privacy: The Information Gatherers*, London: National Council for Civil Liberties, 1977.

Hiebert, Ray Eldon (ed.), *Impact of Mass Media*, 3rd edn, New York: Longman, 1995.

Hooper, David, *Official Secrets: The Use and Abuse of the Act*, London: Secker and Warburg, 1987.

Howitt, D. and Cumberbatch, G., *Pornography: Impacts and Influences*, London: HMSO, 1990.

Hulteng, John L., *The Messanger's Motives: Ethical Problems of the Mass Media*, 2nd edn, Englewood Cliffs, NJ: Prentice-Hall, 1985.

Jones, J. Clement, *Mass Media Codes of Ethics and Councils: A Comparative International Study on Professional Standards*, Paris: Unesco, 1980.

Jones, Nicholas, *Soundbites and Spindoctors*, London: Cassell, 1995.

Kalven, Harry, Jr, *A Worthy Tradition: Freedom of Speech in America*, New York: Harper and Row, 1988.

Kant, Immanuel, *Groundwork of the Metaphysics of Morals*, in H. J. Paton (ed.) *The Moral Law*, London: Hutchinson, 1948.

Kant, Immanuel, *The Philosophy of Immanuel Kant*, Chicago: University of Chicago Press, 1949.

Karnow, Stanley, *Vietnam: A History*, New York: Viking Press, 1983.

Keane, John, *The Media and Democracy*, Oxford: Polity Press, 1991.

Keeble, Richard, *The Newspapers Handbook*, London: Routledge, 1994.

Kellner, Douglas, *Television and the Crisis of Democracy*, Boulder, CO, San Francisco and Oxford: Westview Press, 1990.

Kieran, Matthew, 'Violent films: natural born killers?', *Philosophy Now* 12 (1995): 15–18.

Kieran, Matthew, 'Art, imagination and the cultivation of morals', *Journal of Aesthetics and Art Criticism* 54 (1996): 337–51.

Kieran, Matthew, *Media Ethics: A Philosophical Approach*, Westport, CT: Praeger, 1997.

Kieran, Matthew, 'News reporting and the ideological presumption', *Journal of Communication* 47/2 (1997): 79–96.

Kieran, Matthew, Morrison, David and Svennevig, Michael, *Regulating for Changing Values: A Report for the Broadcasting Standards Commission*, London: BSC, 1997.

Klaidman, Stephen and Beauchamp, Tom L., *The Virtuous Journalist*, New York: Oxford University Press, 1987.

Knightley, Phillip, *The First Casualty: From the Crimea to Vietnam: The War*

Correspondent as Hero, Propagandist, and Myth Maker, New York: Harcourt Brace Jovanovich, 1975.

Knowlton, Steven R. and Parsons, Patrick R. (ed.), *The Journalist's Moral Compass*, Westport, CT: Praeger, 1995.

Koch, Tom, *The News as Myth*, New York: Greenwood, 1990.

Kurtz, Howard, *Media Circus*, New York: Random House, 1994.

Lambeth, Edmund B., *Committed Journalism*, 2nd edn, Bloomington, IN: Indiana University Press, 1992.

Lee, Alan, *The Origins of the Popular Press in England 1855–1914*, London: Croom Helm, 1976.

Lemert, J. B., *Criticizing the Media*, Newbury Park, CA: Sage, 1989.

Lester, Paul, *Photojournalism: An Ethical Approach*, Hillsdale, NJ: Erlbaum, 1991.

Levy, Leonard, *Blasphemy: Verbal Offense against the Sacred from Moses to Salman Rushdie*, New York: Alfred A. Knopf, 1993.

Lewis, Anthony, *Make No Law: The Sullivan Case and the First Ammendment*, New York: Vintage Books, 1991.

Lichtenberg, Judith (ed.), *Democracy and the Mass Media*, Cambridge: Cambridge University Press, 1990.

Limburg, Val E., *Electronic Media Ethics*, Boston, MA: Focal Press, 1994.

Locke, John, *Two Treatises of Government*, Cambridge: Cambridge University Press, 1963.

Locke, John, *A Letter Concerning Toleration*, New York: Prometheus, 1990.

Machiavelli, Niccolò, *The Prince*, New York: Dover, 1992.

MacKenzie, John, *Propaganda and Empire: The Manipulation of British Public Opinion 1880–1960*, Manchester: Manchester University Press, 1984.

MacKinnon, Catherine, *Only Words*, Cambridge, MA: Harvard University Press, 1993.

McLuhan, Marshall, *Understanding Media: The Extensions of Man*, London: Routledge and Kegan Paul, 1964.

McLuhan, Marshall and Fiore, Quentin, *The Medium in the Message*, Harmondsworth: Penguin Books, 1967.

McNair, Brian, *Glasnost, Perestroika and the Soviet Media*, London: Routledge, 1991.

McNair, Brian, *An Introduction to Political Communication*, London: Routledge, 1995.

McNair, Brian, *News and Journalism in the UK*, 2nd edn, London: Routledge, 1996.

McNair, Brian, 'Performance in politics and the politics of performance: public relations, the public sphere and democracy', in J. L'Etang and M. Pieczke (eds) *Critical Perspectives in Public Relations*, London: International Thomson Business Press, 1996, pp. 35–53.

McQuail, Denis, *Media Performance: Mass Communication and the Public Interest*, Newbury Park, CA: Sage, 1992.

Mander, Jerry, *Four Arguments for the Elimination of Television*, New York: Quill, 1978.

Marshall, W. L., 'Pornography and sex offenders', in D. Zillman and J. Bryant (eds) *Pornography: Research Advances and Policy Considerations*, Hillsdale, NJ: Erlbaum, 1989, pp. 185–214.

Meiklejohn, Alexander, *Free Speech and its Relation to Self-government*, New York: Harper and Row, 1948.

Merill, John C. and Barney, Ralph D. (eds) *Ethics and the Press*, New York: Hastings House, 1975.

Metz, Christian, *Psychoanalysis and Cinema: The Imaginary Signifier*, London: Methuen, 1982.

Meyer, Philip, *Ethical Journalism*, New York: Longman, 1987.

Meyerwitz, Joshua, *No Sense of Place*, Oxford: Oxford University Press, 1985.

Mill, John Stuart, *On Liberty*, Harmondsworth: Penguin Books, 1982.

Mitchell, William J., *The Reconfigured Eye: Visual Truth in the Post-photographic Era*, Cambridge, MA: MIT Press, 1992.

Moore, Roy L., *Mass Communication Law and Ethics*, Hillsdale, NJ: Erlbaum, 1994.

Morris, D., *Behind the Oval Office*, New York: Random House, 1996.

Morrison, David E. and Tumber, Howard, *Journalists at War: The Dynamics of News Reporting during the Falklands Conflict*, London: Sage, 1988.

Mulvey, Laura, *Visual and Other Pleasures*, London: Macmillan, 1989.

Newsome, Elizabeth, 'Video violence and the protection of children', Child Development Research Unit, University of Nottingham, March 1994.

Nozick, Robert, *Anarchy, State and Utopia*, Oxford: Blackwell Publishers, 1974.

Olen, Jeffrey, *Ethics in Journalism*, Englewood Cliffs, NJ: Prentice-Hall, 1988.

Paik, Haejung and Comstock, George, 'The effects of television violence on antisocial behavior: a meta-analysis', *Communication Research* 21 (1994): 516–46.

Pally, Marcia, *Sex and Sensibility: Reflections on Forbidden Mirrors and the Will to Censor*, Hopewell, NJ: Ecco Press, 1994.

Patterson, Philip and Wilkins, Lee (eds), *Media Ethics: Issues and Cases*, 2nd edn, Dubuque, IA: Wm. C. Brown, 1994.

Paul, Noel S., *Principles for the Press: A Digest of Council Decisions, 1953–1984*, London: Press Council, 1985.

Perse, Elizabeth M., 'Uses of erotica and acceptance of rape myths', *Communication Research* 21 (1994): 488–515.

Philo, Greg, *Seeing and Believing*, London: Routledge, 1990.

Plato, *Republic*, trans. D. Lee, Harmondsworth: Penguin Books, 1974.

Powes, Lucas A., Jr, *The Fourth Estate and Constitution: Freedom of the Press in America*, Berkeley and Los Angeles, CA: University of California Press, 1991.

Press Complaints Commission, *Code of Practice*, London: Press Complaints Commission, September 1994.

Press Complaints Commission, *Annual Report 1995*, London: Press Complaints Commission, 1995.

Rachlin, Allan, *News as Hegemonic Reality*, New York: Praeger, 1988.

Rawls, John, *A Theory of Justice*, Oxford: Oxford University Press, 1972.

Ricoeur, Paul, *Hermeneutics and the Human Sciences*, trans. J. B. Thompson, Cambridge: Cambridge University Press, 1981.

Ritchin, Fred, *In Our Own Image*, New York: Aperture, 1990.

Robertson, Geoffrey, *Freedom, the Individual and the Law*, Harmondsworth: Penguin, 1989.

Rodgerson, G. and Wilson, E. (eds) *Pornography and Feminism*, London: Lawrence and Wishart, 1993.

Rorty, Richard, *Contingency, Irony and Solidarity*, Cambridge: Cambridge University Press, 1989.

Rosenblum, Mort, *Who Stole the News?*, New York: John Wiley and Sons, 1993.

Rubin, Bernard, *Questioning Media Ethics*, New York: Praeger, 1978.

Schaner, Frederick, 'Uncoupling free speech', *Columbia Law Review* 92 (1992): 1321–57.

Schlesinger, Philip, *Media, State and Nation: Political Violence and Collective Identities*, London: Sage, 1991.

Schlesinger, Philip and Tumber, Howard, *Reporting Crime: The Media Politics of Criminal Justice*, Oxford: Clarendon Press, 1994.

Schoeman, Ferdinand David (ed.), *Philosophical Dimensions of Privacy: An Anthology*, Cambridge: Cambridge University Press, 1984.

Schostak, John, *Dirty Marks: The Education of Self, Media and Popular Culture*, London: Pluto, 1993.

Scruton, Roger. *The Aesthetic Understanding*, Manchester: Carcanet, 1983.

Seib, Philip, *Campaigns and Conscience: The Ethics of Political Journalism*, Vancouver, BC: University of British Columbia Press, 1994.

Seymour-Ure, Colin, *The British Press and Broadcasting Since 1945*, Oxford: Blackwell, 1991.

Shearer, Anne, *Survivors and the Media*, London: Broadcasting Standards Council and John Libbey, 1992.

Shetreet, Simon (ed.), *Free Speech and National Security*, Dordrecht: Nijhoff, 1991.

Singer, Jerome L. and Singer, Dorothy, G., *Television, Imagination and Aggression*, Hillsdale, NJ: Erlbaum, 1981.

Slater, Michael D., 'Processing social information in messages: social group familiarity, fiction versus nonfiction, and subsequent beliefs', *Communication Research* 17 (1990): 327–43.

Smith, Anthony, *The Newspaper: An International History*, London: Thames and Hudson, 1979.

Smith, Anthony (ed.), *Newspapers and Democracy: International Essays on a Changing Medium*, Cambridge, MA: MIT Press, 1980.

Smith, Anthony (ed.), *Television: An International History*, Oxford: Oxford University Press, 1995.

Smolla, Rodney, *Free Speech in an Open Society*, New York: Vintage Books, 1993.

Snoddy, Raymond, *The Good, The Bad and the Unacceptable*, London: Faber, 1992; pbk edn 1993.

Snyder, Joel and Allen, Neil Walsh, 'Photography, vision and representation', *Critical Inquiry* 2 (1975): 143–69.

Sorell, Tom, 'Art, society and morality', in O. Hanfling (ed.) *Philosophical Aesthetics*, Oxford: Blackwell Publishers, 1992, pp. 297–347.

Stephenson, Hugh, *Media Freedom and Media Regulation*, London: Association of British Editors, 1994.

Stocking, S. Holly and LaMarca, Nancy, 'How journalists describe their stories: hypotheses and assumptions in newsmaking', *Journalism Quarterly* 67 (1990): 295–301.

Strossen, Nadine, *Defending Pornography: Free Speech, Sex and the Fight for Women's Rights*, London: Abacus, 1996.

Tester, Keith, *Media, Culture and Morality*, London: Routledge, 1994.

Thompson, M. P., 'Confidence in the press', *The Conveyancer and Property Lawyer* 57 (1993): 347–58.

Thomson, J. J., 'The right to privacy', *Philosophy and Public Affairs* 4 (1975): 295–314.

Tuchman, Gaye, *Making News: A Study in the Construction of Reality*, New York: Free Press, 1978.

Tunstall, Jeremy, *The Media in Britain*, London: Constable, 1983.

Van den Haag, E., 'On Privacy', in J. R. Pennock and J. W. Chapman (eds) *Privacy: Nomos XIII*, New York: Atherton Press, 1979, p. 149.

Vaux, Kenneth L., *Ethics and the Gulf War: Religion, Rhetoric and Righteousness*, Boulder, CO: Westview, 1992.

Wacks, R., *Privacy and Press Freedom*, London: Blackstone Press, 1995.

Wakeham, J., 'The Conservative campaign: against the odds', in I. Crewe and B. Gosschalk (eds) *Political Communications: The General Election Campaign of 1992*, Cambridge: Cambridge University Press, 1995, pp. 3–8.

Waldron, Jeremy, *Liberal Rights*, New York: Cambridge University Press, 1993.

Walton, Kendall, 'Transparent pictures: on the nature of photographic realism', *Critical Inquiry* 11 (1984): 246–77.

Warburton, Nigel, 'Photographic communication', *British Journal of Aesthetics* 28 (1988): 173–81.

Warburton, Nigel, 'Seeing through "Seeing through" photographs', *Ratio* NS 1/1 (1988): 64–74.

Warburton, Nigel, 'Varieties of photographic representation', *History of Photography* 15 (1991): 203–10.

Warren, Samuel and Brandeis, Lewis, 'The right to privacy', *Harvard Law Review* 4 (1890): 205.

Weaver, Paul, *News and the Culture of Lying*, New York: Macmillan, 1994.

Williams, Bernard (ed.), *The Williams Report: Report of the Committee on Obscenity and Film Censorship*, Cmnd. 7772, London: HMSO, 1979.

Index